RD
HOME
HANDBOOKS

VEGETARIAN COOKING

VEGETARIAN COOKING

Contributing editor
Sarah Brown

The Reader's Digest Association, Inc.
Pleasantville, New York

This is an RD Home Handbook
specially created for The Reader's Digest Association, Inc.,
by Dorling Kindersley Limited.

First American edition, 1992

Published in the United States
by The Reader's Digest Association, Inc.,
Pleasantville, N.Y.
Published in Great Britain
by Dorling Kindersley Limited, London
Typeset by Bournetype, Bournemouth
Printed in Singapore

Designed and edited by Swallow Books,
260 Pentonville Road, London N1 9JY

Library of Congress Cataloging in Publication Data

Vegetarian cooking/contributing editor, Sarah Brown — 1st American ed.
    p. cm. — (RD home handbooks)
  Previously published as: Vegetarian cookery.
  Includes index.
  ISBN 0-89577-409-7
  1. Vegetarian cookery, I. Brown, Sarah. II. Vegetarian cookery.
III. Series.
  TX837.V426   1992
  641.5'636 — dc20   91-28308

CONTENTS

INTRODUCTION

Throughout the 1980s, we were bombarded with contradictory information about what food we should be including in our daily diet. We were told facts such as: saturated fat is bad for you, but polyunsaturated fat lowers cholesterol levels; eat plenty of fresh vegetables, but cut down on bananas – they're fattening; avoid eggs, they could contain salmonella. We became more aware of health and diet, but it became harder to sort out the facts from all the advice and differing opinions. When is something really good for you and when is it just a fad or a clever piece of marketing? This confusion extends to the foods themselves: which are really "full of natural goodness," and "wholesomeness," and which are nutritionally sound?

This book explains which foods the body needs in order to remain healthy when eating a vegetarian diet, and how to buy the right balance of ingredients, and cook them with care to retain all of the nutrients. A true vegetarian does not eat any fish, meat, or poultry, and may or may not eat dairy products and eggs.

From the health point of view, the case for vegetarianism is a strong one. Most of the so-called diseases of civilization such as cancer, heart disease, high blood pressure, obesity, and diverticulitis are becoming increasingly linked with diet – more specifically diets that are high in refined sugar, fat and salt, and low in fiber. As long ago as 1916, studies comparing the lowfat diets of Japan to the cholesterol-rich diets of northern Europe and America found a definite correlation between high-fat, low-fiber Western diets and cancer and heart disease. A vegetarian diet not only replaces animal fats with vegetable ones, but often cuts down on the

total fat intake, since in the average diet a third of the fats come from meat and another third from dairy products. Eating cereals, dried beans and peas, fruit, and vegetables will ensure an adequate fiber intake, and if you eat sufficient amounts of whole, or unprocessed foods, you will avoid the high levels of added salt and sugar that many processed foods contain.

A healthier approach
Finding out how the body can get all the nutrients it needs in a vegetarian diet is an important issue, especially if you've just decided to give up meat. The early chapters of the book tell you about the main sources of protein, fiber, vitamins, minerals, fats, and carbohydrates in foods. They tell you what the recommended daily allowances for adult males and females are, and give helpful hints on how you can cut down on saturated fats, salt, and sugar, as well as suggesting appetizing alternatives.

If you walk into a health food store you can be overwhelmed by the variety of goods that are available on the shelves, and be confused as to what to buy. *The Pantry* (see pages 44–99) helps you to find out what grains, dried beans and peas, nuts, fruit, and vegetables you need to keep regular stocks of, and also gives you some useful information on how to prepare and cook them.

Once your cupboards are full to the brim, you'll want to start learning some vegetarian cooking techniques and it won't be long before you're getting the satisfaction of seeing people enjoy your own homemade yogurt (see page 105) or eating your hot, fresh whole-wheat bread (see page 102) straight from the oven.

Cooking vegetarian meals for family and friends might seem a bit tricky at first, but they will soon be amazed at the variety of ingredients that can be used, and the delicious meals that can be created. The main recipe section (see pages 122–81) is divided into course order – soups, appetizers, salads, vegetable dishes, rice and pasta dishes, casseroles and roasts, desserts and puddings – so that you can easily find the dish you are looking for. Each recipe is based on the high-fiber, high-protein, lowfat principle, and has a nutritional profile to help you understand exactly which nutrients are contained in each dish, and in what quantity.

To help you plan how to put meals together, and cater for those special occasions when you want to produce a meal that is a bit fancier, you'll find nine interesting and well-balanced menus (see pages 182–219). Once again, each menu and recipe has a nutritional profile. The menus are all high in fiber and protein, low in saturated fat, and provide a good source of vitamins and minerals.

Once you start using this book you will soon realize that the days of gourmet dinner parties need not vanish, and that food does not taste any less delicious just because it is good for you. The variety of recipes included means that you do not have to miss out on any of the pleasure of well-cooked, interestingly seasoned food. What is more, your concept of what is delicious will eventually change. Even if you used to enjoy sweet, sugary desserts, they will start to taste sickly, while rich, high-fat foods will seem heavy and indigestible.

Follow the principles outlined in the book and you will start to enjoy your food more, while knowing that you're also improving your overall diet and general health.

Shopping for a healthier diet
You will soon begin to enjoy yourself at the fruit and vegetable market, making your selection of ingredients for the week's meals.

CHAPTER ONE

SOURCES OF NUTRIENTS

Which foods are essential to our bodies, and what are we better off not eating at all? The answers to these questions need to be fully understood before you can see whether or not your normal daily diet is a well-balanced and truly healthy and nutritious one.

Protein, fat, carbohydrates, vitamins, and minerals are all essential nutrients to life. This part of the book explains why they are so necessary to us, which foods supply them (including complementary proteins), and the recommended daily allowance of each one.

On the following pages is an easy-to-use photographic guide to the commonly available foods that are the best sources of essential nutrients. Divided by nutrient type, each food item illustrated is shown with the quantity of protein, vitamin, mineral, fat, or carbohydrate per 3½oz (100g).

Nutritious foods
A healthy diet needs to include a good, overall mix of foods such as fresh vegetables, fruit, dried beans and peas, and dairy products.

Protein

Protein has two main functions. Firstly, it promotes growth and forms the basic framework of different body structures such as skin, nails, and hair. A constant supply of protein is needed for the maintenance of body structures and to repair worn-out tissues. Secondly, protein maintains supplies of enzymes, hormones, and antibodies. These regulate many of the body's most important functions, such as the ability to digest food. Excess protein is either changed to fat and stored, or used to produce heat and energy.

Protein is made up of amino acids, which consist of carbon, hydrogen, and oxygen groups, together with nitrogen, which enables the amino acids to string together forming long, complex molecules. Some 20 or so amino acids act like building blocks, combining in different ways to produce a wide variety of proteins. Eight are called essential, because the body cannot do without them and cannot synthesize them for itself. These are leucine, isoleucine, lysine, methionine, phenylalanine, threonine, tryptophane, and valine. Growing children also need arginine and histidine.

Protein from animal sources – meat, milk, and eggs – contains all the essential amino acids in roughly the proportions that the body needs, hence they are called first-class protein. No single vegetable food contains amino acids in the proportions the body needs, so they are referred to as second-class protein. A mixture of vegetable proteins is needed to provide an adequate level of the essential amino acids in the total diet. For example, wheat is low in lysine but contains adequate methionine; beans are low in methionine but contain adequate lysine. Eat the two foods together and the body's amino acid requirements are met – the combination of the protein sources gives a high-quality protein supply. The ability of different proteins to make up for each other's deficiencies is known as their supplementary or complementary value. Most traditional cuisines have recipes based on protein's ability to do this. For example, rice and dhal (lentils) are combined, and pasta (wheat) and chickpeas.

We are currently advised to eat less saturated fat and increase our intake of dietary fiber. Meat and dairy products, although good sources of protein, are also high in saturated fat and lacking in fiber. Plant foods can easily be combined to provide good protein while containing little fat (in the case of dried beans and grains), and plenty of fiber. The soybean is exceptional in being a source of high-quality protein in itself, since it contains good proportions of all eight essential amino acids. The recommended daily allowance is 58–63 grams for adult males and 46–50 grams for adult females. Pregnant and breastfeeding women require larger daily allowances.

Extracts and grains

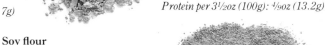

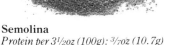

Yeast extract
Protein per 3½oz (100g): 1²/₅oz (39.7g)

Whole-wheat flour
Protein per 3½oz (100g): ⁴/₉oz (13.2g)

Soy flour
Protein per 3½oz (100g): 1²/₇oz (36.8g)

Processed oats
Protein per 3½oz (100g): ⁴/₉oz (12.4g)

Semolina
Protein per 3½oz (100g): ³/₇oz (10.7g)

Wheat germ
Protein per 3¹/₂oz (100g): ⁹/₁₀oz (26.5g)

Rye flour
Protein per 3¹/₂oz (100g): ²/₇oz (8.2g)

Whole-wheat bread
Protein per 3¹/₂oz (100g): ¹/₃oz (8.8g)

Bran
Protein per 3¹/₂oz (100g): ¹/₂oz (14.1g))

Dairy products and eggs

Double Gloucester
Protein per 3¹/₂oz (100g): ⁹/₁₀oz (26g)

Coulommiers
Protein per 3¹/₂oz (100g): ⁴/₅oz (22.8g)

Cottage cheese
Protein per 3¹/₂oz (100g): ¹/₂oz (13.6g)

Parmesan cheese
Protein per 3¹/₂oz (100g): 1¹/₈oz (35.1g)

Eggs
Protein per 3¹/₂oz (100g): ⁴/₉oz (12.3g)

Cheddar cheese
Protein per 3¹/₂oz (100g): ⁹/₁₀oz (26g)

Brie
Protein per 3¹/₂oz (100g): ⁴/₅oz (22.8g)

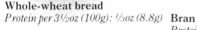

Goat's milk (whole)
Protein per 3¹/₂oz (100g): ¹/₉oz (3.3g)

Skim milk
Protein per 3¹/₂oz (100g): ¹/₈oz (3.4g)

Soy milk
Protein per 3¹/₂oz (100g): ¹/₈oz (3.6g)

Whole milk
Protein per 3¹/₂oz (100g): ¹/₉oz (3.3g)

Yogurt
Protein per 3¹/₂oz (100g): ¹/₆oz (5g)

Nuts

Pistachios
Protein per 3¹/₂oz (100g):
²/₃oz (19.3g)

Almonds
Protein per 3¹/₂oz (100g):
³/₅oz (16.9g)

Peanuts
Protein per 3¹/₂oz (100g):
⁶/₇oz (24.3g)

Walnuts
Protein per 3¹/₂oz (100g):
⁵/₇oz (20.5g)

Brazil nuts
Protein per 3¹/₂oz (100g):
³/₇oz (12g)

Dried beans and lentils

Navy beans
Protein per 3¹/₂oz (100g): ²/₉oz (6.6g)

Splitpeas
Protein per 3¹/₂oz (100g): ¹/₄oz (7.1g)

Lentils
Protein per 3¹/₂oz (100g): ¹/₄oz (7.6g)

Chickpeas
Protein per 3¹/₂oz (100g): ²/₇oz (8g)

Tofu
Protein per 3¹/₂oz (100g): ¹/₄oz (7.4g)

Fiber

Dietary "fiber" is the term used to describe a group of substances that are not broken down by the digestive enzymes. Fiber, which makes up the cell walls of plants, is a form of carbohydrate. It is essential for the efficient working of the digestive system, although it is not actually digested by the body.

All fibers make food chewy, so that you eat less, and more slowly. This is good exercise for the jaws and stimulates saliva production, which helps neutralize acid formed on the teeth, reducing dental decay. Fiber also swells up in your stomach, making you feel more satisfied after eating.

There are five kinds of fiber: pectin, gum, cellulose, hemicellulose, and lignin. Each plays a different role in improving health and preventing disease.

Pectins

These are found in the cell walls of fruits, and in the form of pectose, in the soft tissues of unripe fruits. In the digestive tract, pectins bind some of the bile salts produced by the gall bladder. This may reduce the digestion and absorption of fats and cholesterol, which may in turn help to prevent heart disease.

Gums

These are sticky substances exuded by plants. Like pectin, gum reduces cholesterol uptake. Gums also line the stomach and slow down the absorption of sugar, which is especially useful for people suffering from diabetes.

Cellulose

This comes from the tough outer walls of plant cells. In the digestive tract it takes up water and increases the bulk of partly digested foods. Bulkier food moves more quickly through the body, and takes with it toxins that may have accumulated in the lower intestine.

Hemicelluloses

These come from the cell walls of plants. They also help to bulk out food, making it pass more quickly through the body.

Lignin

This is a woody substance, found mainly in root vegetables. Like cellulose, it adds bulk to stools, making them easier to pass, and may help to prevent hemorrhoids, varicose veins, and possibly cancer of the rectum.

Good sources of fiber

For a range of fiber intake you should eat beans, whole grains, fresh fruit, and vegetables. Meat and dairy products do not contain fiber. Sprinkling bran on top of other food is not the best way to increase fiber intake. An acid in bran combines with minerals, reducing their absorption. Eat fiber as part of a complete food, as this contains a greater quantity of minerals than is found in refined grains. Among the best sources of fiber are bran, apricots, prunes, and whole-wheat bread. There is no recommended Daily Allowance for fiber; experts suggest 20 to 35 grams.

Grains

Soy flour
Fiber per 3½oz (100g): ⅓oz (11.9g)

Whole-wheat flour
Fiber per 3½oz (100g): ⅓oz (9.6g)

Bran
Fiber per 3½oz (100g): 1⁵⁄₉oz (44g)

Whole-wheat bread
Fiber per 3½oz (100g): ³⁄₁₀oz (8.5g)

Ground oats
Fiber per 3¹/₂oz (100g): ¹/₄oz (7g)

Navy beans
Fiber per 3¹/₂oz (100g): ¹/₄oz (7.4g)

Chickpeas
Fiber per 3¹/₂oz (100g): ¹/₅oz (6g)

Pot barley
Fiber per 3¹/₂oz (100g): ²/₉oz (6.5g)

Fruit

Dried peaches
Fiber per 3¹/₂oz (100g): ¹/₂oz (14.3g)

Blackberries
Fiber per 3¹/₂oz (100g): ¹/₄oz (7.3g)

Prunes
Fiber per 3¹/₂oz (100g): ⁴/₇oz (16.1g)

Dried apricots
Fiber per 3¹/₂oz (100g): ⁶/₇oz (24g)

Currants
Fiber per 3¹/₂oz (100g): ²/₉oz (6.5g)

Dried figs
Fiber per 3¹/₂oz (100g): ²/₃oz (18.5g)

Plantain
Fiber per 3¹/₂oz (100g): ²/₉oz (6.4g)

Fresh black currants
Fiber per 3¹/₂oz (100g): ³/₁₀oz (8.7g)

Dates
Fiber per 3¹/₂oz (100g): ³/₁₀oz (8.7g)

Passion fruit
Fiber per 3¹/₂oz (100g): ²/₉oz (6.7g)

Raisins
Fiber per 3¹/₂oz (100g): ²/₉oz (6.4g)

Raspberries
Fiber per 3¹/₂oz (100g): ¹/₄oz (7.4g)

Golden raisins
Fiber per 3¹/₂oz (100g): ¹/₄oz (7g)

Nuts

Vegetables

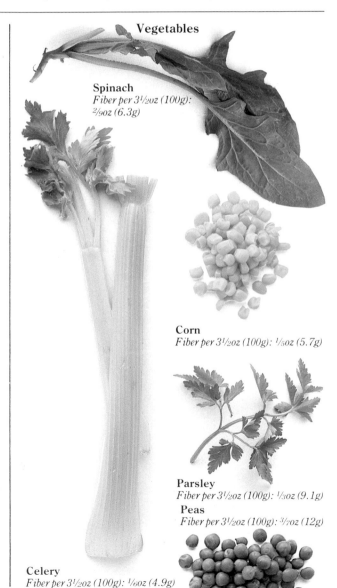

Peanuts
Fiber per 3¹/₂oz (100g): ²/₇oz (8.1g)

Spinach
Fiber per 3¹/₂oz (100g): ²/₉oz (6.3g)

Fresh coconut
Fiber per 3¹/₂oz (100g): ¹/₂oz (13.6g)

Brazil nuts
Fiber per 3¹/₂oz (100g): ¹/₃oz (9g)

Corn
Fiber per 3¹/₂oz (100g): ¹/₅oz (5.7g)

Almonds
Fiber per 3¹/₂oz (100g): ¹/₂oz (14.3g)

Shredded coconut
Fiber per 3¹/₂oz (100g): ⁵/₆oz (23.5g)

Parsley
Fiber per 3¹/₂oz (100g): ¹/₃oz (9.1g)

Peas
Fiber per 3¹/₂oz (100g): ³/₇oz (12g)

Celery
Fiber per 3¹/₂oz (100g): ¹/₆oz (4.9g)

Vitamins

Vitamins are essential chemicals, required by the body in very small quantities. Since the body cannot produce them, they must be supplied by external means, i.e. in food.

Vitamins fall into two distinct groups: water-soluble (the vitamin B group, vitamin C and folate), and fat-soluble (vitamins A, D, E, and K). Water-soluble vitamins dissolve in the blood and tissue fluids; they cannot be stored in the body for long. Any excess is excreted in the urine. Fat-soluble vitamins can be stored by the body in the liver and fatty tissues.

The amount of any vitamin required each day varies according to age, sex, and occupation. Growing children, pregnant women, and lactating mothers all need more vitamins, as do the elderly, and those recovering from illness.

Some chemicals contained in many widely consumed substances – alcohol, cigarettes, coffee, aspirins, birthcontrol pills – use up some of the body's vitamin resources, so people who smoke, drink, or take regular medication need to be sure that their food is rich in vitamins.

Vitamins can be destroyed during the storing, processing, or cooking of food. Refined foods such as white flour and white rice are often "enriched" to make up for the vitamins removed during processing. Water-soluble vitamins are vulnerable to heat; a large amount can be destroyed during cooking. Fat-soluble vitamins are generally more stable but can be sensitive to light and air.

Vitamin A
This keeps skin and mucous membranes healthy. It is essential for vision in dim light.

The B-group vitamins
These are important in the metabolism of carbohydrates, fats, and proteins in the body. Vitamins B_1 (thiamin), B_2 (riboflavin), B_3 (niacin), B_6, Folate (folic acid), Biotin, and Pantothenic acid make up the B-group vitamins. They keep the hair, skin, eyes, mouth, and liver healthy. They are needed for proper functioning of the brain, nervous and circulatory systems, and for red blood cells.

Vitamin C
This is necessary for healthy connective tissue. It promotes the healing of wounds, helps the body to fight against infection, and increases the absorption of iron.

Vitamin D
This is essential for maintaining normal levels of calcium and phosphorus in the blood, and enhances the absorption of calcium, ensuring sound formation of bones and teeth.

Vitamin E
This is a component of all cell membranes. It prevents damage to the components of the cell membranes. It protects unsaturated fats in the body from damage and protects vitamin A from destruction.

Vitamin K
This vitamin is needed to prevent the body from hemorrhaging.

Folate (folic acid)
This, along with vitamin B_{12}, is needed for the successful formation of genetic material in the DNA molecules contained in cells. It also helps in the formation of proteins.

Recommended amounts
The recommended daily allowance for each of these vitamins is as follows: vitamin A, 1,000 mg for adult males and 800 mg for adult females; thiamin, 0.5 mg/1,000 kcal; riboflavin, 1.4–1.7 mg for adult males and 1.2–3 mg for adult females; niacin, 15–19 mg for adult males and 13–15 mg for adult females; vitamin B_6, 2 mg for adult males and 1.6 mg for adult females; vitamin B_{12}, 2 mg for all adults; vitamin C, 60 mg for all adults; vitamin D, 5 mg for all adults; vitamin E, 10 mg for adult males and 8 mg for adult females; vitamin K, 80 mg for adult males and 65 mg for adult females; folate (known as folic acid), 200 mg for adult males and 180 mg for adult females. It is necessary for pregnant and breast-feeding women to take larger quantities of most vitamins.

Vitamin A

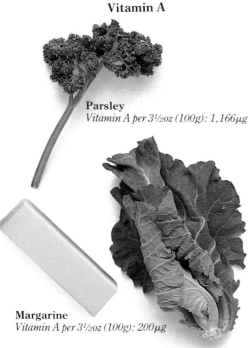

Parsley
Vitamin A per 3¹/₂oz (100g): 1,166µg

Margarine
Vitamin A per 3¹/₂oz (100g): 200µg

Cabbage leaves
Vitamin A per 3¹/₂oz (100g): 83µg

Sorrel
Vitamin A per 3¹/₂oz (100g): 2,150µg

Carrots
Vitamin A per 3¹/₂oz (100g): 2,000µg

Thiamin (vitamin B₁)

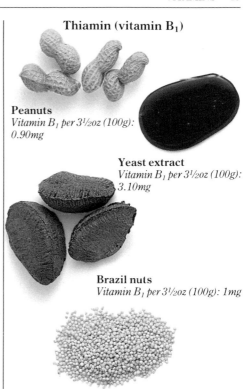

Peanuts
Vitamin B₁ per 3¹/₂oz (100g): 0.90mg

Yeast extract
Vitamin B₁ per 3¹/₂oz (100g): 3.10mg

Brazil nuts
Vitamin B₁ per 3¹/₂oz (100g): 1mg

Millet
Vitamin B₁ per 3¹/₂oz (100g): 0.73mg

Soy flour
Vitamin B₁ per 3¹/₂oz (100g): 0.75mg

Bran
Vitamin B₁ per 3¹/₂oz (100g): 0.89mg

Wheat germ
Vitamin B₁ per 3¹/₂oz (100g): 1.45mg

Riboflavin (Vitamin B$_2$)

Yeast extract
Vitamin B$_2$ per 3^1/$_2$oz (100g): 11mg

Almonds
Vitamin B$_2$ per 3^1/$_2$oz (100g): 0.92mg

Wheat germ
Vitamin B$_2$ per 3^1/$_2$oz (100g): 0.61mg

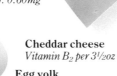

Brie
Vitamin B$_2$ per 3^1/$_2$oz (100g): 0.60mg

Parmesan cheese
Vitamin B$_2$ per 3^1/$_2$oz (100g): 0.50mg

Cheddar cheese
Vitamin B$_2$ per 3^1/$_2$oz (100g): 0.50mg

Egg yolk
Vitamin B$_2$ per 3^1/$_2$oz (100g): 0.47mg

Niacin (Vitamin B$_3$)

Peanuts
Vitamin B$_3$ per 3^1/$_2$oz (100g): 16mg

Yeast extract
Vitamin B$_3$ per 3^1/$_2$oz (100g): 58mg

Wheat germ
Vitamin B$_3$ per 3^1/$_2$oz (100g): 5.8mg

Dried peaches
Vitamin B$_3$ per 3^1/$_2$oz (100g): 5.3mg

Button mushrooms
Vitamin B$_3$ per 3^1/$_2$oz (100g): 4mg

Whole-wheat flour
Vitamin B$_3$ per 3^1/$_2$oz (100g): 5.6mg

Bran
Vitamin B$_3$ per 3^1/$_2$oz (100g): 29.6mg

Soy flour
Vitamin B$_6$ per 3^1/$_2$oz (100g): 0.57mg

Walnuts
Vitamin B$_6$ per 3^1/$_2$oz (100g): 0.73mg

Hazelnuts
Vitamin B$_6$ per 3^1/$_2$oz (100g): 0.55mg

Vitamin B$_6$

Wheat germ
Vitamin B$_6$ per 3^1/$_2$oz (100g): 0.93mg

Bran
Vitamin B$_6$ per 3^1/$_2$oz (100g): 1.38mg

Banana
Vitamin B$_6$ per 3^1/$_2$oz (100g): 0.51mg

Yeast extract
Vitamin B$_6$ per 3^1/$_2$oz (100g): 1.30mg

Vitamin B$_{12}$

Cheddar cheese
Vitamin B$_{12}$ per 3^1/$_2$oz (100g): 1.7μg

Cottage cheese
Vitamin B$_{12}$ per 3^1/$_2$oz (100g): 0.5μg

Egg yolk
Vitamin B$_{12}$ per 3^1/$_2$oz (100g): 4.9μg

Yeast extract
Vitamin B$_{12}$ per 3^1/$_2$oz (100g): 0.5μg

Brie
Vitamin B$_{12}$ per 3^1/$_2$oz (100g): 1.2μg

Parmesan cheese
Vitamin B$_{12}$ per 3^1/$_2$oz (100g): 1.5μg

Vitamin C

Lemon
Vitamin C per 3¹/₂oz (100g): 80mg

Sorrel
Vitamin C per 3¹/₂oz (100g): 119mg

Red pepper
Vitamin C per 3¹/₂oz (100g): 204mg

Black currants
Vitamin C per 3¹/₂oz (100g): 200mg

Parsley
Vitamin C per 3¹/₂oz (100g): 150mg

Green pepper
Vitamin C per 3¹/₂oz (100g): 100mg

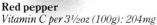

Vitamin D

Egg yolk
Vitamin D per 3¹/₂oz (100g): 5.00µg

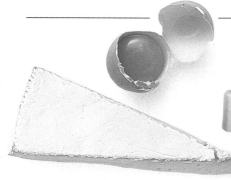

Margarine
Vitamin D per 3¹/₂oz (100g): 7.94µg

Brie
Vitamin D per 3¹/₂oz (100g): 0.18µg

Cheddar cheese
Vitamin D per 3¹/₂oz (100g): 0.26µg

Vitamin E

Peanuts
Vitamin E per 3¹/₂oz (100g): 8.1mg

Almonds
Vitamin E per 3¹/₂oz (100g): 20mg

Hazelnuts
Vitamin E per 3¹/₂oz (100g): 21mg

Brazil nuts
Vitamin E per 3¹/₂oz (100g): 6.5mg

Egg yolk
Vitamin E per 3¹/₂oz (100g): 4.6mg

Margarine
Vitamin E per 3¹/₂oz (100g): 8mg

Vitamin K

Soybeans
Vitamin K per 3¹/₂oz (100g):
190μg

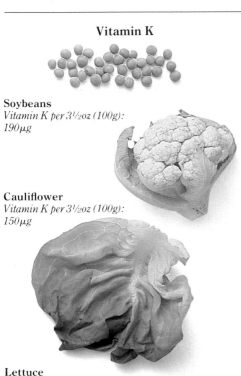

Cauliflower
Vitamin K per 3¹/₂oz (100g):
150μg

Lettuce
Vitamin K per 3¹/₂oz (100g): 200μg

Savoy cabbage
Vitamin K per 3¹/₂oz (100g): 100μg

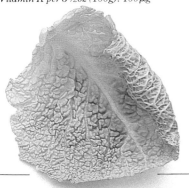

Folate (folic acid)

Watercress
Folate per 3¹/₂oz (100g): 200μg

Bran
Folic acid per 3¹/₂oz (100g): 130μg

Wheat germ
Folate per 3¹/₂oz (100g): 62μg

Yeast extract
Folate per 3¹/₂oz (100g): 83μg

Minerals

Four percent of our body is made up of 100 or so different minerals, of which about 20 are known or suspected to be essential. Six are present in the body in large quantities: sodium, potassium, chlorine, calcium, phosphorus, and magnesium. A sufficient supply of sodium and phosphorus is obtainable from most foods. The other 14 are called trace elements, making up less than 1/10,000th part of our body.

Plants are the main source of minerals, as they absorb them from the soil. Minerals are part of the structural framework of the body, being present in bones and teeth, as well as in muscle fibers and nerve cells. They enable muscles to contract and relax, and impulses to be transmitted through the nerves. As soluble salts, they contribute to the composition and balance of body fluids. Minerals are constituents of enzymes, vitamins, and hormones. They enable many chemical reactions to take place which break down and utilize food.

Apart from their individual functions, minerals also work in groups, this is why taking supplements of only one mineral may cause a deficiency of another, a balanced intake is of the utmost importance.

Modern agricultural and food processing techniques can distort the mineral balance. For example, phosphates are used extensively as fertilizers. A high intake of phosphorus increases the body's need for calcium. Another example is salt. Our intake of sodium is some eight to ten times our requirement due to the salt contained in processed foods and added in cooking; this may upset the sodium/potassium balance. Pollution from car exhausts, cigarette smoke, medication, alcohol, and caffeine all affect our mineral needs. A varied diet of wholefoods, fresh fruit, vegetables, and nuts can help counteract this problem.

Sodium, potassium, and chlorine
These are responsible in different ways for the mechanisms that ensure a constant volume of body fluids. Chlorine (in the form of chloride) is necessary for making hydrochloric acid in the gastric juices of the stomach. This is required for the digestion of protein. Potassium is required for muscle cells and blood corpuscles. Sodium is essential for balancing the quantities of fluids inside and outside each cell.

Calcium, phosphorus, and magnesium
Calcium is a major component of the bones and teeth and is necessary for their maintenance. It is also needed for blood clotting, maintenance of cell membranes, and for proper functioning of the nervous system. Phosphorus teams up with calcium to maintain healthy bones and is also important for energy release. Magnesium is necessary for the utilization of calcium and potassium by the body, and for the correct functioning of the nervous system.

Iron, zinc, and copper
Iron is necessary for the formation in the body of hemoglobin. Vitamin C enhances iron absorption, and a trace of copper is needed for the correct functioning of iron in the body. Zinc is essential for growth and for the synthesis of proteins. It is necessary for wound healing, sexual maturation, and the maintenance of skin, hair, nails, and mucous membranes.

Iodine
Very small quantities of iodine are required for the normal functioning of the thyroid gland.

Recommended daily intake
The recommended daily allowances for the different minerals are as follows: calcium, 800 mg for all adults; phosphorus, 800 mg for all adults; magnesium, 350 mg for adult males and 250 mg for adult females; iron, 10 mg for adult males and 15 mg for adult females of childbearing age; zinc, 15 mg for adult males and 12 mg for adult females; iodine, 150 mg for all adults; selenium, 70 mg for adult males and 55 mg for adult females. Pregnant and breast-feeding women require larger daily allowances. The National Academy of Sciences recommends 2,400 mg as an average daily intake of sodium. There are no official recommendations for daily intakes of manganese, chromium, potassium, chlorine, or copper, but they are essential in the diet.

Magnesium

Bran
Magnesium per 3½oz (100g): 520mg

Almonds
Magnesium per 3½oz (100g): 260mg

Brazil nuts
Magnesium per 3½oz (100g): 410mg

Wheat germ
Magnesium per 3½oz (100g): 300mg

Peanuts
Magnesium per 3½oz (100g): 180mg

Soy flour
Magnesium per 3½oz (100g): 240mg

Millet
Magnesium per 3½oz (100g): 162mg
Oatmeal
Magnesium per 3½oz (100g): 110mg

Walnuts
Magnesium per 3½oz (100g): 130mg

Whole-wheat flour
Magnesium per 3½oz (100g): 140mg

Calcium

Parmesan cheese
Calcium per 3½oz (100g): 1,200mg

Cheddar cheese
Calcium per 3½oz (100g): 800mg

Dried figs
Calcium per 3¹/₂oz (100g): 280mg

Almonds
Calcium per 3¹/₂oz (100g): 250mg

Spinach
Calcium per 3¹/₂oz (100g): 600mg

Parsley
Calcium per 3¹/₂oz (100g): 330mg

Brazil nuts
Calcium per 3¹/₂oz (100g): 180mg

Watercress
Calcium per 3¹/₂oz (100g): 220mg

Brie
Calcium per 3¹/₂oz (100g): 380mg

Soy flour
Calcium per 3¹/₂oz (100g): 210mg

Potassium

Dried apricots
Potassium per 3¹/₂oz (100g): 1,880mg

Blackstrap molasses
Potassium per 3¹/₂oz (100g): 2,927mg

Yeast extract
Potassium per 3¹/₂oz (100g): 2,600mg

Dried peaches
Potassium per 3¹/₂oz (100g): 1,100mg

Soy flour
Potassium per 3¹/₂oz (100g): 1,660mg

Wheat germ
Potassium per 3¹/₂oz (100g): 1,000mg

Dried figs
Potassium per 3¹/₂oz (100g): 1,010mg

Parsley
Potassium per 3¹/₂oz (100g): 1,080mg

Bran
Potassium per 3¹/₂oz (100g): 1,160mg

Golden raisins
Potassium per 3¹/₂oz (100g): 860mg

Iron

Blackstrap molasses
Iron per 3¹/₂oz (100g): 16.1mg

Wheat germ
Iron per 3¹/₂oz (100g): 10mg

Parsley
Iron per 3¹/₂oz (100g): 8mg

Bran
Iron per 3¹/₂oz (100g): 12.9mg

Dried peaches
Iron per 3¹/₂oz (100g): 6.8mg

Millet
Iron per 3¹/₂oz (100g): 6.8mg

Soy flour
Iron per 3¹/₂oz (100g): 6.9mg

Compressed yeast
Iron per 3¹/₂oz (100g): 5mg

Dried figs
Iron per 3¹/₂oz (100g): 4.2mg

Egg yolk
Iron per 3¹/₂oz (100g): 6.1mg

Zinc

Parmesan cheese
Zinc per 3¹/₂oz (100g): 4mg

Bran
Zinc per 3¹/₂oz (100g): 16.2mg

Brazil nuts
Zinc per 3¹/₂oz (100g): 4.2mg

Cheddar cheese
Zinc per 3¹/₂oz (100g): 4mg

Almonds
Zinc per 3¹/₂oz (100g): 3.1mg

Walnuts
Zinc per 3¹/₂oz (100g): 3mg

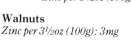
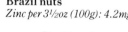

Peanuts
Zinc per 3¹/₂oz (100g): 3mg

Whole-wheat flour
Zinc per 3¹/₂oz (100g): 3mg

Irish oats
Zinc per 3¹/₂oz (100g): 3mg

Brie
Zinc per 3¹/₂oz (100g): 3mg

Compressed yeast
Copper per 3¹/₂oz (100g): 5mg

Copper

Bran
Copper per 3¹/₂oz (100g): 1.3mg

Brazil nuts
Copper per 3¹/₂oz (100g): 1.1mg

Whole egg
Copper per 3¹/₂oz (100g): 1mg

Shredded coconut
Copper per 3¹/₂oz (100g): 0.6mg

Parsley
Copper per 3¹/₂oz (100g): 0.5mg

Currants
Copper per 3¹/₂oz (100g): 0.5mg

Whole-wheat flour
Copper per 3¹/₂oz (100g): 0.4mg

Dried peaches
Copper per 3¹/₂oz (100g): 0.6mg

Fava beans
Copper per 3¹/₂oz (100g): 0.4mg

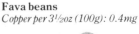

Fat

There are three main types of fat; they are known as saturated, monounsaturated, and polyunsaturated. The type is determined by the number of free "links" in the chemical structure. Saturated fat has hydrogen atoms attached to all of its links, monounsaturated fat has a few links free, and polyunsaturated fat has many free links.

Saturated fat is generally of animal origin, with the exceptions of coconut and palm oils, and hydrogenated (artificially hardened) vegetable fat. Polyunsaturated fat (PUFA) tends to be liquid at room temperature, and is found mainly in plants and in fish. Monounsaturated fat is found particularly in nuts and fruit. No single food contains only one sort of fat; what distinguishes foods is the proportions in which different types of fat are present.

Apart from being a concentrated source of energy, fat has several other functions. Food containing fat is more palatable, since it helps the flavors to mingle and facilitates swallowing. Fat satisfies the appetite, not only because it is high in calories, but also because it slows down digestion, keeping the stomach full for a longer period. The fatty tissues store the fat-soluble vitamins A, D, E, and K. Fat is stored in layers under the skin to help keep the body warm, and it cushions the vital organs to protect them against impact and hold them in place. Stored fat can be used by the body for fuel if the body is deprived of food for any length of time.

Polyunsaturated fat provides essential fatty acids (EFA) – these are linoleic, linolenic, and arachidonic. They are vital constituents of the capillaries and membranes, and are used to regulate blood flow. Linoleic acid needs to come from the food we eat; the other EFAs can also be synthesized by the body.

For optimum health, the American Cancer Society and the American Heart Association recommend that less than 30 percent of calories come from fat.

Polyunsaturated fat

Safflower seed oil
PUFA per 3¹/₂oz (100g): 2¹/₂oz (72.11g)

Brazil nuts
PUFA per 3¹/₂oz (100g): ⁴/₅oz (22.93g)
Peanuts
PUFA per 3¹/₂oz (100g): ¹/₂oz (13.95g)

Sunflower seed oil
PUFA per 3¹/₂oz (100g): 1³/₄oz (49.95g)

Soybean oil
PUFA per 3¹/₂oz (100g): 2oz (56.73g)

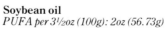

Walnuts
PUFA per 3¹/₂oz (100g): 1¹/₄oz (35.15g)

Soy flour
PUFA per 3¹/₂oz (100g): ⁴/₉oz (13.34g)

Carbohydrates

Carbohydrates are compounds of carbon, hydrogen, and oxygen. The two main types of digestible carbohydrates are sugars (simple carbohydrates) and starches (complex carbohydrates); they are our most important source of energy.

The chief sugars are simple sugars or monosaccharides, consisting of glucose, fructose, and galactose, and double sugars, or disaccharides, comprising sucrose, maltose, and lactose. Sucrose is the most commonly eaten sugar, yet it provides no nutrients at all.

Starches are an example of polysaccharides, or complex carbohydrates. It is recommended that we should eat more starches (contained in potatoes, whole-wheat bread, and flour products) and fewer simple carbohydrates.

Before being used by the body, carbohydrates must be broken down into simple sugars, which can then be absorbed through the walls of the small intestine into the bloodstream. They are then either broken down to produce energy, or stored in the liver as glycogen. This forms a reserve to help maintain blood sugar levels between meals or during exercise. Excess carbohydrate is stored as fat.

Apart from giving us energy, carbohydrates are needed to metabolize protein so that it can be used to build and repair body tissues. The central nervous system also requires a steady supply of carbohydrates.

To release the energy that is stored in carbohydrates, the body requires sufficient quantities of vitamins. Especially important in this respect are vitamins in the B-complex group, used to regulate the production of energy from glucose.

The best sources of carbohydrates are illustrated here. There is no recommended daily intake of carbohydrates in the U.S.

Grains and dried beans, peas, and lentils

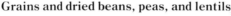

Rice
Carbohydrate per 3¹/₂oz (100g):
3oz (86.8g)

Pot barley
Carbohydrate per 3¹/₂oz (100g):
2⁹/₁₀oz (83.6g)

Rye flour
Carbohydrate per 3¹/₂oz (100g):
2²/₃oz (75.9g)

Processed oats
Carbohydrate per 3¹/₂oz (100g):
2⁴/₇oz (72.8g)

Split peas
Carbohydrate per 3¹/₂oz (100g):
1⁹/₁₀oz (54.7g)

Lentils
Carbohydrate per 3¹/₂oz (100g):
1⁴/₅oz (50.8g)

Butter beans
Carbohydrate per 3¹/₂oz (100g):
1⁵/₈oz (46.2g)

Whole-wheat flour
Carbohydrate per 3¹/₂oz (100g):
2¹/₄oz (63.5g)

· CHAPTER TWO ·

HEALTHY EATING

"Eat less fat, less salt, and less sugar. Eat more fiber and complex carbohydrate, especially from whole grains, dried beans and peas, fresh fruit, and vegetables." This is the message from nutritionists. These guidelines sound straightforward, but if it were simple to follow them, no doubt we would all be healthier tomorrow.
Change is not easy. People become rooted in their eating habits, and find it hard to believe that a change to their diet can really improve their health and general well-being. However, if you approach change gradually, the transition to good health can be relatively painless! It will also give you time to change to new shopping and cooking routines. Remember, while it is important to aim for meals that reflect the lowfat, low-salt, low-sugar, high-protein, high-fiber principle, do not worry if every dish does not contain the perfect balance. What counts is your average intake of nutrients over a week. This chapter shows you how to change to a well-balanced diet.

The right choice
By combining well-chosen ingredients for starters: Top left: Papaya and lime salad (see p.190); main courses: Bottom left: Celebration roast (see p.186); Top right: Radicchio salad (see p.213); and desserts: Bottom right: Mango and orange sorbet (see p.211), you can create perfectly balanced meals for friends and family.

Changing to a healthy diet

L ook carefully at your present diet. Ask yourself: Do I eat enough fresh fruit? Do I eat a lot of fats? Do I eat too much canned or processed food? Only you can decide what changes need to take place. Then think about which of the foods that you normally buy could be replaced with something more healthy.

The key to a healthy diet is to eat a variety of foods each day. Foods for a healthy diet should be wholesome and nutritious, and should not contain dangerous chemicals or additives. The term "whole foods" applies to foods to which nothing has been added and nothing taken away. The benefit of these types of food is that they retain nutrients that would be lost in refining or food processing.

Today, whole foods are not restricted to health food stores. Many supermarkets offer a range of products that are largely additive-free, using good-quality, natural ingredients. Some stock whole wheat products – flours, breads, pastas, crackers, and cereals – as well as preservative-free yogurts and fruit juices, and unrefined oils.

Next, start looking at the labels on any processed food that you buy – look particularly for the sugar, salt, and fat contents. Start buying sugar-free breakfast cereals, watch out for hidden sugar in products such as canned soups and baked beans, and note the salt content in canned vegetables – and some frozen ones. In fact, try to cut down on canned food altogether. Think about some of the processed foods that you buy, and consider making them yourself. Mayonnaise, sweet-and-sour sauces, and soups can all be made quite easily at home, and by doing this you can be sure there are no unwanted additives.

Consider the quality of the fresh food you are eating. If you are able to grow your own fruit and vegetables, you can eat really fresh produce that has been cultivated without chemical sprays and pesticides. If you cannot grow your own fruit and vegetables, choose quality produce; go to a reputable store, preferably one supplying organic fruit and vegetables. You might also find organic produce at a farmers' market.

Think about your meals
Once you have the correct ingredients, small changes to your menus can make huge differences to your diet.

Breakfast: Make your own Swiss-style muesli or choose a sugar- or fat-free cereal. If you prefer a hot breakfast, try oatmeal, homemade muffins, or homemade baked beans, broiled tomatoes, or mushrooms on whole-wheat or rye toast. Drink unsweetened fruit juices, and coffee substitutes or herbal teas (see *Drinks*, p.43).

Lunch and supper: There is a wide range of staple foods for you to draw from. Grains and dried beans should be eaten for their carbohydrate, fiber, protein, vitamin, and mineral content; nuts and seeds for protein (remember they have a high fat content); vegetables and fruit for their fiber, vitamins, and minerals. Within these groups different foods have different nutritional values (see pp. 12–31).

Change the emphasis so that the main part of your meals is unrefined carbohydrate, which is satisfying, and provides energy – do not rely on high-calorie, low-nutrient processed foods to fill you up. Alter the way you cook your meals: broil or bake instead of frying, and steam or stir-fry your vegetables.

Try to include some raw fruit or vegetables in at least one of your main meals to obtain maximum nutritional benefit. This could be a salad appetizer or main course – there are plenty of ideas in the book to choose from. You could also serve a fresh fruit salad instead of a rich dessert which is just as satisfying and nutritionally far better for you.

Snacks: Fresh vegetables and fresh fruit make nourishing snacks. Replace candies with dried fruit, and savory nibbles with nuts and seeds. Eat sugar-free or low-sugar cookies or cakes until you can give up traditional snacks, or, try whole-wheat bread spread with miso for a savory snack.

Eating out
Health food restaurants are burgeoning, and they generally have a good range of dishes to choose from. Eating in a conventional

Unusual salads

Fresh salads of vegetables and dried beans make light nourishing meals, such as corn salad (see p.191), and green bean julienne (see p.199). Alternatively, for a more exotic flavor, mix dried apricots with bulgur wheat and pumpkin seeds, or chopped Brussels sprouts with red cabbage, nuts, and fruit.

restaurant is sometimes more difficult. If the appetizers are more imaginative than the main courses, order several plus a salad. Select steamed rather than fried vegetables.

Eating in other people's houses is often more difficult because you will rarely be given a choice of dishes or meals to eat. Just remember that no food is completely forbidden in a healthy diet; it is really up to you to balance your diet on a weekly basis.

Meals for children

If your children have always eaten whole foods at home, problems start only when they go out or go to school. It is up to you to make sure that the rest of their diet is balanced. If you are changing to a whole food diet yourself, your children may be more resistant to change, but again it is a question of introducing new foods gradually. Remember to let them have the odd treat occasionally as well.

Main courses are relatively easy because most children like pizzas, pastas, and grain dishes, particularly rice and millet. For desserts try the trifle (see p.176), cranachan (see p.177) or just yogurt with fresh fruit.

If you are packing lunches for school or picnics, vary the type of bread you use, and fill sandwiches with imaginative spreads such as ricotta cheese, golden tofu pâté (see p.138), or a sweet tahini spread. The latter two are especially good for children because they are high in protein, which is essential for their growth and development. Make pastries with a light yeast pastry or use a whole-wheat piecrust dough for pies.

Snacks are a particular problem with children because raw fruit and vegetables do not have the same appeal as a bar of chocolate or a piece of cake. However, dried fruit can make a good substitute for candy, and there are several recipes in the book for sugar-free cakes and cookies, for example, carob cookies (see p.180) and fruit and nut bars (see p.181). Avoid giving very young children small nuts and seeds because they can easily choke, and avoid fruit drinks, which are high in additives – offer fruit juices mixed with sparkling mineral water as an alternative.

Healthy alternatives

This section is intended as a guide to the foods to avoid or cut down on, with suggestions for alternatives to help you ease into a new and healthier way of eating, without really missing the old way. First steps might be to reduce your fat intake by replacing whole milk with skim milk, and butter with polyunsaturated margarine, to eat whole-wheat bread and pasta, and brown rice instead of polished white rice.

Fat

Fatty foods were once extremely expensive, now they are the cheapest form of calories available. This is because weight for weight they contain almost twice as many calories as carbohydrates and proteins. In 1800, fat accounted for about 10 percent of the calories in our diet. Today, it can account for 40 percent of the calories in American diets.

Variety salads
Try mixing fresh fruit and nuts in your salads. The mixtures featured here are beets with apple, zucchini with an orange and tahini dressing, strawberry with cucumber, orange with olive, and coleslaw with apricots or a fennel.

Fat and disease
There are now clear links between fat and various so-called Western diseases. Too much fat can make you fat, leading to obesity. This brings a greater likelihood of illness such as diabetes, arthritis, gall-bladder disease, high blood pressure, and heart trouble. Even without obesity there are clear links between fat consumption and heart disease, and because high-fat diets tend to be low-fiber diets, they are thought to be a contributory factor in colin cancer.

Reduce consumption
We urgently need to cut down our consumption of fat to 30 to 35 percent of our total calorie intake. Although we need some fat in our diet for energy, and to supply essential fatty acids and fat-soluble vitamins, an average adult needs only about 3 ounces (85g) per day.

Saturated vs. unsaturated fat
It is not just a matter of how much fat we eat but also the type of fat (see p. 30). Saturated fat can cause fatty deposits on artery walls. These fatty deposits are largely cholesterol, a normal component of most body tissues, found only in animal and dairy products. The deposits may build up and block the arteries, thus obstructing the flow of blood, a process called atherosclerosis. If this occurs in a heart artery it can cause a heart attack. Blockage in other regions can cause strokes, angina, or other circulatory problems. Low blood cholesterol levels reduce the risk of heart attacks, and it is known that cholesterol levels fall when less saturated fat is eaten. Unsaturated fat is thought to offer some protection against atherosclerosis by lowering blood cholesterol levels. The best protection, however, is to eat less fat altogether – particularly saturated fat.

Avoiding fats

In practical terms, this means cutting down on animal-derived products such as lard, eggs, butter, hard cheese, cream, and whole milk. This can be very hard to do unless you make everything you eat so that you can see exactly what goes into things. Processed foods may be loaded with unsuspected fats and the only way to tell is by reading the labels: the label will give the amount of fat (in grams) for a specific serving size (ie: by weight, and sometimes also by wet weight). It may also list the percentage of calories provided by the fat, and specify the amounts of saturated, polyunsaturated, and monounsaturated fat. Ingredients are listed in descending order of weight. This means if you learn which ingredients are high in fat, as well as which ones contain primarily saturated or polyunsaturated fat, you should be able to assess the overall fat content. As a general rule, avoid foods which list oil or fat as the first ingredient, or list several oils or fats.

Blended oils should be avoided as they may well be made from a mixture of palm or coconut oil (both containing saturated fat) and an unsaturated oil such as sunflower. Buy the unblended, unsaturated oils such as corn, sunflower, and safflower, and get them cold-pressed if possible because the heat used in other methods of processing can destroy some of the important nutrients they contain, such as lecithin and Vitamin E. Many margarine

manufacturers start with cheap ingredients such as beef suet and whale oil and rely on extensive processing, coloring, and additives to produce palatable results. Moreover, they use the process of hydrogenation to solidify the fat, thus turning unsaturated fat into saturated fat. The best margarines are made with cold-pressed, unsaturated oils that have not been hydrogenated, and can be found in health food stores.

HOW TO CUT DOWN ON FAT
• Eat more vegetarian meals.
• Have fresh fruit salads, fruit compotes, or yogurt instead of desserts.
• Use yogurt as a salad dressing instead of oil.
• Broil or bake rather than fry.
• Use non-stick pans so you use less oil.
• Use gentle heat when cooking, because high temperatures change unsaturated fats into saturated fats.
• Use polyunsaturated oil and margarine in place of butter and lard.
• Use fresh herbs on food instead of butter.
• Change from whole milk to skim milk.
• Moisten sandwiches or crackers with lettuce and tomatoes or a savory spread rather than butter.
• Avoid blended oils made partly with saturated fats; use cold-pressed oils instead.
• Eat cakes, pastries, chocolate, potato chips, cookies, and ice-cream rarely, even homemade low-fat ones.
• Avoid food where fat is high on the label.

Dairy products

About a third of our fat intake comes from meat and a third from dairy products. Together, these make up about 40 percent of our saturated fat intake, so it makes sense to cut down on these products or to use less fatty alternatives. Although dairy products contain high proportions of proteins, vitamins, and minerals, we can, in fact, make do with less butter, milk, cream, and cheese because all these nutrients can be found in other sources (see *Sources of Nutrients*, pp. 10–31).

There are, however, other reasons, apart from a high fat content, for cutting down on dairy products. Milk contributes to a number

of complaints, and milk allergies are common. There are two types of milk allergy: some people are allergic to milk protein, which can result in breathing difficulties, catarrh, or eczema; others have an enzyme deficiency known as lactose intolerance that hinders the breaking down of milk sugars in the body. Lactose is one of the milk sugars and it is broken down by an enzyme called lactase. If lactase is not present, the lactose accumulates in the intestine, ferments, and causes cramps and diarrhea.

After chocolate, the most likely causes of migraine headaches are cheese and other dairy products. They also cause the formation of mucus and may contribute to various sinus problems and bronchitis.

Baked potatoes
Potatoes are a good source of protein and fiber, and are not especially fattening, except when served with butter or sour cream..Try serving potatoes with a sauce made from yogurt and chopped chives, or chilis and beans. Alternatively, scoop out the inside and mix it with another vegetable such as spinach or broccoli.

Alternatives to dairy products

There are many ways in which you can cut down on your consumption of dairy products. Start by using skim milk. If you cannot drink cow's milk, try goat's milk or soy milk.

Skim milk: Whole milk is between 3 and 4 percent fat; skim milk is less than ½ percent fat. Lowfat milk contains 2 percent fat. One quick way to reduce your daily fat intake is to use skim milk for coffee and cereals. Skim milk does taste different and it can take time to get used to it, but when you become adjusted, whole milk will seem too rich.

Goat's milk and soy milk: Those allergic to cow's milk can substitute goat's milk or soy milk. Goat's milk has a higher phosphate, copper, and magnesium content than cow's milk but beware, because it also has a much higher fat content and it is very difficult to obtain lowfat goat's milk. Soy milk also has a higher fat content than skim milk. Both soy and goat's milk are available in powdered form.

Lowfat milk products: It is easy enough to cut down on fatty dairy products by substituting some of the lowfat ones listed below. Some of the products have highfat versions, or versions containing water and salt, so it is important to check the labels carefully.

Lowfat cottage cheese is similar to curd cheese but made from skim milk so it is low in fat, yielding about 30 calories per ounce. Some varieties contain salt and preservatives, so check the label carefully. Curd cheese is made from the separated curd of whole cow's or goat's milk, so it is about 11 percent fat and gives 40–45 calories per 1 ounce. Lowfat ricotta is another soft, white cheese, but it is made from milk and does not contain salt. The fat content is generally low but can be up to 40 percent, so it is wise to check the label.

Reduced fat sour cream looks like cream and tastes similar to sour cream but is made from lowfat dairy products. Its fat content varies from 5 to 10 percent. Check the label if you buy it or make your own (see p. 107). Yogurt can be made from skim or whole milk but is acidic enough to break down milk protein into a more easily digested form. You can make your own (see pp. 105–6).

**HOW TO CUT DOWN ON
HIGHFAT DAIRY PRODUCTS**

- Use skim milk instead of whole milk.
- Serve yogurt as a dessert.
- Use yogurt or reduced fat sour cream instead of cream when you are cooking creamy dishes.
- Make yogurt-based dressings for salads.
- Soak muesli in fruit juice instead of milk.
- Try herbal teas instead of tea with milk.
- Sprinkle cooked vegetables with herbs such as parsley instead of butter.
- Use a good-quality margarine made from polyunsaturated fat instead of butter.
- Avoid butter in sandwiches; moisten the bread with tahini, yeast extract, or a similar savory spread.

Salt

We need less than 1/7th of an ounce of salt per day and we can get this from whole, fresh foods, yet we add salt to our food and take in about ten to twelve times as much as we need. There are links between intake of salt and high blood pressure, a condition which can lead to other circulatory problems, such as heart disease and strokes.

Salt is sodium chloride. Sodium and potassium together help to regulate the body fluids, and the balance is a delicate one (see *Minerals*, p.24). Too much salt can upset the balance and cause fluid to be retained in the body. The kidneys also have to work harder to get rid of the excess salt.

Avoiding salt
Most of the salt we eat comes from processed foods. Canned vegetables, for example, may have as much as 200 percent more sodium than fresh ones, so it is not just obvious things like potato chips that you have to watch. High-salt foods include many canned and packaged soups, pickles, sauces, butter, and margarine, as well as plenty of unexpected ones, such as breakfast cereals. Many of the additives contained in processed foods are sodium-based.

The best strategy is to cut out all processed foods and, when cooking, simply leave salt out of a recipe, or use one of the alternatives listed at right. Give your taste buds a chance to get the flavor of a dish. Adding salt at the table is often just a habit, sometimes an addiction; you will probably find it easier to give up salt if you reduce the amount you add gradually.

HOW TO CUT DOWN ON SALT
• Use a low-sodium salt. • Use gomasio or herb salt instead of ordinary, table salt. • Use miso as a savory spread. • Sprinkle vegetables with fresh herbs, spices, or lemon juice instead of adding salt during cooking. • Use miso, shoyu, tamari, or low-sodium soysauce instead of salt to flavor soups and stews.

Alternatives
Even though there are very few low-sodium salt substitutes, there are several substitute flavorings. Some of them are highly flavored and because of this, they will help you cut down on your daily intake of salt.

Low-sodium salt: Half-sodium salt and half-potassium salt, this is helpful in making the transition between using salt and not using it.

Herb salt: This is salt with herbs. While it is just as salty, it has more flavor and will, therefore, help you to use less salt.

Gomasio: A mixture of toasted, crushed sesame seeds and salt.

Miso: A seasoning made from soybeans fermented with salt and wheat or barley, which has the consistency of a dense spread. It can be stored for several months but should not be subjected to extremes of temperature.

Shoyu and tamari: Dark liquids with a salty taste (see *Seasonings and flavorings*, p.90), these can be added to any savory dish. Shoyu is made from soybeans, wheat, salt, and water. Tamari is usually made without wheat.

Low-sodium baking soda: This is a useful substitute for baking soda, which is high in salt. Mix equal parts of rice flour or arrowroot, cream of tartar, and potassium bicarbonate.

Sugar

We know that refined sugar can make us fat, rot our teeth, and that it is linked with diabetes. So why do we in the Western world eat on average 2 pounds of refined sugar a week each? Is sugar addictive? The culprit is sucrose in the form of white or brown sugar. The way that nature packages sugar, along with fiber, vitamins, minerals, and water – as, for

example, in fresh fruit and vegetables – ensures that we do not eat too much. Refined sugar, on the other hand, gives only calories.

Whatever we eat raises the level of blood glucose (blood sugar). Provided glucose is released slowly and steadily during digestion, the blood sugar level is maintained within normal limits, sustaining mental and physical ability, helping us to concentrate and keeping our emotions balanced. All goes well when unrefined, high-fiber carbohydrates (both

Sugar-free desserts
Many delicious desserts – such as baked millet pudding with stewed apricots, and poached pears with carob sauce – can be made by using honey and other natural sweeteners in place of refined sugar.

starches and sugars) are eaten because these are digested slowly, but a concentrated supply of refined sugar is absorbed quickly and raises blood sugar to high levels. The pancreas sends insulin to lower the sugar level, causing a rapid fall, which leaves a craving for more sugar. It is a vicious circle, causing bursts of energy followed by fatigue and moody ups and downs. If the pancreas cannot cope with so many sudden demands for insulin, this may lead to diabetes. The acid-producing bacteria that attack teeth love sugar, since it reacts with saliva to produce just the right environment.

Sugar is also a drain on nutrients, especially B vitamins and calcium, which are used in metabolizing sugar. Naturally sweet foods like dates often contain enough of the B vitamins to compensate, as do unrefined carbohydrates. Refined sugar, which lacks nutrients, draws more nutrients away from the body's supplies.

There appear to be links between sugar intake and hyperactivity in children, and heart disease. Too much sugar also increases the level of triglycerides (fats) in the blood, and increase in fats may be associated with circulatory disorders such as arterial sclerosis.

As much as three-quarters of the sugar we eat is found in manufactured foods, and not just obvious ones like carbonated drinks. A surprising number of savory foods contain sugar, among them soups, sauces, pickles, ready-made salads, and canned vegetables.

Alternatives to sugar

It is possible to avoid packaged sugar altogether by using unrefined natural sweeteners.

Honey: This contains fructose and glucose. It has slightly fewer calories than sucrose and is sweeter, so you use less. It contains traces of vitamins and minerals. Honey can be used as a sweetener in drinks, on food such as yogurt, or in cooking.

Molasses: This is the residue left after extracting sugar from cane or beet, which contains minerals, especially calcium and iron, and vitamins. It is sucrose, not fructose, but it has a strong flavor so you will find that you do not need to use very much.

Maple syrup: This is not as sweet as honey and is largely sucrose, but it does contain calcium and potassium.

Malt extract: A product of beer-making, malt extract contains maltose, which is far less sweet than sucrose. It has a strong flavor and contains iron and some of the B vitamins. Other grain syrups have a similar taste.

Fruit juice concentrates: Undiluted, these can be used instead of sugar in cakes and cereals. In the refrigerator, these will keep, undiluted, for about 3–5 weeks.

Dried fruit purées: These make excellent sugar substitutes in baking – the sweetest is date purée. To make fruit purée, chop the fruit finely, cover it with water and simmer, for 10–15 minutes, until the fruit is soft enough to mash. Cream it in with the fats as you would sugar. 1 to 2 ounces dates is equal to about 1 ounce of sugar.

HOW TO CUT DOWN ON SUGAR

- Do without sugar in hot drinks.
- Buy sugar-free breakfast cereals or make your own Swiss-style muesli at home.
- Avoid fruit drinks and instead drink unsweetened fruit juice or mineral water.
- Use less sugar than called for in recipes.
- Eat ice cream and candies only rarely.
- Replace desserts with fruit, lowfat cheese, or yogurt, perhaps with an unrefined natural sweetener.
- Eat fresh fruit and raw vegetables.
- Avoid processed foods as much as possible.
- Buy sugar-free or reduced-sugar jams, or switch to savory spreads such as miso (see p. 89).
- Check labels on processed foods.

Additives

While most nutritionists caution against too much fat, salt, and sugar in your diet, many also advise cutting down on the consumption of food additives. What are food additives? Any substance that does not naturally occur in the food we eat. This includes preservatives, colorings, flavorings, flavor enhancers, stabilizers, emulsifiers, and sweeteners.

Most food additives have no nutritional value and are added to commercially-prepared food to prolong its shelf life, add flavor, color or texture, or assist in the processing. Different laws exist from country to country governing the use of food additives, the general rule being that additives must be safe and not used in greater quantities than necessary.

Are additives dangerous? That's a question that has been hotly debated for years by doctors, nutritionists, and consumer advocates. Nearly 3,000 additives are considered "safe" by the United States Food and Drug Administration (FDA), the government agency responsible for keeping the foods we eat safe. But many health-conscious individuals question the safety of FDA guidelines and prefer to limit their intake of food additives.

Avoiding Additives

Additives are now so commonplace that the best way to avoid them is to eat as many whole, fresh foods as possible. As it is not always possible, or practical, to avoid processed foods, be sure to carefully read the ingredient labels of the foods you buy. Compare different brands and purchase the products which contain the smallest amount of food additives.

Common food additives

Antioxidants: BHA (butylated hydroxytoluene) and BHT (butylated hydroxyanisole) are two of the most commonly used antioxidants. These preservatives prevent fats from turning rancid and prolong shelf life. There have been new studies done that have linked both BHA and BHT with cancer, stunted growth in children and other ailments. *Artificial Sweeteners:*

Saccharin, sorbitol and aspartame (NutraSweet) add sweetness to foods and beverages without adding calories. As with now-banned cyclamate sweeteners, their safety is questionable.

Bleaching agents: Used to whiten flour, bleaching agents such as potassium bromide and sodium stearyl fumarate destroy most of the nutrients not already removed in refining.

Emulsifiers & Stabilizers: By preventing the separation of fats, liquids and solids, these improve the texture of prepared foods. Many are derived from natural sources, such as alginates and carrageenan (seaweed derivatives), guar gum (a thickening agent made from a soy-bean like legume), lecithin (a dairy-based product), pectin (a thickener prepared from fruits) and vegetable gums. Artificial additives in this category include diglycerides, monoglycerides, polysorbates, and sorbitan monostearate.

Flavorings: New regulations require manufacturers to spell out each flavor additive by name. This will help those allergic to milk or wheat-derived flavorings.

Flavor Enhancers: The two most commonly used flavor enhancers are Monosodium glutamate (MSG) and Hydolyzed vegetable protein. Both are used to improve the taste of everything from baby food to canned soups. MSG has been known to cause headaches, dizziness, and chest pains.

Food Dyes: Only five artificial dyes have been approved as safe, yet they appear in products as diverse as smoked fish and after-dinner mints. Colorings extracted from natural sources include annatto, caramel, carrot oil and dehydrated beets. The safety of caramel, a burnt sugar extract, is currently under review by the Food and Drug Administration.

Humectants: Used to retain moisture, freshness and texture, glycerol monostearate, propylene glycol and sorbitol can be found in cake mixes, baked goods, candies, marshmallows and shredded coconut.

Preservatives: Considered "justifiable" additives by many nutritionists, preservatives let us enjoy out-of-season foods, prevent oils and fats from turning rancid and protect us against ailments associated with consuming spoiled foods. Unfortunately, many of these additives are of questionable safety. Commonly used preservatives include nitrates, nitrites, calcium propionate, sodium benzoate, sodium propionate, and sulfites.

Nitrates and nitrites: Nitrates are used in bacon, frankfurters and luncheon meats in order to turn meat pink, and prevent the growth of bacteria that causes botulism, (commonly known as sausage poisoning). However, during digestion, nitrates may become nitrites which decrease the level of oxygen being carried around the body by the red blood cells. There is also evidence that nitrates and nitrites both readily convert to cancer-causing nitrosamines during cooking and digestion.

Sulfites: These help preserve vitamin C, but destroy vitamins B_1 and E, and have now been banned from use on fresh fruits and vegetables except potatoes. Sulfites can cause hives, shortness of breath, and on rare occasions, death for asthmatics. All other products containing sulfites (including wine and beer) must list the additives on the label. To avoid sulfites, do not consume products that contain sulphur dioxide, sodium metabisulfite, potassium metabisulfite, potassium bisulfite, sodium bisulfite, and sodium sulfite.

Additives in alcohol

Sulphur dioxide occurs naturally in wine as a by-product of the fermentation process. In addition, it is added to wine during the bottling process to prolong its shelf-life. Under US law, all wine labels must indicate that sulfites are included. However, producers do not have to state the amount. Sulphur dioxide in wine has been found to cause an allergic reaction known as urticaria or nettle rash. Sulfites in wine can provoke attacks in asthma sufferers, since the fumes are inhaled as the wine is swallowed. Sulphur dioxide may also aggravate the more painful symptoms of a hangover.

Casein, a protein derived from cow's milk, which is commonly used to clarify both red and white wine, can cause allergic reactions.

Other additives found in alcohol include *kieselguhr*, a powder derived from fossils, and *bentonite*, a clay which contains aluminium. When taken internally, aluminium is considered to be a potential health risk.

One additive, DEPC (diethyl pyrocarbonate) has been banned in alcoholic beverages by the Food and Drug Administration (FDA) because it forms urethane, a known carcinogen in animals. Urethane is, in fact, produced naturally in the fermentation and distillation processes of alcoholic drinks, although the amounts are small, the effects may be cumulative.

The highest quantities of urethane are found in liquors such as bourbon, sherry, and fruit brandies. There is, however, some controversy surrounding this issue: Whilst the American Council on Science and Health consider the evidence inconclusive, the FDA consider urethane to be more hazardous.

Whilst complete labeling is not compulsory, at least it is possible to make an informed choice when purchasing alcohol. It is worth trying organic wines. Although they are not as easily available, they may contain substantially less sulphur dioxide. However, there is no actual legal definition of an organic wine, so look for a certification label on the bottle.

Cakes and cookies
Whole-food cakes and cookies are full of vitamins and fiber from the fruit and whole-wheat flour, as well as being satisfyingly filling and full of flavor.

HOW TO AVOID ADDITIVES

- Avoid all processed foods.
- Wash all fresh fruit and vegetables thoroughly before eating raw or cooking.
- Look out for new additive-free products in health food stores and supermarkets.
- Use whole-wheat flour. Until you are used to baking with whole-wheat flour, use half whole-wheat and half all-purpose.
- Buy organically produced food whenever possible.
- Buy bread from stores you know do not use additives, or make your own.
- Read food labels carefully.

Drinks

Drinks are another potential problem area. Carbonated drinks, fruit drinks, and mixers contain additives and sugar, while tea and coffee contain caffeine and tannin.

Caffeine and tannin

I have never heard of a caffeine death, but the lethal dose is said to be about ⅓ ounce. To take in 250mg, the point at which caffeine qualifies medically as a stimulant, you would need to drink 19 cups of cocoa, four to six cups of tea or instant coffee, three to five 12-ounce bottles of Cola beverages, or only one to two cups of freshly ground coffee. Caffeine makes the heart beat more rapidly and irregularly. It makes you feel more alert when you drink it, but too much can cause anxiety, restlessness, and sleeplessness. It raises blood pressure and levels of fats in the blood. It also makes the pancreas produce more insulin, which lowers blood sugar levels, and makes the stomach more acid.

Sensitivity to coffee and tea varies from one person to another. Caffeine is suspected of preventing iron from being properly used, and of causing deficiencies of certain B vitamins. It may also reduce the absorption of some other vitamins and minerals. Unexplained allergic reactions, including rashes and migraine, sometimes stop when caffeine is excluded from the diet. As well as caffeine, tea contains tannin, which tends to cause constipation.

Alcoholic drinks

A little alcohol may not be a bad thing because it acts as a tranquilizer, or relaxant, and may lessen the likelihood of heart disease. Alcohol is not, as some people think, a stimulant. Alcohol-tolerance is related to size, so women often take less than men; a recommended safe amount is either two glasses of beer, two glasses of wine or sherry, or a double measure of liquor per day. Too much alcohol causes dehydration, puts a strain on the liver, and exhausts supplies of B vitamins. Heavy drinkers can suffer malnutrition because alcohol, like sugar, offers no nourishment, only calories. Pregnant or lactating women should be wary of alcohol because it crosses the placenta and also passes into breast milk.

Alternatives

If you want to cut down on your intake of additives, sugar, caffeine, tannin, or alcohol, try one of the drinks below.

Decaffeinated coffee and low-tannin tea: This coffee is available as beans or instant coffee. It contains minute traces of caffeine – no more than 3mg per 3½-ounce jar – but it can cause digestive disorders. Low-tannin tea is made in the same way as ordinary tea but has a lower tannin content.

Cereal coffees: These are made up of roasted grains such as wheat or barley, and sometimes dandelion or chicory, all of which are good for the digestion.

Herbal teas: These come in a vast range and are best drunk without milk or sugar. You can add lemon juice, or sweeten them with fruit juice concentrate or honey, if you prefer.

Carob: A cocoa substitute, this makes a good milky drink when flavored with cinnamon and honey. Make it with skim milk.

Yogurt drink: To make a refreshing drink, beat yogurt until it is frothy, then dilute it with water or orange juice and garnish it with mint.

Fruit juices: These are available from a wide variety of fruit. Look out for those made with organically grown fruit, but if you cannot find them, buy pure, unsweetened juices.

Mineral water: This can be bought either carbonated or still, and makes a refreshing drink. Mix it with unsweetened fruit juice.

Chapter Three

The Pantry

One of the joys of trying out a different style of cooking is undoubtedly discovering a fresh range of dishes with new combinations of tastes and textures. Based as it is on the cuisines of many different countries, vegetarian cookery draws on a wide variety of ingredients, some of which will be familiar; others, such as sea vegetables and soy products, less so. This section is intended as a guide to those ingredients that play a central part in vegetarian cooking, and that feature in the recipes in this book, from the everyday staples such as cereals and dried beans and peas, to different seasonings and flavorings.

Naturally, there is no need to buy every type of bean or cereal product shown here – you can gradually add to your supplies as you try out different recipes. A selection of fresh foods is also illustrated, including some of the less-common vegetables and whole food or vegetarian substitutes for animal products.

Keeping stock

Once you have changed to a vegetarian diet, it is well worth stocking up on the vegetables, dried beans and peas, fruits, herbs, spices and special flavorings that are needed to cook the dishes.

Grains

Wheat, rice, barley, oats, millet, rye, and corn (maize) are the world's major food grains or cereals, and all belong to the immense family of grasses. Another grain of culinary interest, buckwheat, is the seed not of a grass but of a herbaceous plant. Wheat, millet, and oats are the richest sources of protein, but all unrefined grains provide fiber, carbohydrate, minerals, and vitamins – especially the B vitamins.

For thousands of years grains have been the staple foods that have kept people alive: wheat, rye, barley, and oats in temperate climates; rice, corn, and millet in the tropics, and subtropics. Most of the world's populations still eat the staple produce that grows in their back yards, but in the affluent countries meat has pushed grains out of their primary position. In these countries grains are often refined and processed to the point where all of the fiber and many of the essential nutrients have been lost, along with two other very important ingredients: taste and texture.

Unrefined whole grains still contain the germ, an important source of oils, proteins, and minerals and bran, a valuable source of fiber. They may be bought whole or cracked, flaked, parboiled, steamed or toasted, all of which help to shorten cooking time and make them easier to digest.

Buying
Most health food and whole food stores sell grains in bulk form from berries to flour. Choose a store where you can rely on the stock being fresh. Supermarkets often stock a variety of packaged grains. Read the labels and make sure that you are getting the whole grain or its product. Also, if you care about organically grown food, check for this information. With bread, for example, be sure to buy only the loaves labeled "whole-wheat" because they will be made from flour containing the whole grain. Bread simply labeled "wheat bread" can contain a varying proportion of white and whole-wheat flours. The brown color can come from "caramel coloring," which will be listed on the label.

Storing
Whole grains keep indefinitely in cool, dry conditions in an airtight container, but the longer they are stored the longer they take to cook. Flakes and flours do not keep so long and are best used within 3–6 months because the milling process exposes the oil contained in the germ, which eventually goes rancid, particularly in oats, and the vitamin E content is lost. Unstabilized wheat germ, that is wheat germ that has not been heat-treated to remove the most volatile oils, should be kept in the refrigerator. Stabilized wheat germ keeps longer, but should be used quickly.

Cooking
To cook whole grains, first rinse them to remove surface dust. Choose a pan with a tight-fitting lid, or use a pressure cooker. Rub a little oil around the pan to prevent the grains from sticking – this will also make the pan easier to clean. One cup of grains is enough for 2–3 people.

Put some water in the pan (see the table opposite for quantities) and bring to a boil. Put in the grains, bring to a boil again, then cover the pan and simmer very gently until the water is absorbed. Do not stir unnecessarily because this tends to make the grains sticky, and do not toughen the grains by adding any salt until just before the end of the cooking time.

There are simple ways to vary the basic method. Sauté the grain lightly in a little oil or shoyu before adding boiling water (this is good with barley, buckwheat, and millet in particular); add spices and vegetables for flavor, particularly saffron, ginger, coriander, garlic, or onions. Mix different grains – rice with wheat or barley – for more texture and taste.

The softer grains – millet, rice, and buckwheat – make excellent croquettes. Rice, barley, and millet are good for sweet puddings, and buckwheat, wheat, and oats for substantial breakfast porridges. Cracked grains absorb water more easily and cook quickly. Bulgur wheat, which is steamed, cracked, and toasted, needs soaking but no further cooking. It is ideal in salads such as the Middle Eastern

PREPARATION AND COOKING TIMES FOR WHOLE GRAINS				
Type of grain	Preparation before cooking	Amount of liquid per 1 cup of grain	Average cooking time	Pressure cooking
Wheat	soak overnight (8–12 hours)	4 cups	50–60 minutes	20 minutes
Rice long-grain short-grain	can be toasted or lightly fried	1¾–2 cups 1¾–2 cups	25–30 minutes 20–25 minutes	10 minutes 8–10 minutes
Wild rice	–	3 cups	50–60 minutes	20 minutes
Corn	–	plenty of water	5–10 minutes	
Barley	toast	4 cups	50–60 minutes	20 minutes
Oats	can be toasted	3 cups	30–35 minutes	12 minutes
Rye	soak overnight (8–12 hours)	3 cups	50–60 minutes	20 minutes
Millet	can be toasted or lightly fried	2½–3 cups	20 minutes	8 minutes
Buckwheat	toast or lightly fry	2–2½ cups	20 minutes	8 minutes

Taboulleh, where it is mixed with herbs, oil, lemon juice, onions, and tomatoes. Flakes are used in breakfast cereals (Swiss-style muesli or granola) and as versatile toppings for either sweet or savory dishes. You can vary the proportions of flakes to flour. Substitute granola for the flakes if you want a sweeter tasting crumb topping.

Swiss-style muesli is generally a combination of various flakes, mainly oats, with seeds, nuts, and dried fruit. A good version is one nearer to the original Swiss formula muesli, with more emphasis on fresh fruit. For one person, soak 2 tablespoons rolled oats in 2 tablespoons water for 1–2 hours (or overnight). Just before eating, stir in the juice of an orange, 1 tablespoon ground almonds, and a whole unpeeled apple, grated.

Leftover, cooked, grains make excellent salads when mixed with beans or vegetables, or they can be added to soups or casseroles. Cooked grains will keep for two days in the refrigerator and can be successfully frozen. To reheat, first thaw, either overnight in the refrigerator, or for several hours (the exact time depends on how large a portion you are thawing) at room temperature.

Turn the grains into an oiled dish, cover with foil, and heat in a moderate oven 350°F for 15–20 minutes.

Of the grains, wheat, millet and oats are the richest source of protein, but all unrefined grains also provide fiber, carbohydrate, minerals, and vitamins.

YEAST

Yeast for baking is available both fresh and dried. Active dry yeast can be found in the baking supplies section of most supermarkets. The ¼-ounce (7g) packages have a shelf life of one to two years, but be sure to check the expiration date, which is stamped on the package. Compressed fresh yeast is sold in 2-ounce (15g) cakes and is harder to find. Look for it in the refrigerator case of your supermarket. As fresh yeast is viable for only two to three weeks, it is important to check the freshness date on the wrapper. Fresh yeast must be kept dry and stored in the refrigerator. One package of active yeast is equal to one cake of compressed fresh yeast. Both types yield equally good results, the main difference being the temperatures and liquids required to dissolve them. Dry yeast requires hot water (110°F to 115°F). Fresh yeast dissolves in lukewarm water or milk (80°F to 90°F).

VARIETIES OF WHEAT

The whole berry or grain is by far the most nutritious form of wheat; when cooked, it is chewy and substantial. It retains its outer covering, or bran, which contains valuable vitamins, minerals, and fat, as well as being high in fiber, and the germ, which is only 2 percent of the grain but contains the bulk of the nutrients. The rest of the grain, some 70 percent, is the endosperm and consists mostly of the starch used to make flour. When the grain is milled a rich brown flour is obtained.

Wheat flakes

Bulgur wheat

Whole-wheat berries

Cracked wheat

Wheat germ

Semolina

Whole-wheat flour

Unbleached all-purpose flour

Bran

Whole-wheat and white flours

Couscous

Wheat

The most universally grown and the most important of all food grains, wheat (*Triticum vulgare*) is available in a wide variety of forms, from the whole berry to flour, and wheat flour is used more than any other for making bread, cakes, pastry, and pasta. Both wheat germ and bran can be bought separately and added to breakfast cereals, breads, and cakes or just used as toppings.

Cracked or kibbled wheat is produced by cracking whole-wheat berries between rollers so that they will cook more quickly, in only 20 minutes, in fact. If they are then hulled, steamed, and roasted they are known as bulgur wheat, or burghul, and need little or no cooking. Wheat flakes are similar, but rolled flatter and often toasted to a golden brown.

All the above are variants on the whole-wheat berry, which is often subjected to further milling to produce lighter, more widely appreciated results. During this process, the two valuable constituents of wheat germ and bran are lost.

Flour is the form in which wheat is most easily available. Most of today's flour is produced by roller-milling, a process that involves high temperatures and consequent loss of vitamins and flavor. For this reason, stone-ground flour is generally considered preferable, although it is more expensive and slightly coarser in texture.

Whole-wheat flour is made from the whole berries, retaining all of the nutrients. White all-purpose flour has had all the bran and germ removed; unbleached white flour is preferable in whole-food cooking if you do not want to use all whole-wheat flour, because it has not been chemically treated.

Bread is the end product of most of the world's flour. Leavened bread is made mainly from wheat, the only grain high in gluten, a protein that stretches to form an impermeable skin over the thousands of bubbles of gas formed when yeast ferments. Bread made with hand or strong flour has a lighter consistency than bread made with soft flour. Whole-wheat flour gives a rather dense loaf, unbleached all-purpose flour produces one with a light texture, which has some percentage of the nutrients still intact. A mixture of the two is often considered a good compromise.

Semolina is produced from the starchy part of the grain, the endosperm. It is available as medium or coarse meal and used for desserts or gnocchi. Semolina from durum wheat is used for making commercial pasta, which would be otherwise difficult to make with "soft" flour. Fine semolina grains coated with flour are known as couscous, the basis of the North African dish.

Rice

Rice can be divided into two main categories, long-grain and short-grain. Properly cooked, long-grain rice has dry, separate grains. It goes well with curries, pilafs, stews, and chicken or meat dishes. Short-grain rice has a softer texture and is stickier when cooked, making it particularly suitable for use in Japanese and Chinese cooking.

Brown (whole grain) rice has a chewy texture and nutty flavor that makes white rice seem bland, stripped as it is of the outer layers and germ, and with them most of the nutrients. It contains bran which gives additional protein, iron, calcium, and vitamin B, but it can take quite a lot longer to cook than white rice.

Rice can also be found in the form of flakes and flour; the flour has a light consistency and small quantities are good in bread and cakes. The bran and germ removed when rice is milled are sold as rice bran, an excellent source of vitamin B, as well as minerals and protein. Small quantities can be added to cakes, cookies, or be mixed in with crumble or nutty toppings.

Wild rice is not actually a rice but a grain. Nevertheless, it looks like rice and is used in the same way. It is also a member of the grass family. Originating in North America, it is gray-brown in color. It is often served on its own so as not to submerge its characteristically delicate, subtle flavor, a little like that of artichokes. Wild rice can also be served mixed with some brown rice and used as a stuffing for various bakes and roasts.

Basmati rice
This has the finest flavor of most white rice, although, like all white rices, a high proportion of nutrients have been removed by milling. Brown basmati is also available.

Oryza sativa
Rice
Brown rice is, like the wheat berry, the whole natural grain, unprocessed. The type most commonly found is long-grain or indica *rice, much grown in India.*

Rice flour
This is usually made from white rice. Because of its lack of gluten, it is useful for those on low-gluten diets.

Rice flakes
These have been processed so that they cook quickly, in about 10 minutes. They can be used to thicken soups, stews, and casseroles.

Zizania aquatica
Wild rice
Wild rice is not a rice, although it looks like one. Its grains are longer and more slender, dark gray-brown when raw, turning slightly purplish when cooked. It is native to North America.

Japonica
Short-grain rice
As its Latin name indicates, this is popular in Japan as well as in parts of China. Another type of short-grain rice is grown in Italy and is generally used to make delicious risotto dishes.

Corn (maize)

This originated in Central America, where it was the staple grain of the Incas, Mayas, and Aztecs. Its popularity has spread not only to North America but also to Europe, where it is used for such national dishes as polenta in Italy and mamaliga in Romania. Unlike other whole grains, it is not usually dried but is eaten fresh. There are three main varieties: dent corn, which supplies commercial cornmeal;

corn on the cob, or sweetcorn, the form in which we know it as a fresh vegetable; and popcorn, the popular snack.

Cornmeal is available finely or coarsely ground. Stone ground or water ground is best, because the germ is not removed. It is too low in gluten to make leavened bread, but mixes well with wheat to give muffins and pancakes a distinctive taste and color. Other important corn products are cooking oil (see p. 94) and corn syrup, which is used for sweetening in many baked goods (see p. 93).

Coarse cornmeal

Fine cornmeal

Zea mays
Corn
Known as maize in Europe, corn originated in Central America. Popcorn is a variety of it with a very hard endosperm, which explodes when heated.

Cornmeal
Another variety of corn is used to produce cornmeal, both coarse and fine: this is sometimes bolted, or sieved. This process removes the bran and some of the fiber but makes little difference to the product nutritionally.

Oats

Still a popular food in Scotland, northern England, and Ireland, oats probably originated in northern Europe. They are made into oatcakes and parkin, or used for soups, as well as for the traditional porridge. They are higher in protein and fats than other grains and rich in B vitamins and iron.

Oats are most often found as rolled oats which cook quickly. Rolled oats can be used for oatmeal, granola, Swiss-style muesli, and crumb toppings, as well as for oatcakes, to which they add a crunchy texture. Steel-cut oats are used for oatmeal and as a crunchy coating for croquettes. Mixed with wheat flour, oats improve the taste of bread.

Avena sativa
Oats
The whole oat grain is known as a groat. It can be used for oatmeal, but it requires a fairly long cooking time.

Rolled oats
Rolled oats come from groats that have been broken by rolling; heat can also be applied to prevent the oil from going rancid, and thus improve shelf life.

Processed oats
These are now generally available in three grades: coarse, medium, and fine. A little added to wheat flour gives flavor to bread.

Old-fashioned jumbo oats
These are similar to rolled oats but, as their name implies, larger. They are also heat-treated to reduce the cooking time.

Rolled oats

Old-fashioned jumbo oats

Processed oats

Barley

The hulled grain is sometimes called pot barley. Pearled barley has been polished and has lost most of the bran, germ, and vitamin B.

Low in gluten, barley flour will not make leavened bread (unless mixed with wheat flour), but the grayish, flat bread made from it is sweet-tasting and delicious to eat. Barley syrup, sometimes known as malt extract, is used as a sweetening agent in cooking.

Hordeum vulgare
Whole barley
Barley is still important for food in some parts of the world, particularly Japan, although elsewhere it has been superseded as a food crop and is used mainly

for brewing. It compares well with other grains nutritionally, and is particularly high in niacin. Like other grains, it is available in flakes and as flour. The inclusion of barley flour adds sweetness to bread. It is an old food crop known to the Greeks and Romans.

Barley flakes

Barley flour

Millet

Richer than other grains nutritionally, millet is a particularly good source of iron and the B vitamins. Its delicate flavor can seem bland at first, but it mixes well with other flavors and makes an excellent alternative to rice in risotto or milk pudding. Millet flour is often used to make unleavened breads and pancakes, and the grains can be mixed with dried beans and peas, and used in soups and stews.

Panicum miliaceum
Millet
This grain is prolific and easy to grow but has only recently been considered suitable for growing in the West, although it has long been an important crop in Africa and Asia, especially northern China. It is related to sorghum, a type of millet which is an important crop in Africa, and is the staple food of the Hunzas, the Himalayan tribe who are well known for their longevity.

Millet flakes
These can be used like other flakes in cereal and sprinkled on food as a topping.

Buckwheat

This is not a cereal grain at all but the seed of a herbaceous plant related to dock and rhubarb. It is supposed to have originated in China and is now a staple food in Russia and Poland. The iron and mineral content is high and it contains all the B vitamins and rutin. The seeds need to be roasted by stir-frying before they can be cooked and served in the same way as rice. Kasha, a porridge-like cooked cereal, is popular in many parts of the Soviet Union.

Buckwheat can also be ground into a flour that can be used to make pancakes and crisp, thin crêpes. Hulled and crushed buckwheat is called groats or kasha. It comes in fine, medium and coarse grains, and can be added to soups or served with gravy.

Fagopyrum esculentum
Whole buckwheat
This is also sometimes called Saracen corn or wheat as it was supposed to have been introduced to Europe by the Crusaders.

Roasted buckwheat
Buckwheat is popular for its delicious flavor;
roasting is the usual way of preparing the grains
for cooking.

Buckwheat flour
This is strong and dark, and is often mixed with wheat
flour. It is a good flour for making crêpes, and soba,
which are a type of Japanese noodles.

Rye

The whole berries can be treated like rice or
wheat berries, or cracked to produce grits or
flakes, which cook quicker. Rye is a good
source of B vitamins, especially B_2 and B_3, and
the minerals potassium and magnesium. It also
contains rutin, once known as vitamin P, which
is good for helping circulatory complaints.

Rye flakes

Secale cereale
Rye
Rye is popular in northern and eastern Europe, and
parts of Russia, where its distinctive sour taste is much
appreciated, particularly in bread. The berries can be
made into dark rye flour, or they can be partially
hulled and made into light flour. Although rye contains
gluten, it is not the same sort as that found in wheat
and will not leaven bread, so that most rye bread is, in
fact, made from a mixture of rye and wheat.

Rye flour

Beans, Peas, and Lentils

Collectively known as dried beans or legumes, these have the advantage that they are cheap to buy, readily available (although some of the less common ones may not be so easy to find), and keep well. Most tend to be bland in taste, but cooked in combination with other ingredients they have a capacity for amalgamating with them, especially with stronger flavors, and enhancing them: chickpeas with tahini (sesame seed paste), lentils with spices, and lima or fava beans with onions, tomatoes, and peppers. Cooked dishes generally improve on being left for several hours or overnight for the full development of flavor before reheating. They may not be the answer if you need to prepare a meal or a snack in a hurry, but they are ideal if you prefer to do the preparation beforehand.

Dried beans and grains take the place of meat in a vegetarian diet because, used together, they make high-quality protein. Apart from soybeans, no one bean or grain has all the amino acids in sufficient amounts to make a high-quality protein by itself, but when grains and beans are eaten together, what is lacking in one can be made up by what is in the other.

Dried beans and peas are also good sources of protein, fiber, carbohydrate, minerals, and vitamins. They may lack vitamin C, but that can be obtained by sprouting them. The vitamin content increases dramatically with sprouting (as much as 600 times for vitamin C). Depending on the dried bean or pea chosen, sprouts are often a good source of vitamins A, B, D, E, and K.

Soybeans are higher in calories than other beans because they have a higher fat content. They also contain some carbohydrates, calcium, and B vitamins. Tofu (bean curd), made from soybeans, is a cheap, nourishing food from the Far East. It is tasteless, so it needs to have flavor added. The firmest kind, which is like white cheese, is often eaten like a piece of meat with a tasty sauce over it, or it may be added to main course vegetable dishes. Softer, custard-like kinds are used to enrich and thicken, much as non-vegetarians use cream or yogurt. Tofu keeps for a month in a vacuum package but, once opened, it should be used within a week. Store it in water (which needs to be changed daily) in the refrigerator.

One common objection to legumes is that they tend to cause gas. The best way to counter this is to accustom yourself to eating them gradually, making sure that they are thoroughly cooked. Lentils and smaller beans are often found to be more digestible.

Buying and storing
It is becoming easier nowadays to find good-quality dried beans and peas. Buy them from a shop with a good turnover; although these do keep well, if they have spent a year sitting on a shelf they will take a very long time to cook. Choose beans or peas that look plump, brightly colored, and unwrinkled; these will be the freshest. Dried beans and peas are worth buying in bulk as they will keep in good condition for up to six months. All legumes keep best in cool, dry, dark conditions in airtight containers. They can be kept in glass jars, as long as they are not exposed to full sun, which impairs flavor and nutrients.

Preparation
All dried beans and peas, but especially lentils, need to be picked over for stones and sand and given a rinse to wash off the surface dust. Lentils and split peas are then ready to cook, but beans and whole peas should be soaked overnight before cooking. Use plenty of water, remembering that dried beans and peas absorb water and will swell up to between two and three times their original bulk. There is a quick method, which is the equivalent of an overnight soak: bring the beans or peas to a boil in plenty of water, boil hard for 3–5 minutes and leave to stand in the water for an hour.

Cooking
After soaking, drain and rinse again. Some vitamins will be lost in the soaking water, but this is not crucial. Put in a saucepan, cover with plenty of fresh water, and bring to a boil. Skim off any scum. Do not salt the water; salt toughens the outer skins and cooking will take

SOAKING AND COOKING CHART FOR BEANS, PEAS, AND LENTILS

"Overnight" here means approximately 8–12 hours. All times given are only a rough guide, as cooking times can vary considerably depending on the age and origin of the crop. The first 10 minutes' cooking of all except lentils and split peas should be done at a fast boil, uncovered, to destroy any toxic elements on the outer skin, except soybeans,* which should boil hard for the first hour. Although lentils and split peas do not need not to be soaked overnight, they will cook faster if they are first steeped in boiling water for 15–30 minutes. Drain well before cooking them.

Type of bean	Recommended soak overnight	Average cooking time	Pressure cooking
Adzuki beans	yes	45 minutes	15 minutes
Black-eyed peas	yes	45–50 minutes	15 minutes
Black beans	yes	50–60 minutes	20 minutes
Cannellini	yes	45–50 minutes	15 minutes
Fava beans	yes	1½ hours	40 minutes
Flageolets	yes	45–50 minutes	15 minutes
Lima beans	yes	60–90 minutes	25–30 minutes
Mung beans	yes	30–45 minutes	15 minutes
Navy beans	yes	50–60 minutes	20 minutes
Pinto beans	yes	60–90 minutes	25–30 minutes
Red kidney beans	yes	45–50 minutes	15 minutes
Soybeans	yes	2–2½ hours*	45–50 minutes
Chickpeas	yes	60–90 minutes	25–30 minutes
Whole green peas	yes	60–90 minutes	25–30 minutes
Split peas	no	40–45 minutes	–
Whole lentils	no	30–45 minutes	12–15 minutes
Split lentils	no	15–30 minutes	–

longer. Vegetables, herbs, spices, or flavorings can be added: onions, garlic, carrots, other root vegetables, black pepper, ginger, or chili peppers. The addition of aniseed, dill, fennel, or caraway seeds – 1 teaspoon for 1⅓ cups dried beans – or a strip of the sea vegetable kombu (see p.92) helps digestion.

Soaking and cooking times vary. Lentils cook quite quickly without any soaking – red lentils cook in about 15 minutes, green lentils take slightly longer – but kidney beans need an hour or more after soaking. Soybeans need to boil for one hour. All but lentils and split peas need an initial ten minutes of boiling to destroy toxins found in the skins. After the preliminary boiling, turn the heat down until the water just simmers and cover the pot, but not too tightly. If you add a little oil this will prevent the beans or peas from boiling over and also give them a smoother texture. The cooking time also depends on how long the legume has been stored, and whether you want it for a salad or a purée: those for salads should be just tender, while those for a purée need longer cooking. Use the times given in the chart as a guide, and test the beans or peas for tenderness by pinching them lightly. An alternative cooking method is to use a pressure cooker. It cuts the cooking time by about two-thirds, and there is no need to worry about boiling as this happens automatically. Do not cook more than about 1 pound at a time, or they may froth up and block the safety valve. Timing needs to be precise: even a little overcooking may result in a purée, so use an ordinary saucepan if you are making, say, a bean salad, where the appearance is important.

Serving and keeping

All beans, peas, and lentils can be used as a basis for casseroles, and can be served as a simple side dish, perhaps as a purée: adzuki beans, flageolets, or mung beans have a subtle taste and are particularly suitable. Lima or fava beans, and the kidney beans, are often cooked with spices, herbs, and vegetables for a contrast of flavor. For croquettes, the most suitable are adzuki beans, lentils, mung beans, and black-eyed peas. All can also be used in soups, and this is the most common use for peas, both split and whole. Almost all beans and lentils are good eaten cold in salads, particularly with a vinaigrette dressing. Once cooked, beans, peas, and lentils will keep well for several days in a covered

container in the refrigerator, or they can be frozen – they retain their flavor excellently. Cool and open freeze them, then pack in rigid containers and label. For soups, a handful or two can be removed from the freezer and put straight into the soup near the end of the cooking time. For salads, allow them to thaw for about an hour at room temperature, or overnight in the refrigerator, then mix with the other vegetables or herbs and the dressing. Croquettes, cooked or uncooked, also freeze well: shape into patties, open freeze on trays, and pack in boxes with waxed paper between them. Thaw overnight in the refrigerator, or for 2 hours at room temperature.

The cooking liquid is well worth keeping. Any toxins will have been destroyed, and it makes an excellent base for soups, stews, and sauces. It will keep for 4–5 days in the refrigerator, and can be frozen.

Phaseolus angularis
Adzuki beans
These tiny, round, hard, dark red beans, also known as aduki beans, are very popular in the Far East, especially Japan. Rich in protein, they can also be made into flour.

Phaseolus vulgaris
Black beans
The shiny black outside contrasts with the white inside. Popular in Latin America, these are not the same as the Chinese black bean, a type of soybean, fermented, salted, and used as flavoring. Also called turtle beans.

Vigna unguiculata
Black-eyed peas
Also known as cowpeas, these are native to Central Africa, but were taken to the New World in the

sixteenth century. Not only the seeds are eaten: the immature pods can be cooked and the young shoots and leaves can be boiled like spinach or eaten raw in salads.

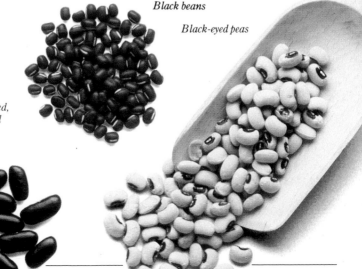

Black beans

Black-eyed peas

Adzuki beans

Vicia faba
Fava beans
Once eaten in quantity – they are no longer as popular – possibly because fava beans contain substances which, if eaten in quantity, can cause a blood disease which is known as favism.

Lima beans

Butter beans

Phaseolus lunatus
Lima beans and butter beans
Originating from tropical America, these are very similar, but lima beans tend to be smaller and sweeter and are an ingredient of the traditional Indian corn dish called succotash.

Whole green peas

Phaseolus vulgaris
Flageolet beans
Very popular in both France and Italy, flageolet beans have an unusually delicate, subtle taste and an attractive pale green color.

Split yellow peas

Phaseolus vulgaris
Cannellini
This is a white variety of the kidney bean which is much appreciated in Italy. A similar bean is widely grown in Argentina.

Phaseolus vulgaris
Navy beans
Navy beans are also known as small white beans or peas; larger white kidney beans are called Great Northern beans. Navy beans are the original beans used to make Boston baked beans.

Split green peas

Pisum sativum
Peas
Common peas are available fresh, canned, or frozen. They were formerly valuable as a dried vegetable, and in this form are available split or whole.

Lathyrus sativus
Ful medames
These small dark-brown beans are especially popular in Egypt, where they have given their name to a national dish in which they are baked with eggs, cumin, and garlic.

Whole mung beans

Split red lentils

Split mung beans

Phaseolus vulgaris
Pinto beans
Pinto beans are not unlike the speckled Italian borlotti beans. The name means "colored." They turn pink when cooked and are important in Mexican cooking.

Phaseolus aureus
Mung beans
Native to tropical Asia, the mung bean is still one of the most widely grown legumes. They can be used as a vegetable but are most popular as the source of bean sprouts.

Green lentils

Brown lentils

Glycine max
Soybeans
These are the most nutritious beans of all, containing all the essential amino acids. Originally from China, where their value has been recognized for nearly 5,000 years. The popular yellow and black beans can be cooked fresh, sprouted for salads, or turned into curd, paste, sauce, or milk. It can be used as a textured meat substitute.

Phaseolus vulgaris
Red kidney beans
Like all kidney beans, these are native to North America. This variety is particularly popular in Mexican cooking. It is also called the chili bean.

Lens esculenta
Lentils
One of the oldest crops, cultivated since prehistoric times, lentils are originally from the eastern Mediterranean, but can now be found all over the Middle East and India. They are available whole or split and come in a variety of colors.

Cicer arietinum
Chickpeas
Popular all over the Mediterranean, Middle East, and India where they are known as Bengul gram (the Indian word "gram" means dried bean). They are also known as garbanzos or garbanzo beans. High in protein, they are very nutrtious, and can be ground into flour.

Chickpeas

Nuts and Seeds

Botanically, nuts and seeds are the same: both have kernels containing the whole future plant in embryo and are a concentrated source of food.

A combination of mixed nuts and cereals with green vegetables makes a nutritionally adequate main course, and nuts give taste and texture to salads, cooked vegetables, and grains. By themselves, or with sunflower or pumpkin seeds, they make a good, satisfying snack. Watermelon and pomegranate seeds are also edible.

Buying

It is better to buy nuts in their shells: this protects the kernels and keeps them fresh. If you do want them shelled, buy loose nuts, preferably whole, as these tend to be of better quality. Avoid nuts that have already been coated in fat and salted. Seeds should always be bought whole.

Storing

Store in a cool place. Unshelled nuts will keep up to six months. Whole shelled nuts will stay in good condition for up to 3 months. Avoid storing in a warm place or their high fat content will turn the nuts rancid. Split, chopped, or ready ground nuts will go stale more quickly still and should be eaten within a 4–6 week period. Keep seeds in an airtight jar.

Preparation

Nuts can be blanched to remove the dark skin, roasted or toasted to improve their flavor (although there is a certain amount of nutrient loss), ground, which also makes them easier to digest, or, in the case of coconut, grated. Seeds, especially sunflower and sesame, are also good-toasted.

To blanch nuts, except for hazelnuts (filberts), put them in a bowl, cover with boiling water, and leave for a few minutes or until they can be popped out of their skins when gently pressed. If you are not using the skinned nuts immediately, drop them in cold water to keep them white. Hazelnuts should be baked in the oven (or toasted under the broiler) for 5 or 6 minutes. If they are then rubbed in a cloth, the fibrous skin will easily come away.

To roast nuts or seeds in the oven, spread them out in a single layer on a cookie sheet or baking pan. Sprinkle with a little oil. Put in a medium oven for about 10 minutes, and shake the pan two or three times to turn them and ensure even browning. You can also fry them, if you prefer. Use a heavy skillet and just enough oil – peanut, for preference – to grease the bottom lightly. Shake or stir the nuts or seeds over gentle heat until evenly browned. If you are prepared to watch them carefully, they will toast under a hot broiler in 2–3 minutes, but must be turned before they burn.

To skin chestnuts, slash each one with a sharp knife (take care, as the skins can be tough), drop them in boiling water and leave them for about 10 minutes. At the end of this time both the outer and inner skins should come away easily. If you prefer, use dried chestnuts which do not need shelling.

Nuts are easily ground: use a small grater, a nut mill, or a blender. A coffee mill, kept especially for the purpose, is ideal. Nuts tend to grind unevenly and it is easier to do a few at a time. Walnuts and Brazil nuts have a tendency to be greasy, and you may need to scrape around the sides of the mill once or twice to remove the ground mixture.

Cooking

As well as being eaten raw, nuts and seeds are used in loaves, croquettes, and casseroles, in cereal mixtures, and in crumb toppings. Peanut butter is the best known nut butter, but cashews, hazelnuts, and almonds also make good spreads and dips. Blend them with a little oil and salt to taste. Alternatively, mix equal quantities of nuts and water with a little oil and salt and blend. Nut butters will keep in the refrigerator for 4–6 weeks if made with only oil, for 3–4 days if made with water. They can also be frozen.

Nut creams and milks are easy to make and can form the basis for sauces or substitutes for cream to serve with desserts or cakes. Almond milk can be made by blending together

1½ tablespoons blanched ground almonds, ¾ cup water and 1 teaspoon honey. Cashew cream is made by blending ⅔ cup cashews, ½ cup cottage cheese, 1–2 tablespoons honey and up to ⅔ cup water until smooth. Both will keep in the refrigerator for up to 3–4 days.

COCONUT MILK

For fresh coconut milk empty 2 cups of grated coconut into a blender with 1¼ cups of very hot water. Blend for a few seconds. Pass the contents through a muslin-lined sieve. The milk will be thick. Unsweetened canned coconut milk is also available from Latin American and East and South Asian grocers.

Nuts

Shelled hazelnuts

Whole hazelnuts

Corylus avellana; C. maxima
Hazelnuts, cobs, filberts
Widely grown in Italy, France, and Turkey, these are low in fat and high in vitamins B and E.

Whole pistachios

Shelled pistachios

Ground almonds

Pistacia vera
Pistachios
Native to the Mediterranean and Middle East, where they are eaten as a snack, pistachios are prized for their bright green color.

Whole almond   *Slivered almonds*

Shelled almond   *Blanched almond*

Prunus amygdalus
Almonds
These are the most popular nuts of all. The sweet variety is the kind normally used; bitter almonds are toxic, but the unpleasant taste is a deterrent. Almonds have the highest protein content of any nut and are also rich in minerals, especially calcium.

Shelled peanuts, with and without skins

Whole (unshelled) peanuts

Arachis hypogaea
Peanuts
Peanuts are not true nuts but underground legumes.

Whole walnut

Anacardium occidentale
Cashews
The unusual fruit looks like an apple with the kidney-shaped nut hanging beneath it. The nutshell contains an acid and is removed before the nuts are sold.

Whole Brazil nut

Shelled Brazil nuts

Shelled walnuts

Bertholletia excelsa
Brazil nuts
From the Amazon basin, the nuts cluster like orange segments inside a woody fruit. They have the highest fat content of any nut and are also rich in minerals.

Juglans regia; J. nigra
Walnuts
These nuts are good sources of protein, vitamins, minerals, and unsaturated fat. Black walnuts are especially tasty. Green or unripe walnuts are rich in vitamin C; they are delicious pickled.

Desiccated coconut

Cocus nucifera
Coconut
The coconut palm is a source of fiber, soap, and animal fodder as well as oil and other edible products. The dried flesh may be compressed into blocks or shredded.

Fresh coconut

Compressed dried coconut

Whole pecans

Shelled pecans

Whole chestnut

Shelled chestnut

Shelled and peeled chestnut

Carya pecan
Pecans
Related to walnuts, but richer, milder, and subtler in flavor, pecans are much appreciated in pies and turkey stuffings. Hickory and bitternut are also related to them.

Eleocharia tuberosa
Chinese water chestnuts
These are not true nuts, but tubers of a sedge, although with their crisp texture they can be used as nuts.

Castanea sativa
Chestnuts
These are native to southern Europe and unlike most other nuts in that they are very starchy and low in protein. Both the hard shell and the thin inner skin need to be removed. Chestnuts are often also available dried.

Seeds

Pinus pinea
Pine nuts
These are the seeds of various pines, chiefly the stone pine of the Mediterranean, and also known as pignolias or pine kernels.

Helianthus annuus
Sunflower seeds
Rich in proteins and minerals and containing 40 percent unsaturated oil, these make an excellent snack.

Sesamum indicum
Sesame seeds
Of African origin, sesame is now an important crop in the Middle and Far East as well as in Mexico. Sesame seeds are an excellent source of oil.

Cucurbita maxima
Pumpkin seeds
These seeds from the native North American plant are eaten roasted. They provide a good source of proteins, fats, and minerals, especially zinc. The seeds are also used as a source of oil.

Linum usitatissimum
Linseeds
These are the nutritious and flavorful seeds of the flax plant The Greeks and Romans used them as food.

Dried Fruit

Dried fruits are a concentrated form of sugar so they are relatively high in calories, but they are also better for you than candy because the minerals and vitamins are concentrated, too. There is less likelihood of over-indulging because, being full of fiber, they fill you up. Dates are about two-thirds sugar and figs about half, while prunes come out best with about two-thirds the calories of most dried fruits. Prunes and figs are useful natural laxatives, too. Dried fruits can be reconstituted in water and used to make many different types of interesting desserts.

Apples and dessert pears are fairly easy to dry at home. You halve the pears and peel, core, and cut the apples into rings, then put them on racks in a slow oven. Leave for several hours at 150°F, or with the door open a little.

Sulphur dioxide is often used as a preservative in dried fruit to slow down browning and prevent spoiling. It helps keep vitamin C but destroys B_1 and is suspected of being a factor in genetic mutations, a serious cause for alarm (see p. 42). Figs and dates are free of it and some stores carry other dried fruits which have not been sulphured. The pale fruits are very likely to have been sulphured. The shiny appearance of some dried fruit may be due to a coating of mineral oil, something else to avoid if possible. Mineral oil in large quantities can interfere with absorption of calcium and phosphorus in the body; it also picks up oil-soluble vitamins (A, D, E, K) as it passes through the body, which are then excreted. Estrogen and the adrenal hormones also dissolve in mineral oil and are lost in the feces.

Buying and storing

Buy pliable dried fruit rather than anything that is really hard. It will keep up to a year in an airtight container but after six months it is a good idea to add some orange or lemon peel to keep it moist. Frozen dried fruit also lasts a year but if the fruit has been reconstituted and is then frozen, it will only keep for about two or three months maximum.

Preparation

Much fruit sold these days is already cleaned, but it is still advisable to rinse it again under running water to remove any traces of preservative, and drain well. If it is for a cake batter, where the fruit may sink if damp, clean it by shifting with some flour.

To plump raisins and currants, soak them in hot liquid – water, fruit juice, or wine – for 5 minutes. Drain, pat dry and use at once. Plumped vine fruits give a juicy texture to cakes and puddings. To reconstitute tree fruits, cover with liquid and leave to soak for 8–12 hours. You may need to add more liquid. A quicker method is to put the fruit in a pan, cover it with liquid and bring it to a boil; simmer, covered, for 10–15 minutes and leave for an hour. It may be eaten at this stage or cooked until soft, whichever you prefer.

Cooking

Stew or cook the fruit for 30–40 minutes or until tender: use the soaking liquid, which now contains valuable nutrients, for cooking. It will keep for 3–4 days in the refrigerator.

Cooked fruit can be eaten hot as fruit compote, puréed for use as a sweet pastry filling or in cakes or quickbreads, or it can be added to breakfast cereals, salads, vegetable stuffings, and savory dishes, such as curries.

Apples are unusual in that they do not lose vitamin C in the drying process. They are mostly used in fruit compotes.

Apricots are sold whole, halved, or in pieces. The pieces are cheaper and are good for purées and jams. Hunza apricots, from the Himalayas, are small, unsulphured, and pale beige in color. They are sold whole and unpitted. Apricots contain more protein than other dried fruit.

Bananas have an excellent flavor. Good mixed with dates and figs for rich fruit purées to use in sauces or cakes, they can also be baked in pies or tarts.

Dates should be plump and moist with thin skins. Cooking dates are compressed into blocks; break them up before use to check that there are no pits left inside.

Figs are high in calcium and potassium, as well as sugar. They can be stuffed: soak them first to reconstitute them and use a cottage cheese stuffing or one based on almonds – figs and almonds go well together and are a traditional combination.

Peaches and *nectarines*, usually available halved, are used in the same way as apricots.

Pears keep their distinctive slightly gritty texture when dried, and are a good addition to fruit dishes such as compotes.

Prunes (dried plums) are lower in sugar and calories than dates or figs. Use in whole-grain breakfast cereals, such as Swiss-style muesli, muffins or quickbreads. They are also excellent in fruit compotes or stewed and served with yogurt. Ready-made prune purée (lekva) can also be bought; this is popular in France, where it is used in confectionery, pastries, and cakes.

Raisins, golden raisins and *currants* are all dried grapes, widely used for fruit cakes and mincemeats. Look for organically grown, non-treated raisins such as Lexia, which are sold with the seeds removed, and Muscatel raisins.

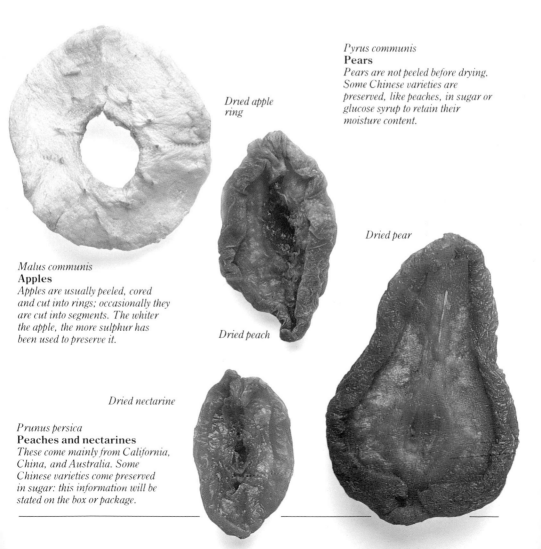

Dried apple ring

Pyrus communis
Pears
Pears are not peeled before drying. Some Chinese varieties are preserved, like peaches, in sugar or glucose syrup to retain their moisture content.

Dried pear

Malus communis
Apples
Apples are usually peeled, cored and cut into rings; occasionally they are cut into segments. The whiter the apple, the more sulphur has been used to preserve it.

Dried peach

Dried nectarine

Prunus persica
Peaches and nectarines
These come mainly from California, China, and Australia. Some Chinese varieties come preserved in sugar: this information will be stated on the box or package.

Half sun-dried apricot

Half unsulphured apricot

Prunus armeniaca
Apricots
Mainly grown in California, the Far East and North Africa. The best variety is considered to be the Hunza apricots from the Himalayas. Apricots have a higher protein and fiber content than other fruits.

Hunza apricot

Whole sulphured apricot

Dried Lerida fig

Ficus carica
Figs
Valued according to size, figs should be rich brown with a thin skin. The thinner the skin, the more likelihood of sugaring on the surface; this therefore indicates quality. Lerida figs are the best.

Muscat raisins

Dried banana

Musa, spp.
Bananas
These dry most successfully when fully ripe with a high sugar content; they may be dried in pieces or slices. Drying helps to concentrate the delicious banana taste.

Phoenix dactylifera
Dates
Dates are very high in sugar (66 percent) and also contain vitamin A and some B vitamins. Dessert dates (shown here) are sold unpitted; the best variety is "Deglet Nour." Dried dates for cooking are sold in blocks.

Prunus domestica
Prunes
The type of plum grown for drying is usually late-ripening and black-skinned. Prunes are sold pitted or unpitted.

Vitis vinifera
Golden raisins
These come from seedless white grapes. Unlike currants, they are often treated chemically – sulphured to preserve color and sprayed to give them an attractive gloss.

Vitis vinifera
Currants
These come from small black seedless grapes grown near Corinth (hence their name) and other parts of Greece. They are not chemically treated. Vostizza is considered the best variety.

Vitis vinifera
Raisins
Look for raisins that are not chemically treated. They make a good snack, especially if mixed with nuts, and are also used in all kinds of baking.

Thompson's seedless raisins

Jumbo raisins

Fresh Fruit

Fresh fruit, preferably eaten raw, is part of any healthy diet. Most fruits contain vitamin C (which cannot be stored in the body). They also contain a high proportion of natural sugars (fructose), carbohydrates, and fiber as well as minerals and other vitamins.

Buying
Buy fresh, firm, plump fruit that is not shrunken or damaged. Fruit with pits, such as peaches, plums, and cherries, should be yielding, neither rock-hard nor too squashy. Melons are ready to eat when they smell ripe and are a little soft at the stem end. Pineapples should be more golden than green, with leaves that pull off without much struggle. Mangoes, papayas (pawpaws), kiwi fruit, and figs should be soft, but if you buy them hard they will ripen at room temperature. Ripe passion fruit has wrinkled skin. Kumquats, like tiny oranges, are ripe when they become quite yielding to touch. Lychees are ripe when they turn rosy red. When buying persimmons, check with your greengrocer; some can be eaten straight away, some are far too bitter and must be kept until squashy. Guavas turn a light yellow color and are very fragrant and soft.

Storing
Fruits with good protective skins, such as citrus fruit, kiwi fruit, apples, and bananas, can be kept at room temperature, but others should go in the refrigerator as soon as they ripen to avoid destruction of vitamins A, B_2, and C. Lychees keep up to three months in the refrigerator. Once fruit is overripe, and especially if it is bruised, these vitamins quickly disappear. Guavas lose four-fifths of their vitamin C content in a day when overripe.

Pears in particular have only a day or so when they are at their best, and strawberries, raspberries and other soft fruits are best eaten as soon as possible after picking. Ripe figs and persimmons should also be eaten quickly. Melons, pineapples, mangoes, papayas, and guavas should all be eaten within a few days of ripening; this also applies to grapes and fruit with stones, such as peaches.

Soft fruits, such as strawberries, should go into the refrigerator without washing or stemming because handling can bruise, and bruises increase enzyme action and vitamin losses. If strawberries are handled when well chilled, damage is minimized. Firm fruit, which is less likely to bruise, can be washed before chilling, but avoid soaking and dry it well.

Preparation
Scrub fruit if you think it needs it, but try not to peel unnecessarily. Citrus fruit are often sprayed to give them a healthy shine. This should not affect the fruit inside, but if you are going to use the peel (or eat them whole, as you can with tiny kumquats, the smallest of the family) they will need to be scrubbed.

Fruit salad should be prepared at the last moment because cutting exposes more surface to the harmful effects of air, and discoloration and vitamin losses result. Toss cut fruit in lemon juice to prevent discoloration. Apricots and peaches (and tomatoes) are easy to peel if you pour boiling water over them and leave to soak for 1 minute.

Section oranges and grapefruit by cutting along on each side of the membranes to get skinless segments. For zesting, use a special zester if you have one; otherwise use a potato peeler or a small sharp knife, but as the strips of peel will be a little thicker than true zest, they can be simmered in water for 5–6 minutes to soften them.

A cherry pitter can also be used for olives. Grapes can be halved and the seeds hooked out with a hairpin or paperclip.

Melons are usually halved or cut into segments, and pineapples can be halved lengthwise, when the flesh can be removed easily. Alternatively, slice pineapples across and remove the peel and core.

Kiwi fruit look prettiest when sliced crosswise. Figs can be halved or sliced. Lychees should be peeled. Persimmons look attractive when sliced crosswise, or the kind that must be allowed to ripen, can have their tops sliced off and the insides scooped out; passion fruit can be served in this manner also.

Soft fruit needs to be picked over carefully and any moldy specimens removed; hull, or top and tail, them as necessary. This can be done a few hours in advance and they should then be kept cool. Papayas can be eaten in the same way as melons. Guavas are usually peeled and the seeds discarded.

Mangoes are not the most accommodating of fruit to prepare. Remember that the pit is flat and oblong, and examine the fruit to work out how the pit is lying. Cut down on each side of the pit and close to it and you will have two shallow pieces, the flesh can be scooped out and chopped or diced. The mango pit will yield a few more cubes.

Cooking

It seems a shame to do anything to fruit because it tastes so good just as it comes. But if you must, cook it according to the same rules that apply to vegetables, to keep as much of the goodness and flavor as possible. Cook in the shortest possible time and serve in its own liquid to get nutrients that dissolve into the water. Very few need sweetening.

Apple crumble is a basic recipe, and can be varied by using different fruit. Stew peeled, sliced apples in a little water for 5 minutes or until soft with sugar, honey, or dried dates to taste. Add a crumb topping and bake at 350°F, for 40 minutes.

Malus, spp.
Apple
The many varieties of apple that are available can be divided into two groups: eating and cooking. Crisp, firm, and juicy with a sweet taste, Rome is a delicious eating apple, and is also a good variety to cook.

Cucumis melo
Charentais melon
This is a cantaloupe with a sugary and fragrant flesh. It can be eaten as a dessert or appetizer. It keeps well when stored in a cool, dry place and ripens after several days in a warm room. When ripe, it is fragrant even before being cut. Although best freshly cut, it can be stored in the refrigerator for up to 2 days if covered.

Citrus sinensis
Orange
The best known of the citrus fruits, this is native to China and south-east Asia. There are both bitter and sweet oranges available. Both types are rich in vitamin C.

Citrus reticulata
Tangerine
Native to southern China and Laos, the tangerine is a small, sweet orange containing numerous pits. These fruits are good eaten on their own or in fruit salads.

Ananas comosus
Pineapple
The pineapple is really a cluster of fruits of the ananas tree, which all combine to form one "multiple fruit." Pineapples can be bought slightly unripe and left to ripen at room temperature.

Prunus, spp.
Nectarine
A smooth-skinned member of the peach family, nectarines have sweet, juicy flesh and are usually served as a dessert fruit. They are normally sold ripe and therefore should always be eaten within a day or two of purchase.

Ficus carica
Fig
There are several varieties of white, purple, and red figs. All are very good eaten fresh. Figs are also excellent in baking and desserts, and good when stewed.

Musa nana
Banana
Bananas are usually eaten raw, either on their own or incorporated in fruit salads, although they can also be gently baked or flambéed with some brown sugar.

Fragaria × ananassa
Strawberry
Native to the United States, strawberries are available fresh and frozen. They should be handled with care, as they bruise easily, which accelerates enzyme action.

Passiflora edulis
Passion fruit
The fruit of a perennial climbing plant native to Brazil, passion fruit (or purple granadilla) can be eaten fresh when the skins are deeply wrinkled and the fruit is juicy, or be used to make preserves.

Carica papaya
Papaya
The papaya, or pawpaw, has a fairly sweet taste when ripe (similar to apricots and ginger) and, like melon, makes a good dessert or breakfast fruit.

Williams

Comice

Pyrus communis
Pear
Pears ripen and are harvested during an extremely short period and, once ripe, go bad very quickly. Bosc pears keep for a slightly longer period than the other types. Bartlett and Anjou varieties are available in Spring and Summer. Comice are usually sold from August through October.

Actinidia sinensis
Kiwi fruit
The kiwi fruit, or Chinese gooseberry, has a slightly sour taste and a hairy skin, which should be removed before eating. It may be poached and sprinkled with lemon juice, but more commonly is eaten fresh, either on its own or in fruit salads.

Vegetables

Vegetables contain minerals and fiber and are excellent sources of vitamins, particularly vitamin C. Root vegetables supply starch and natural sugars for energy. They complement beans, grains, and nuts, providing taste, color, and texture, as well as the vitamins and minerals we need.

If you want vegetables grown organically without artificial fertilizers or sprays, expect to pay a little more. They may be smaller and less perfectly shaped, but that is nothing compared to their superior flavor and nutritional value. For vegetables grown the usual way, find a good greengrocer who will let you select the freshest – go for plumpness and good color. Nutrients are lost in storage no matter what precautions you take, so it is best to use vegetables as soon as possible.

A growing number of exotic vegetables are available and, if you haven't already tried them, try and sample three in particular. Radicchio, which is a kind of Belgian endive eaten raw as a salad vegetable; Chinese cabbage, a cross between celery and greens; and snowpeas, young peas in their shells, which are eaten shells and all.

Buying
Freshness is all-important, and being wrapped in plastic does nothing for a vegetable's flavor, so wherever possible buy unpackaged, loose produce. Look for plumpness and a fresh, bright color; avoid vegetables that are damaged, wrinkled, faded, or limp.

Storing
As soon as you get vegetables home, wash, dry and refrigerate them. This applies to all but salad vegetables and vegetables with skins thick enough to protect against light and air. The point of washing and refrigerating is to stop enzyme action. Enzymes help synthesize vitamins during plant growth but, once the plant is gathered or overripens, enzymes become destroyers. Enzyme action thrives at room temperature but is inhibited by cold or heat, or lack of light, or oxygen. Acid will retard the process but alkali will encourage it.

The following should be eaten as soon as possible: salad vegetables and those to be eaten raw; green vegetables; peas and string beans; vegetables such as zucchini, peppers, and eggplants (but tomatoes are often picked unripe and allowed to continue to ripen); sprouts; mushrooms; and, above all, corn. If any of these vegetables do have to wait, remove any plastic wrapping at once, store in a cool, dark place as light and heat destroy crispness and nutrients, particularly vitamins B_2 and C. Greens can lose up to 50 percent of their vitamin C in one day if kept at room temperature.

If kept in cool, well-ventilated conditions, carrots and onions will keep longer – several weeks – and potatoes will keep for several months but will tend to lose much of their vitamin C content.

Some fresh vegetables are especially suitable for freezing and this causes very little loss of nutrients. Corn, spinach, broccoli, carrots, peas, and beans (green and lima) are all good.

To freeze, prepare the vegetables as directed below and blanch them by plunging into boiling water for a minute; do about 1 pound at a time, so that the water does not cool down too much. (Blanching destroys the enzyme that causes deterioration.) Drain the vegetables and plunge immediately into cold water to prevent further cooking. Drain again, using a salad spinner or dryer. Freeze on a tray in a single layer, covered with a plastic bag. Pack in boxes or bags. They will keep for up to a year. Use straight from the freezer and do not thaw first, or the vitamin content will be significantly reduced.

Preparation
Many vegetables are best eaten raw, for both flavor and nutrition. If you have any suspicion that your vegetables may have been treated with chemicals, it is advisable to wash or scrub them.

Avoid soaking vegetables in water. Water leaches out sugars, vitamins, and minerals, so foods should be exposed to as little as possible, whether by washing or cooking. Apart from destroying vitamins, a mere 4 minutes' boiling of whole vegetables will cause 20 to 45 percent of the mineral content and 75 percent of the sugars to wash away. With cut and peeled food it is even worse. Unless the water is used in soups and sauces all those nutrients go down the drain.

Oil-soluble vitamins such as A are less likely to be lost in cooking but they, too, are sensitive to heat and oxygen. Left at room temperature, green and yellow vegetables slowly lose their A, B_2, and C vitamins.

You may not realize how delicious uncooked vegetables can be until you try, say, a bit of raw turnip or cauliflower. Raw plants are such important sources of fiber, minerals, and vitamins (especially C) that salad should be on the menu every day. Green ones are best because deep green leaves have higher concentrations of nutrients than most fruits and other vegetables. Cooked greens are good but they do lose nutrients, so salads play a very important role in our daily diets. Salad foods must be kept dry, chilled, and uncut until soon before serving. Toss them in a dressing to keep oxygen from the surfaces once cut.

Root vegetables and tubers should be scrubbed and cooked in their skins. In general, do not peel first: scrubbing removes most pesticides, and much of the goodness of root vegetables is contained in or near the skin. Potatoes can lose up to 25 percent of their protein if peeled too coarsely. Celery root is the exception, it requires peeling before cooking. Peel others (except potatoes) after cooking and chop, slice, or dice them. Jerusalem artichokes, small turnips, especially the young white ones, and small kohlrabi can also be left whole, and all can be mashed or puréed.

Some vegetables (Jerusalem artichokes, celery roots, potatoes) go brown when cut. To prevent this, drop them in water, preferably lightly acidulated by adding 3–4 teaspoons of lemon juice or vinegar to each 5 cups of water, or rub with lemon juice. Eggplants also go brown, but this does not matter as when cooked it will not show. It is really not necessary to salt them to draw out their bitter liquid, as many books recommend.

With okra, cut off the conical cap at the stem end, salt and leave them for an hour, then rinse carefully and dry. Cut fennel in thin slices across, discarding the stems and, if particularly tough, the bottom.

Spinach and other leaf vegetables should be well washed and drained before cooking. Do not discard the outer leaves, they are often the most nutritious, but must, of course, be well washed to remove any pesticides.

Cooking
When choosing vegetables for a meal, calculate about ½ pound per person for a main dish, but a bit less for a side dish.

The most nutritious way to eat vegetables is raw because the more a food is processed the greater the loss of nutrients. Of course some vegetables, such as potatoes, are unpalatable unless cooked, but there are ways of cooking that minimize nutrient losses.

Of the many different ways of cooking vegetables, boiling is one of the most popular. However, it is the least desirable, as up to 45 percent of the minerals and 50 percent of the vitamin C may be lost. If you must boil vegetables, use the minimum amount of water and make sure it is boiling when you add the vegetables. Never add baking soda, it may keep the color in, but it destroys vitamin C. Instead, use a drop of vinegar to acidify the water. Salt draws out nutrients and is not good for you, so avoid that, too. For green vegetables, ½-inch water should be enough. If spinach has been thoroughly rinsed and not too well drained, it will need no further liquid. Root vegetables should be barely covered. Keep the pan tightly covered – this will also help prevent vitamin loss – and cook as shown on p. 75.

Steaming is a good way to hold on to nutrients because if little water is used, if there is a tight-fitting lid, and if heat is kept so low that no steam gets out, nutrients that escape into the steam are reabsorbed into the food by the time it is cooked. Put the vegetables in a steamer basket and place them into a pot of boiling water. If you use a pressure cooker, time it carefully.

Coating with oil is another way to avoid contact with oxygen. Frying is not good for the health but stir-frying and sauteing are better because so little oil is used – 2 teaspoons oil is enough to coat the vegetables and keep juices in while cooking. Make sure the food is dry or the oil will not cling, and stir it into hot oil. Cover the pan, lower the heat once food is heated through, and it will cook in its own moisture.

You can also coat vegetables with milk. Milk covers the surfaces as oil does and food cooks in its own juices, keeping its color beautifully. The taste is sweeter and milder than cooking with water, and the milk is lovely in soup.

Vegetables can be baked or broiled but oil them first to stop oxygenation and loss of vitamin C, aggravated by long, slow heating. Baking or roasting is particularly suitable for root vegetables and potatoes. Prick the skins first to prevent them from bursting. Green vegetables can also be baked successfully, particularly Brussels sprouts, but first brush both the sprouts and the baking dish with a little oil. This produces a crisp cooked vegetable, the leaves on the outside well cooked and the inside tender.

To braise vegetables, brown them lightly in a little oil and bake in the oven, adding a little hot liquid, in a covered dish. Pre-heat both oven and casserole before adding vegetables with hot liquid. Unless the liquid covers the food, keep the lid on.

Asparagus is best cooked with the stems in boiling water but the tops out of it, so that the tender tips cook in the steam.

Cooking vegetables in the microwave is similar to steaming; vegetables cook quickly, they keep their bright color and crunchy textures, and vitamin loss of water-soluble vitamins like vitamin C is minimal. Cooking times vary, but leaf vegetables normally need 2 tablespoons water for 1 pound, and take about 6–8 minutes on High in a 700W oven. Beans and peas need the same amount of water for 1 pound and take 5–10 minutes on High in the same oven. Consult a microwave vegetable cooking chart for full details.

Most B vitamins disappear when the temperature is above boiling, as in frying or pressure cooking, but E and K seem to survive. Aromatic oils that give foods flavor are lost in proportion to how long the cooking takes, so serve vegetables firm, not mushy.

VITAMIN LOSSES IN COOKING

Overcooking as well as peeling, results in substantial vitamin loss. The water-soluble vitamins, such as vitamin C, are destroyed most readily by cooking and other processing. See what happens to the vitamin C content in a 3 ounce serving of peas:
- fresh or frozen, uncooked: 25mg
- fresh or frozen, boiled: 15mg
- home canned: 9mg
- canned processed: trace only
- freeze dried: trace only

Even if left untouched at room temperature, leafy vegetables can lose half their C in a day, and light destroys half their B_2. Cutting exposes more surface to destructive contact with light and air, and cooking can have a devastating effect. This is what happens to the most important vitamins in spinach when prepared:

	B_1	C	folic acid
raw, shredded	no loss	30% loss	25% loss
steamed	30% loss	50% loss	75% loss
boiled	total loss	total loss	total loss

PREPARING AND COOKING VEGETABLES

Washing vegetables
- Clean quickly in cold water. Never soak.
- Brush root vegetables. Do not scrape.
- Dry thoroughly.
- Store in bags in the vegetable compartment of the refrigerator.

Preparing vegetables
- Cut food while still chilled.
- Peel only when you absolutely have to.
- Save peelings for soup.
- Save tops (for example, radish and carrot tops) for soups or salads, or to cook as a vegetable.
- Toss cut foods in a little lemon juice or vinegar to prevent discoloration and preserve nutrients.

Cooking vegetables
- Do not cook in copper or iron pans.
- Never add baking soda.
- Add a drop of vinegar to hard water.
- Steam if possible. Otherwise, boil very little water, add food, return to boil. Cover pan tightly, then simmer.
- Cook on High in the microwave with 2 tablespoons water or as recommended.
- Cook until barely tender.
- Save vegetable water for soups, sauces, or other recipes.

COOKING TIMES AND METHODS FOR DIFFERENT VEGETABLES

Eggplants are usually sauteed and/or baked, often with a stuffing: see detailed recipes for specific cooking directions.
Tomatoes can be broiled for 3–4 minutes. No times have been giving for frying or sautéing as these will be found in specific recipes.

Spinach* is not strictly speaking boiled, but cooked in the water adhering to it after rinsing.
All the times listed below give *very lightly cooked* vegetables, many with a crisp, crunchy texture. If you prefer softer vegetables, you will need to increase the cooking time.

Vegetable	Steam	Boil	Bake (whole)	Braise	Stir-fry
Potatoes	25–30 minutes	20 minutes	1–1½ hours	15–20 minutes	–
Carrots	20 minutes	10–15 minutes	45–60 minutes	15–20 minutes	yes
Turnips	25–30 minutes	10–15 minutes	–	15–20 minutes	yes
Rutabagas	25–30 minutes	20 minutes	–	15–20 minutes	yes
Parsnips	–	15–20 minutes	45–60 minutes	15–20 minutes	–
Celery root & kohlrabi	20 minutes	10–15 minutes	–	15–20 minutes	yes
Salsify & scorzonera	30–40 minutes	20–30 minutes	–	–	–
Sweet potato & Yam	25–30 minutes	20 minutes	1–1½ hours	–	–
Jerusalem artichokes	–	15–20 minutes	–	–	–
Radish/daikon	–	–	–	–	yes
Beets	–	40–60 minutes	–	–	–
Asparagus	–	10–15 minutes	–	–	–
Fennel	12–15 minutes	10–12 minutes	–	15–20 minutes	yes
Onions	–	–	45–60 minutes	–	–
Leeks	15–20 minutes	10–15 minutes	–	8–10 minutes	–
Celery	12–15 minutes	8–10 minutes	–	10–12 minutes	yes
Globe artichokes	–	30–40 minutes	–	–	–
French beans	4–8 minutes	–	–	–	yes
Lima beans	–	10–15 minutes	–	–	–
Peas	–	8–12 minutes	–	–	yes
Snowpeas	6–8 minutes	–	–	–	yes
Okra	–	15–20 minutes	–	–	–
Corn	–	8–15 minutes	–	–	yes
Mushrooms	–	–	–	–	yes
Cabbage	4–6 minutes	–	–	–	yes
Red cabbage	–	–	–	45–60 minutes	–
Brussels sprouts	6–10 minutes	–	25–30 minutes	–	yes
Cauliflower	4–8 minutes	–	–	–	–
Spinach*	–	*6–8 minutes	–	–	–

Continued overleaf

COOKING TIMES AND METHODS FOR DIFFERENT VEGETABLES					
Vegetable	Steam	Boil	Bake (whole)	Braise	Stir-fry
Broccoli	4–8 minutes	–	–	–	yes
Bok choy	4–8 minutes	–	–	–	yes
Spinach beet	10–12 minutes	–	–	–	–
Swiss chard	10–12 minutes	–	–	–	–
Chicory	–	–	–	10–12 minutes	–
Belgian endive	–	–	–	–	yes
Chinese cabbage	4 minutes	–	–	–	yes
Zucchini	4–8 minutes	–	–	–	yes
Squash	10–20 minutes	–	45–60 minutes	–	yes
Peppers	–	–	–	–	yes
Cucumbers	5–10 minutes	–	–	–	–

Salad Vegetables

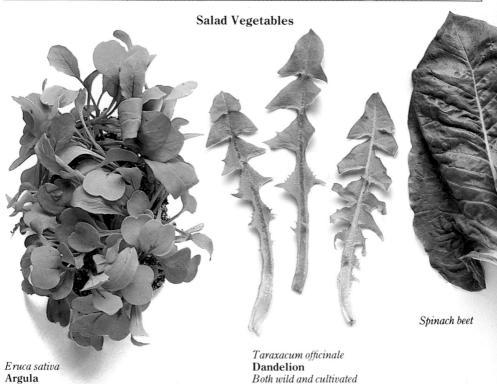

Spinach beet

Eruca sativa
Argula
Argula is deservedly popular in Italy and parts of France. The young, tender leaves add a taste to a salad.

Taraxacum officinale
Dandelion
Both wild and cultivated dandelions add a distinctive flavor to salads. If picking your own, be sure to avoid those that have been sprayed with pesticides.

Valerianella olitoria
Lamb's lettuce
*Also known as corn salad and
mache. Delicious in mixed green
salads.*

Belgian endive

Cichorium intybus
Belgian endive
*Chicory and Belgian endive have
a similar slightly bitter taste.
Both are usually blanched by the
grower to reduce this bitterness.
Belgian endive can be eaten raw, or
stir-fried.*

Swiss chard

Beta vulgaris
Chard; Spinach beet
*Swiss chard and spinach beet are
the same species; they resemble
spinach, but lack its distinctive
flavor. The firm central stalks of
Swiss chard are often cut out and
cooked separately. Rinse well.*

Radicchio

Escarole

Cichorium endivia
Chicory
*The chicory family includes several
delicious salad greens; curly
French "Frisée", tart escarole, and
red-tinged radicchio.*

Chicory

Levisticum officinale
Lovage
*The young, reddish leaves (above)
are good in salads; the older leaves
(bottom) and the stems are used
sparingly as herbs.*

Brassica chinensis
Bok choy
*Less well known than some other
leaf vegetables, bok choy, or
Chinese cabbage, is crisp and
delicate-tasting and needs little or
no cooking at all.*

Rumex acetosa
Sorrel
Wild sorrel is high in oxalic acid. This gives it a fresh, sharp taste but also impedes assimilation of minerals, notably calcium and iron. Garden sorrel is less acid.

Sprouts

Easy and quick to grow at home, sprouts provide fresh, green vegetables of outstanding nutritional value: they contain valuable amounts of protein as well as vitamins A, B complex, C, and E, minerals, and enzymes.

The changes that take place as the seed grows are incredible. The total vitamin content can increase by 800 percent in a few days.

Buying
Buy untreated seeds from a health food store or a firm specializing in organically grown produce, because almost all seeds sold for planting will have been treated with fungicides and pesticides. Split beans or seeds will not sprout.

Growing
If you do not have tiered sprouting trays, fine strainers, or mesh trays, or a wide-necked jar with a cheesecloth cover or other porous substance, will do very well. Pick over the seeds, removing tiny stems and stones.

Put 2 tablespoons of seeds in a jar and soak in lukewarm water overnight, to encourage them to germinate more quickly. Next day, drain off the water. Put the seeds on a suitable tray or leave them in the jar. Put in a warm place but not in direct sun. They need good ventilation and a constant temperature of 55–70°F. Remember to allow space in the container for the growth of the sprouts; they will increase in volume by 4–6 times.

Every night and morning pour warm water over the seeds. Turn the jar, if you are using one, upside down so the water can drain away completely. If not properly drained the sprouts can get moldy, but be careful not to rinse them so vigorously that you damage the delicate shoots. Grain sprouts take 2–3 days, beans and lentils 5–7 days, to be at their best. When ready, give the sprouts a final rinse.

Storing
Sprouts keep in the refrigerator for up to 4 days. Use an airtight container with a double layer of paper towels or cheesecloth at the bottom, to absorb the excess moisture.

Using
All garden sprouts can be eaten raw in salads. The delicate green leaves of mustard, types of cress, and alfalfa look particularly pretty and can also be used as a garnish. Adzuki beansprouts have a distinct flavor of peanuts; mung beans taste a little like delicate peapods, but if grown for too long will lose some of their nutritive value. Fenugreek sprouts taste spicy.

The best known and easiest to sprout are mustard, mung beans, and alfalfa. Sprouts are good used on bread: use wheat sprouts, or alfalfa sprouts, which have been grown to only ¼-inch tall.

Sprouts

Mung beans
(Phaseolus aureus)

Alfalfa *(Medicago sativa)*   Wheat *(Triticum vulgare)*

Growing sprouts
Sprouts from wheat (and other grains such as rye) and from lentils are best when grown to about the length of the seeds. Adzuki bean sprouts should be about ½-inch long, mung beans can be grown to 1-inch. Mustard and garden cress are eaten at the two-leaf stage, when 1–1½-inches long, so are alfalfa sprouts, which take 5–6 days. Fenugreek sprouts are best when not more than 2–3 times the length of the seed, which normally takes 3–6 days.

Garden cress *(Lepidum sativum)*   Mustard *(Sinapis alba)*

Adzuki beans
(Phaseolus angularis)   Fenugreek *(Trigonella foenum-graecum)*   Lentils
(Lens esculenta)

Vegetables

Hibiscus esculentus
Okra
This is also known as gumbo. The edible part is the pod, picked and eaten while still unripe, as when fully ripe it becomes fibrous and indigestible. It is very mucilaginous and when added to soups and casseroles gives them a rich, thick consistency.

Oriental radish

Raphanus sativus
Oriental radish
A useful vegetable for winter salads, much grown in China and Japan. The large roots are crisp, but not quite so tender as spring radishes. It is excellent when used in stir-fries.

Okra

Brassica oleracea
Kohlrabi
A variety of cabbage, also called turnip-rooted cabbage, although the apparent root is actually the swollen stem. Both green and purple varieties are good when young, crisp and tender, they can then be eaten raw and have a delicate, slightly turnip-like flavor. Weight for weight, they have more vitamin C than oranges.

Kohlrabi

Foeniculum vulgare var. *dulce*
Fennel
Often known as Florence fennel, the "bulb" is the swollen leaf-base and has a pronounced aniseed flavor. It is usually served raw in salads or in soups.

Fennel

Jerusalem artichoke

Helianthus tuberosus
Jerusalem artichoke
No relation to globe artichokes, but a cousin of the sunflower, this has a sweet, nutty flavor.

Raphanus sativus
Daikon
A large winter radish, also known as Japanese white radish or mooli. It has a crisp texture and a milder flavor than ordinary winter radishes. It is used like them, in salads and stir-fries. All winter radishes have slightly more nutritional value than spring ones.

Daikon

Salsify

Tragopogon porrifolius
Salsify
Also called oyster plant, as its subtle taste is supposed to resemble that of oysters. "Black salsify" is the related scorzonera, which is similar in appearance but black-skinned.

Ipomoea batatas
Sweet potato
Similar in taste to the yam, these vitamin-rich tubers can be used interchangeably.

Sweet potato

Herbs and Spices

The word "herb" comes from the Latin word "*herba*," meaning grass or herbage. Herbs are usually annual plants and are mostly grown from seed. The flowers, leaves, seeds, stems, and roots are used as flavorings in cooking, or for medicinal purposes. The amount used in cooking depends partly on individual taste, and partly on the type of herb. Strongly flavored herbs should be used only sparingly. Many herbs, such as parsley, basil, fennel, marjoram, or thyme, do not grow too vigorously and can easily be kept in small pots on the windowsill.

Buying and storing herbs
Most herbs should be bought and used fresh whenever possible, although a few (principally oregano, marjoram, sage, bay leaf, and dill) keep their aroma well when dried. Buy small amounts of dried herbs, if possible, from a whole food store or somewhere where there is a high turnover of stock.

To dry your own herbs, pick them when the leaves are dry, preferably just before flowering. Tie the items in bunches and hang them upside down in a cool, dark place. When dry, crumble the leaves, leaving out the stems, then put them into small jars.

Some herbs can also be frozen for use as a flavoring rather than as a garnish: parsley, cilantro leaves, chives, tarragon, and chervil are all suitable. Blanch in boiling water for a few seconds. (Otherwise they will lose their color and look unappetizing. Blanching also helps to retain flavor and aroma.) Drain them, leave in sprigs and open freeze. Wrap in plastic bags and keep for 3–4 months. Keep dried herbs away from light or heat, in airtight containers to prevent any deterioration in the flavors.

Using herbs
To get the best flavor from fresh herbs, tear or snip them rather than chop them, except parsley. Dried herbs are more pungent in flavor than fresh, so use only 1 teaspoon of the dried herb where you would need to use at least 2–3 teaspoons of the fresh variety.

SPICES
Even a small amount of spice, judiciously used, alters the whole character of a dish. The term generally refers to the dried roots, bark, pods, berries, or seeds of aromatic plants. Most spices come from countries in the East, but allspice, chili peppers, and vanilla originated in the New World.

Buying and storing spices
Buy spices whole whenever possible as they keep their flavor and freshness much better. Turmeric, pepper, cayenne, and paprika are generally sold ready ground, but red dried chili peppers can be bought whole and then ground. Keep in airtight containers, in a dark place.

Preparing spices
Some spices can be crushed in a mortar and pestle: they include allspice, cardamom, cloves, coriander, cumin, dill and fennel seed, juniper, black peppercorns, and saffron. Poppy seeds are tough and require a nut mill, which can, of course, also be used for other spices. Aniseeds, capers, caraway, celery, dill, and fennel seeds are generally used whole. Green peppercorns are not strictly speaking a spice, as they are not dried. They are easily crushed or mashed. Nutmeg needs grating: a cheese grater does perfectly well. Ginger can also be grated, especially when fresh, or it can be sliced thinly or chopped. Always prepare spices just before they are to be cooked.

Fresh chili peppers can be chopped (remove the seeds unless you are sure you like the chili hot), or kept in a jar of oil to impart their flavor. Keep topping off with oil as you use it – you will need only a few drops at a time.

Saffron threads are often mixed with a little warm water, or milk to extract the most color and flavor. Saffron may also be lightly crushed and put in a warm oven for a few minutes, or powdered in a grinder.

Using spices
Many spices benefit from being lightly fried in a little oil before being added to the dish they are to flavor. This seems to bring out and

COOKING WITH HERBS CHART						
Herb	Soups	Stews	Sauces	Salads	Garnish	Other remarks
Basil	yes		yes	yes	yes	Goes particularly well with tomatoes; an essential ingredient of pesto.
Bay leaf	yes	yes	yes			A bay leaf, a sprig of thyme, and some parsley make a *bouquet garni*.
Cilantro leaves	yes	yes	yes	yes	yes	Use like parsley.
Chervil	yes	yes	yes	yes	yes	The mixture known as *fines herbes* is made of finely chopped chervil, parsley, tarragon, and chives.
Chives			yes	yes	yes	Particularly good with potato salad.
Dill leaves			yes	yes	yes	Good with potatoes and green vegetables.
Garlic	yes	yes	yes			Extremely versatile and enhances other flavors.
Lemon balm	yes	yes				Use to flavor summer drinks and salads.
Sweet marjoram	yes	yes				Goes well with nuts, eggs, and tomatoes.
Mint			yes	yes	yes	Use to flavor young vegetables, especially peas and new potatoes, or add to yogurt or bean dishes. Also good with fruit and summer drinks.
Oregano	yes	yes	yes			Indispensable to many Greek and Italian dishes.
Parsley	yes	yes	yes	yes	yes	Use generously both as flavoring and as garnish.
Rosemary	yes	yes				Good with potatoes and squash. Add to marinades.
Sage		yes				Use sparingly: very pungent.
Savory	yes	yes		yes	yes	Use like thyme or marjoram; good with beans.
Tarragon	yes	yes	yes		yes	Particularly good with cheese, cream, eggs, sauces, and some vegetables.
Thyme	yes	yes				Good with most vegetables, such as tomatoes, zucchini, eggplants, and peppers.

reinforce their aroma, and applies particularly to coriander, cumin, cardamom, ginger, and fenugreek.

Cinnamon sticks and whole mace, being difficult to grind, are often used to flavor liquids – sauces or drinks – from which they can be easily extracted once they have yielded their aromatic flavors. In the same way, a vanilla bean can be used to flavor drinks, syrups, custards, and other sweet desserts. Coriander, cumin, cardamom, peppercorns, turmeric,

cloves, ginger, and chili peppers are the most important spices for curry. Some recipes call for "garam masala," a combination of spices. This can be bought, or you can make your own: there is no standard recipe (the name means "hot mixture"). It is a starting mixture rather than a complete curry powder. A mixture could consist of 4 parts coriander, 1 part cumin, and 1 part chili. This is to be then lightly roasted or fried and added to 1 part ground black peppercorns.

Herbs

Petroselinum crispum
Parsley
Available curled (left) or flat (above), parsley is a good source of both Vitamin C and iron. Flat parsley is thought to have a finer taste than curled parsley.

Salvia officinalis
Sage
There are many varieties. It dries well, but can become musty if it is kept for too long.

Allium sativum
Garlic
Sold all the year round, a garlic bulb is separated into cloves which are used one or two at a time. An essential ingredient in many casseroles, curries, and soups.

Origanum vulgare
Oregano
This is wild marjoram, which for the best flavor must be grown in strong sun. Luckily it keeps its aroma when it is dried.

Coriandrum sativum
Cilantro
Also known as Chinese parsley, it is used lavishly in Mexican, Middle Eastern, and Asian recipes.

Laurus nobilis
Bay leaf
Good in milk puddings as well as savory stews and sauces. A bay leaf (left) kept in a package of grains will give them a delicate taste.

Anthriscus cerefolium
Chervil
Very popular in France, chervil can be used in the same way as parsley but has a more delicate taste with a hint of aniseed.

Satureja montana
Winter savory
Its German name means "bean-herb," which indicates its traditional use. Summer savory (S. hortensis) is similar and even more aromatic.

Artemisia dracunculus
Tarragon
If possible, make sure that you are getting French tarragon (left), not Russian, which is tasteless.

Rosmarinus officinalis
Rosemary
A wonderfully aromatic herb with a strong flavor. The spiky needles, however, can be a menace when dried.

Thymus vulgaris
Thyme
This popular herb contains an essential oil, thymol, which helps to digest fatty foods.

Melissa officinalis
Lemon balm
The crushed leaves give off a wonderful lemony scent. They can be used generously in salads.

Ocimum basilicum
Basil
If you cannot find fresh, do not use dried; substitute another herb. A pot of basil in the kitchen will help keep flies away.

Mentha spp.
Mint
There are many species of this popular herb, from spearmint to the fresh-tasting peppermint used for making soothing teas.

Anethum graveolens
Dill
The dried leaves are known as dillweed, one of the most popular herbs used in Scandinavia.

Allium schoenoprasum
Chives
Mostly eaten raw, but also good in omelettes, chives are widely used from China and Japan to Europe and America.

Origanum majorana
Marjoram
Sweet marjoram, native to the Mediterranean, is very fragrant and can be dried successfully.

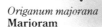

Apium graveolens
Celery seeds
The distinctive bitter taste of celery seeds goes well in bread, egg dishes, dressings, and salads.

Pimenta officinalis
Allspice
Also called Jamaica pepper; the taste combines cloves, cinnamon, and nutmeg.

Capsicum frutescens
Chili
Ripe chili peppers dry and keep well. "Chili powder" often includes other spices.

Pimpinella asinum
Aniseed
This is popular in Mexico and all over the Mediterranean for its licorice flavor.

Coriandrum sativum
Coriander
Mild but aromatic, coriander seed is an important ingredient in Arab and Eastern food.

Carum carvi
Caraway
Looks like cumin seed and often confused with it, but the taste is quite different.

Cuminum cyminum
Cumin
The pungent seed is often combined with coriander seeds to make a basic curry mixture.

Capsicum frutescens
Cayenne
A very hot, pungent red chili sold ready ground. Use sparingly.

Vanilla planifolia
Vanilla
Fruit of an orchid plant from Mexico, traditionally used to flavor chocolate. Expensive, but good in many sweet dishes.

Anethum graveolens
Dill seeds
Popular in dips and cheese-spreads, dill seed is much used in pickle making.

Capsicum annuum
Paprika
Made from very mild, sweet peppers, grown in Hungary and Spain. Use generously.

Foeniculum vulgare
Fennel seeds
Like the bulb, fennel seeds have a slight aniseed flavor. Good with fruit and salads.

Piper nigrum
Pepper
Unripe whole peppercorns are green. When dried they turn a brown-black color.

Trigonella foenum-graecum
Fenugreek
Produces spicy sprouts. Use the ground seed sparingly.

Papaver rhoeas; P. somniferum
Poppy seed
White poppy seed is often used in curries, dark, deep blue is popular in pastries and bread.

Brassica alba; B. nigra
Mustard
The white (or yellow) seed is milder in flavor than the black (or brown) seed.

Curcuma longa
Turmeric
Always sold ground. Avoid contact with clothing, as tumeric is a powerful dye.

Myristica fragrans
Nutmeg
Always buy whole and grate as required: ready ground nutmeg quickly loses its aroma. Sometimes coated with lime to repel insects.

Crocus sativus
Saffron
Always buy the stigmas or "threads" of this extremely expensive spice, as the powder is often impure.

Juniperus communis
Juniper
The berries have a pungent, slightly resinous flavor. They go well with cabbage and add a light touch to oily or heavy dishes.

Myristica fragrans
Mace
Mace is the outer net-like covering of nutmeg. It is sold both in blades and ready ground, as it is difficult to grind at home.

Eugenia caryophyllata
Cloves
These are buds of an evergreen tree, widely used in curries, marinades, mincemeat, fruit dishes, and mulled wine. Use sparingly, as the taste is very strong.

Capparis spinosa
Capers
The buds of a small Mediterranean bush, these are usually sold pickled in vinegar and should not be allowed to dry out. Capers are used mostly in sauces and salads.

Elettaria cardamomum
Cardamom
The flavorless pod encloses black aromatic seeds used in curries and pastries and to flavor drinks, including tea and coffee.

Zingiber officinale
Ginger
Fresh gingerroot is firm and juicy. It needs peeling before being grated or chopped for use in curries, stir-fries, or puddings.

Cinnamomum zeylanicum
Cinnamon
The "quills" of dried bark can flavor drinks and syrups; the powder is widely used in breads, cookies, and desserts.

Seasonings and Flavorings

Any well-stocked vegetarian pantry should contain a wide range of flavorings and seasonings, from spices and vinegars, seaweeds and syrups, to flavorings made from nuts and vegetables and, finally, the indispensable soybean.

Soybean products

The soybean, difficult to digest when whole, is easily assimilated when fermented and provides nutrients as well as flavorings. The best known fermented products are soysauce, shoyu, tamari, and miso.

Miso is a living food rather in the same way that yogurt is, and contains bacteria and enzymes which are destroyed by boiling. It is therefore usually added as a flavoring at the end of cooking, often mixed with a little warm water so it dissolves easily. Dark miso tends to be saltier and it has a stronger flavor than lighter varieties. Shiro, or white, miso has a pale yellow color and mild taste. Genmai miso, made with rice, is lighter and sweeter.

Tamari, shoyu, and miso all keep well but should not undergo sudden changes of temperature. Miso may develop a white mold: this is a natural yeast by-product and can simply be mixed straight back in. Rock salt, held by some to have the finest taste, and sea salt are preferable to refined table salt, which may have additives. Both can be used for cooking and at the table. Salt

substitutes often consist of potassium salts. One of the most successful combinations of salt with other flavorings is gomasio, or sesame salt, whose nutty flavor complements many dishes. It will keep for up to two weeks.

Both the strong dry mustard and the gentler, more aromatic, prepared mustard have their place in the kitchen. With dry mustard, make up only as much as you are going to need at any one time.

Pungent sauces can be made using prepared horseradish or freshly grated root. Dried horseradish can also be used.

Nuts and seeds provide useful flavorings, from peanut butter to tahini, a beige paste of similar consistency made from sesame seeds.

Dried mushrooms add rich natural flavoring and are popular in Japan and China. They keep well in an airtight container and are reconstituted by soaking in warm water for at least half an hour.

Vegetable concentrates, stock cubes, and yeast extracts are all quick ways of adding flavor. Yeast extracts in particular are rich in nutrients, but high in salt so should not be used too generously. They are sold in screwtop jars and will keep for at least six months.

Soysauce/Shoyu
Look for naturally fermented sauces. Always read the label to be sure you are buying a sauce without preservatives, colorings, or sweeteners.

Tamari
True tamari, a liquid made from the manufacture of miso, contains no wheat and is therefore suitable for people on gluten-free diets.

Dried mushrooms
These are available in several varieties, from the strongly flavored cep (Boletus edulis) to the ordinary cultivated mushroom (Agaricus bisporus) shown here. Even this kind makes a valuable contribution of flavor.

Japanese gomasio
Also called sesame salt, this is available from health food stores, but it is easy to make by grinding four or five parts roasted sesame seeds with one part salt. Keep in an airtight container and use instead of salt.

Grated horseradish
When fresh, grated horseradish is very pungent, and much liked in Germany and Scandinavia, as well as Britain. It can be used in the same way as mustard.

Brewer's yeast
This is exceptionally high in protein as well as in calcium, iron, and B vitamins. It can be sprinkled over cereals or used as part of a topping, and adds an interesting flavor as well as nourishment.

Mugi miso

Hatcho miso

Vegetable concentrates
Like stock cubes, vegetable concentrates are a quick way of adding flavor to stocks, soups, and casseroles, and for making hot drinks. They can also be used as a spread on toast.

Yeast extracts
Yeast extracts are made from a mixture of brewer's yeast and salt, which produces a highly flavored brown residue, full of protein, iron, potassium, and B vitamins, some with added B_{12}.

Genmai miso

Miso
Like shoyu and tamari, miso is a product of the fermented soybean, a little like peanut butter in texture. All misos have quite a high salt content, although lighter colored miso has slightly less.

Peanut butter
This is not only a nutritious spread but can be adapted to other uses, particularly as a flavoring for sauces and dressings.

Vegetable stock cubes
These are quite widely available, but make sure they do not contain any artificial additives. They should be a concentration of vegetables, yeast, and vitamins.

Whole-grain mustard
Available dry or prepared, this contains the whole mustard seed. It adds texture as well as taste.

Tahini
Tahini is sesame seed paste, widely used in the Middle East. It can be used as a dip, on its own, or to flavor other dips, salad dressings, and sauces.

Mustard powder
Made mainly from black mustard seeds, its clean, sharp taste makes it ideal for flavoring sauces, dressings, and dips.

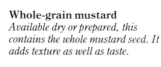

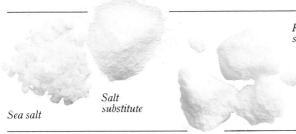

Sea salt

Salt substitute

Rock salt

Sodium chloride

Salt

Salt comes from the sea, either as sea salt or as bay salt, which is directly evaporated from sea water, or as rock salt deposits left by vanished prehistoric seas. Salt alternatives are also available.

Sea Vegetables

Most seaweeds are like salty rubber but there are, surprisingly, around 70 edible species. We would do well to know about them because they provide an excellent, cheap, seemingly inexhaustible supply of protein, vitamins, and minerals. As a source of B vitamins they are unusual in having B_{12}, not often found in vegetables. They are hard to beat for their mineral content, supplying all we need, and are particularly rich in calcium, potassium, sodium, iodine, and iron.

We eat some seaweed without knowing it – it is used in manufactured vegetable gelatines, ice cream, salad dressings, soups, sauces, and sausage skins. Those who eat it knowingly are the Celts, Chinese, and Japanese. A variety eaten in Wales is red seaweed called laver, which smells like cabbage and looks like spinach. In the Far East, kelp, or brown seaweed, is particularly popular, used as a garnish for rice or as a seasoning.

Buying and storing

Available in natural food stores and Oriental markets, sea vegetables are sold cleaned, dried, and packaged. Unopened, they will keep indefinitely; once opened, they will last up to four months in an airtight container.

Preparation

Dried nori, dulse, kombu, wakame, and arame need a preliminary brief soaking for 5 minutes or so to soften them, although this is not necessary if they are to be added to a soup or stew. The exception is dulse, which needs to be rinsed and then soaked again for 10 minutes. Nori does not need to be softened if it is to be crumbled over a salad. Carrageen should be rinsed before use.

Nori, intensively farmed in Japan, is similar to laver and normally sold in sheets. It is traditionally toasted and wrapped around small rice balls which are then dipped in shoyu. After its preliminary soaking, it can be used to flavor soups or as a salad ingredient, when it should be rinsed and boiled for 15 minutes.

Dulse can be eaten raw, or, if dried, simmered for 30 minutes after being soaked. Widely available, it is a dark, leafy vegetable with a sweet, tangy taste and is particularly good with cooked cabbage.

Kombu, valued and cultivated in Japan, is eaten both raw and cooked. The flavor is sweet and it is used to enhance stocks and soups (see page 121).

Wakame should have the central vein cut out after soaking. It can then be either simmered for 10 minutes, or cut into small pieces and served as a salad.

Arame has a broad leaf and is usually shredded into hair-like threads. It is similar to hijiki, which is shredded more coarsely. Both can be steamed, sauteed, or eaten as a salad. Arame is a good introduction to seaweeds because of its mild taste.

Agar is a vegetable, available in powder or flake form. The powder is easier to use and ensures better results. Make sure it is thoroughly dissolved in boiling water or liquid before use, otherwise it will not set. Use 2 teaspoons of agar powder to 2½ cups of boiling liquid for a delicate jelly.

Carrageen, or Irish moss, is still enjoyed in Ireland, where it is most often used to make carrageen mold or blancmange. Soak ½ ounce dried carrageen in water for 15 minutes. Drain, rinse and cover with 2½ cups milk; bring to a boil and simmer, covered, for 20–30 minutes. Strain, cool slightly, sweeten to taste, pour into a wet mold and leave to set. This method can be adapted to fruit desserts.

Sea Vegetables

Agar flakes   *Agar powder*

Agar
Agar (or agar-agar, from a Malay word meaning jelly) is obtained from several different species of sea vegetables. Also called Japanese or Ceylon moss, it is used as a substitute for animal gelatine.

Rhodymenia palmata
Dulse
Dulse grows in the North Atlantic and is eaten in Ireland and New England, as well as Iceland and parts of Canada.

Laminaria spp.
Kombu
This is much cultivated in Japan and considered suitable for offering to people as a gift.

Chondrus crispus
Carrageen
Also called Irish moss, carrageen is still eaten in Ireland, and used to be valued as a cure for bronchial diseases and tuberculosis.

Porphyra spp.
Nori
Nori is intensively grown in Japan, where it is usually sold in sheets which can be wrapped around rice. Laver, still used in Wales, is a similar sea vegetable.

Eisenia bicyclis
Arame
This has a mild taste that blends well with other flavors, and is a good introduction to sea vegetables. It is rich in iron.

Undaria pinnatifida
Wakame
This is another Japanese favorite. Softer than kombu, it can be used in many of the same ways, particularly in soup.

Sweeteners

Rather than substituting one kind of sugar for another, it is important to monitor your intake of sugar and cut down on the total. There is little difference nutritionally between white and brown sugar, but brown sugar does contain a little fiber.

A product of cane sugar, molasses, especially blackstrap molasses, contains small amounts of minerals, including calcium and iron, and some B vitamins. Its strong flavor makes it suitable for fruit breads. It will keep for up to six months in an airtight jar.

Honey is twice as sweet as sugar, so you need to use only half the amount of sugar given in a recipe (reduce the liquid elsewhere to allow for the water content of honey). Look for the word "pure" on the label: blended honey may contain sugars, syrups, and possibly additives. A jar of clear honey may crystallize if stored at a low temperature. Simply warm gently and the honey will become clear again.

Maple syrup is not as sweet as honey, but it does contain some minerals, especially calcium. Other syrups available include corn syrup, rice syrup, sorghum syrup, and barley syrup, also known as malt extract.

Fruit juice concentrates are very useful flavorings and can be combined with other sweetenings, such as honey, to reduce the total amount of sweetener needed in cakes and pastries – on their own the taste is too strong.

Bottles of concentrates are available in some health food stores. Unsweetened frozen juices can also be used.

Carob powder, or carob flour, made from the seeds of the Mediterranean carob tree, tastes very similar to chocolate. Naturally sweeter than cocoa, it has no caffeine, a lower fat content and also contains some vitamins. When substituting carob for cocoa, use about half the quantity suggested for cocoa.

Corn syrup
Corn syrup, or glucose syrup, is made by heating cornstarch and water with a little sulphuric or hydrochloric acid.

Molasses
Sometimes called black treacle, molasses is the residue left when cane sugar is refined. It has some vitamins and minerals.

Maple syrup
This comes from the sugar maple and black maple. It takes 50 gallons of sap to make 1 gallon of syrup, so it is a very concentrated form of sweetener.

Apple juice concentrate
Concentrated and plain fruit juices are useful flavorings for fruit salads, sauces, and cereals.

Malt extract
Sometimes also called barley syrup, this is not so sweet as sugar; it is used to flavor drinks and malted breads and cakes.

Muscovado sugar
This is a dark, moist, partly refined sugar with a strong distinctive flavor. It is sometimes called Barbados or raw sugar.

Demerara sugar
Demerara can be white sugar dyed with caramel. If the country of origin is stated on the package, it is less likely to be dyed.

Light brown sugar
Has a more delicate flavor than darker brown sugar.

Carob powder
Carob pods, the size of a banana, but flat and dark brown, contain small black seeds, so uniform in size that the word "carat" as a weight measure derives from them.

Oils, Fats, Dairy Products, and Alternatives

Oils are used mainly as a cooking medium for frying and sauteing, as a condiment for salads, and as shortening in baking. Fats are solids, a good source of energy, and unrefined contain many vitamins and minerals.

Dairy products like milk provide protein, vitamins, and minerals such as calcium and phosphorous. Nutritious soybean products have evolved from the Chinese pantry and provide excellent lowfat alternatives.

Oils

There are three main types of oil that are obtained from seeds, beans, and nuts.

Cold-pressed oil is still extracted using the ancient method of hydraulic pressing. Much of the oil remains in the pulp, but that which is extracted is high quality and full of flavor. Unfortunately true cold-pressed oil is very expensive to buy.

Semi-refined oil requires greater pressure and higher temperatures. The extraction rate is higher, but the vitamin content suffers.

Refined oil, confusingly labeled "pure," is produced by a method called solvent extraction, which removes most of the goodness as well as bleaching and deodorizing the oil. Many of the vitamins are then added back artificially along with preservatives to prevent the oil from going rancid. This is generally the cheapest type available.

Buying

This depends on what you want your oil for: dressing salads, frying vegetables and grains, or baking. For salad dressings, use cold-pressed or unrefined oil: it tastes much better to most palates and nutritionally is the most valuable.

Olive oil has a rich flavor, but one that varies widely depending on the country of origin. "Virgin oil" means oil from the first pressing.

It is the best quality of oil and is highly recommended for use in uncooked sauces and salad dressings.

Safflower oil is pale in color, with a delicate flavor, high in linoleic acid and low in cholesterol, which justifies its high price.

Sunflower oil is perhaps the best all-purpose oil. It is high in linoleic acid, second only to safflower oil, and slightly cheaper.

Sesame oil does not go rancid quickly, and food containing it will not go stale, which makes it a good oil for baking.

Corn oil is cheap to produce, almost tasteless and popular as a cooking oil. It is also widely used as an ingredient in margarine.

Peanut oil is another very popular oil. It is particularly good for frying as it can be heated to very high temperatures without burning. *Soy oil* is also cheap and popular.

Walnut oil has a strong, nutty taste and is very expensive to buy, so it is used chiefly for dressing salads.

Storing

Cold-pressed oils, apart from sesame oil, do not keep well. They are not heat-treated or otherwise stabilized and may go rancid, so buy comparatively small quantities (enough for a month or two) and keep in a cool, dark place. If it is too cold and the oil congeals, do not worry – the oil will liquify very quickly when brought to room temperature. Semi-refined oils will keep for up to three months.

Fats

Butter is high in saturated animal fat and as such should not be overindulged in. Since most of us could do with reducing our total fat intake, this leaves a comparatively small amount of butter available, but still an appreciable one. You also have the option of substituting butter with vegetable oils or margarine. Butter addicts maintain that there is no real substitute, either for taste or quality. So unless you need to keep to a low-cholesterol diet use butter (preferably unsalted) for cooking where taste matters.

Margarine is often presented as the healthy alternative to butter. In fact, many margarines are highly refined and contain additives. Soft margarines contain about 30 percent polyunsaturated fat. In hard margarines the original polyunsaturated fat have been hydrogenated, so they are not much better for you than butter, from the point of view of fat content. If you do not eat any animal product, then you will want a vegetable-based margarine; if you do eat butter but want to cut down on cholesterol, an excellent compromise is to mix equal parts of butter and good quality oil (safflower or sunflower). Covered, this will keep for several days in the refrigerator.

Ghee is clarified butter, popular in cooking because any impurities have been removed and it can be heated to a much higher temperature than ordinary butter without burning. To make your own, simply melt butter and filter it through cheesecloth. Vegetable ghee is also available. This is vegetable oil that has been hydrogenated to make it solid at room temperature. So has *solid vegetable shortening*, which is used for baking. Neither will do anything to lower your cholesterol level, but they should not contain any unwelcome additives either.

Milk products

Milk is a very useful product that contains the essential vitamin B_{12}, which is lacking in a strictly vegetarian diet. Milk is a very good source of protein, vitamins, and minerals, particularly calcium and phosphorous. However, it also contains saturated fat. Skim milk has had most of the fat content removed. Goat's milk is often a good substitute for people who find it difficult to tolerate drinking cow's milk.

Buttermilk is another easily digestible milk product, has a similar protein and mineral content to whole milk, but contains less vitamin A and the fat content is much lower. It is useful in baking.

Yogurt is a living food, in which bacteria act on the milk sugars to produce lactic acid. It is easy to assimilate, and eating it regularly helps the digestion. Many commercial yogurts contain additives, preservatives, and coloring agents, so it is worth making your own. There are yogurt-makers available that can maintain the milk at exactly the right temperature while it ferments. (See *Making Yogurt*, pp. 105–106.)

Soybean products

Soybean foods have become very popular recently because of their varied uses for vegetarians. *Soy milk* is an easily digested substitute for dairy milk and recommended to sufferers of milk allergies. To make it, soak soybeans in water overnight (1 cup of beans will produce about 8 cups soy milk). In the morning, strain them and grind them with the same volume of water (each cup will have roughly doubled in size, so add 2 cups of water for each original cup of beans). Put this in a large pot and add the same quantity of water (another 4 cups for each original cup). Bring to a boil and boil for 20 minutes, uncovered. It should be rapidly boiled to ensure that all toxins are destroyed. You will find that the water froths up considerably – sprinkling cold water on top will help to settle it. Strain before use. Soy milk makes an excellent substitute for milk in custards, puddings, and milk shakes.

Tofu is soybean curd. This is another way of utilizing the soybean. Its high-protein content (it is also rich in iron, calcium, and B vitamins, while containing few calories or saturated fat, and no cholesterol) makes it a nutritious substitute not only for meat and fish, but also for dairy products. The Chinese hardly use milk in their daily diets. In Chinese and Japanese cooking, tofu is a most versatile ingredient, whether marinated, stir-fried, or deep-fried, whisked into dressings and sauces, or added to soups, burger mixes, and even some desserts.

It is available in various forms. Silken tofu is the softest, a mixture of some curds and whey, with a consistency like firm junket. It is best for mashing, or blending for dips, dressings, and sauces. It is usually sold in a carton, which will keep unopened and unrefrigerated for 6 months. Once opened the tofu should be consumed within 2 days.

Firm tofu is a heavily pressed version, with a dense texture like firm cheese; it can be cubed, sliced, and marinated. When sold loose, you will usually find it refrigerated, submerged in water. It will keep fresh for a week immersed in water in the refrigerator, with the water changed daily. It is also sold in vacuum packs, which keep, if not opened, for 3–4 weeks. Once opened, keep the tofu under water and treat it just like loose tofu, otherwise it will develop a fresh skin. Soft tofu, with a texture between firm and silken, can be treated in the same way as firm tofu.

Tofu can be frozen, which drastically changes its look and texture. Squeeze out thawed tofu to get rid of excess water.

Fats

Solid vegetable shortening
This is the only vegetarian alternative to lard or suet. Vegetable oils are hydrogenated to make them solid at room temperature.

Ghee
Ghee generally denotes clarified butter but a vegetable version (above) made from hydrogenated vegetable oils is also available.

Milk products

Buttermilk
This is the liquid remaining after fresh cream has been churned to make butter. Much of the buttermilk sold today is cultured and soured by adding bacteria to form lactic acid.

Yogurt & Strained Yogurt
One of the most popular fermented milk products, yogurt is a natural antibiotic, the acid in it killing almost all harmful organisms. It is easily digested, especially goat's milk yogurt (below).
Strained yogurt (below right), popular in Greece, is much smoother, creamier and sweeter than ordinary yogurt, not unlike crème fraîche. It is an excellent substitute for cream.

Yogurt

Strained yogurt

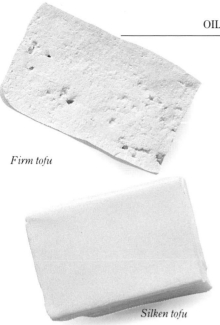

Firm tofu

Soybean products

Soy milk
Soy milk can be used as a substitute for dairy milk. Commercial soy milk sometimes contains sugar.

Silken tofu

Tofu
This product of the soybean is generally available as silken tofu, made from lightly pressed soybean curd, and firm tofu, which is more heavily pressed. Soft or regular tofu has a texture in between the two.

Soft tofu

Cheese and Eggs

Strict vegetarians eat only cheese made with non-animal rennet. These can be found in health food stores and include cheddar and other hard cheeses, as well as the soft cheeses such as cottage cheese, ricotta, and feta, some varieties of which do not use rennet anyway. Although a good source of protein, cheese made from whole milk is high in fat and cholesterol, so use it sparingly and substitute lowfat cheese wherever possible.

Eggs
Most commercially available eggs are produced by cooped-up chickens fed synthetically enhanced diets. Free-range eggs come from chickens that are fed more natural foods.

Eggs, particularly the yolks, are an excellent source of protein and contain all the essential amino acids. They are also high in fat and cholesterol, which is why many people are advised to limit their consumption of eggs.

Store eggs in a cool place. If the shell is soiled, wipe it with a dry cloth; washing removes the protective film. Do not use eggs with cracked shells as these could easily be contaminated with bacteria.

Substitutes for eggs
Eggs in cooking can be replaced in a number of ways. All the following variations will alter the texture and flavor to a certain extent, but it is worth experimenting if you want to cut down on cholesterol or have any particular allergy problems.

Where eggs are used to enrich a dish such as pastry or bread dough, use soy flour instead. One to two tablespoons mixed with 2–2½ cups flour gives a richer pastry; ½ cup soy flour in 4 cups flour gives a rich bread dough. Soy flour mixed to a cream with water can be used instead of an egg-wash, or glaze. One to two tablespoons of soy flour can be added to savory bakes as a substitute for an egg, but will not bind the mixture in the same way, tahini (see page 90) can be used as a binding agent.

Cheeses

Hard cheeses

All the cheeses on these two pages are made without animal rennet: Hard goat's cheese, cheddar, Monterey Jack; farmhouse cheese made with celery seeds; Botton (an English farmhouse cheese from Yorkshire) made with chives; and Double Gloucester (considered one of the great English cheeses). Other hard cheese available include Gouda and Munster.

Farmhouse

Cheddar

Botton

Double Gloucester

Hard goat's cheese

Cream cheese
Made, as the name indicates, from cream, this cheese therefore has a very high fat content. It is valued for its smooth, rich taste and creamy texture.

Curd cheese
Soft cheese made from whole cow's milk, this is usually set without using rennet. It is sometimes known as lactic curd cheese.

Cottage cheese
Cottage cheese is a type of lowfat curd cheese made from cooked skim cow's milk. It is drained, washed, and coated with thin cream, and has a granular appearance.

Sapsago
A Swiss whey cheese, this is also known as Geska, Schabzieger, or Glärnerkäse. It can be used instead of Parmesan. The greenish color comes from a special clover.

Coulommiers
Coulommiers is a mild French cheese, similar to Brie (it is also called Brie de Coulommiers). Usually eaten unripened, it is often sprinkled with paprika or herbs.

Chèvre
Chèvre, or French goat's cheese, is a traditional soft cheese with a distinctive taste. It is usually found in the shape shown here, or as a small cylinder.

Ricotta
This is a very lowfat soft cheese made from whey, not from pressed curds. It is sometimes available in mature hard form for grating.

Feta
This is the best known Greek cheese: with tomato and cucumber, it becomes "Greek salad." Traditionally made from sheep or goat's milk, it is curdled naturally without the addition of rennet.

Chapter Four

Basic Vegetarian Cooking Techniques

If you are switching to a healthier diet, you may wish to make your own basic foods – bread, for example, is easy to make and better than anything bought from a store, even a health food shop, as you will know exactly what ingredients have been used in your loaf. Nothing can beat the delicious smell of a newly baked loaf of bread, fresh from the oven!

No special equipment is needed in order to make yogurt; a vacuum bottle will do very well. In fact, basic kitchen equipment and some cheesecloth is all that you will need for making reduced fat sour cream (p. 107), curd cheese (p. 108), thickened yogurt (p. 106), and tofu (p. 115).

Most pastry is made out of refined flour and is not very nutritious, but there are healthier ways of making it. Hot water crust pastry, basic piecrusts, yeasted pastry, and strudel pastry can all be made using whole-wheat flour and less fat.

Vegetarian cookery involves the frequent use of dried beans, peas and lentils and dried fruit, and you will need to know how to reconstitute these. Grains, too, are easy to cook once you know how.

Home produce
Foods cooked, or made at home always taste that much better. Top left: Using a yogurt maker (see p. 106); Top right: Making strudel pastry (see p. 113); Bottom left: Making tomato sauce (see p. 119); Bottom right: How to stir-fry (see p. 121).

Making bread

It is worth making your own bread, as many of the so-called wholesome and healthy whole-wheat loaves available in the stores are neither. Often the flour used is mixed whole-wheat and processed white so much of the fiber is lost. Even the distinctive brown coloring may come from caramel. Many such loaves often have as many additives as white bread, and are manufactured in much the same way, having no real fermentation time to enhance the flavor.

When making your own bread, choose a hard, stoneground, 100 percent whole-wheat flour. Hard flours, usually made from American or Canadian wheat, have a high gluten content, thus ensuring a strong, elastic dough which is

needed for good results. It is possible to add a soft, low-gluten flour like soy for extra flavor and protein, which the dough might otherwise lack. You can also add a little oil as this will improve the texture.

Once you have got used to making the basic loaf, try a variety of flours, also adding nuts, seeds, or wheat germ, cooked grains or even beansprouts for different flavors and textures. Richer bread doughs can be made using milk, yogurt, or eggs as part of the mixing liquid. For naturally sweet loaves, use honey, molasses, or dried fruits. If you are on a strictly salt-free diet, you can leave out the salt from the basic recipe, but the taste and texture of the loaf will be quite different.

Whole-wheat bread

Along with grains and dried beans, whole-wheat bread is one of the staples of a vegetarian diet – it is high in protein, fiber, vitamins, and minerals. It is also very easy to make at home. Bake in a preheated oven at 425°F for 35–40 minutes. Once cooked, the bread should sound hollow when tapped a couple of times on its bottom.

Ingredients
1 ounce compressed yeast
¼ cup soy flour
2 cups warm water
4½ cups whole-wheat flour
up to 1 teaspoon salt
Makes two 1-pound loaves

Making whole-wheat bread

1 *Beat the yeast and soy flour with ⅔ cups of the warm water. Leave in a warm place for 5 minutes or until the mixture becomes frothy.*

2 *Mix most of the flour and salt in a large bowl. Pour in the yeast mixture and add the remaining flour. Mix all the liquids in with a wooden spoon.*

3 *Draw up the flour with your hands to form a dough, turn out onto a floured surface and knead thoroughly until the dough has a smooth, velvety surface.*

4 *Put into a clean bowl and leave covered in a warm place for 1 hour to rise. This process is called "proving." It also enhances the flavor of the bread.*

5 *After an hour, turn the dough out onto a floured surface, punch your fist into the dough, and knead it again thoroughly for a few minutes.*

6 *Divide the dough and shape it into two loaves. Put these into two greased loaf pans and leave them to rise again for another 10 minutes before baking.*

Sourdough bread

This is a delicious sharp-tasting bread popular in the San Francisco area whose flavor is enhanced if it is kept for one day before cutting. Mix together the rye flour, milk, and salt. Leave at room temperature for 48 hours. Blend the yeast with half the water and the sourdough starter. Mix in half the rye flour, and leave overnight at room temperature. Mix the remaining rye flour with the salt. Add to the dough with the remaining water, then add the whole-wheat flour and knead well. The dough should be moist, but not sticky. Form into a loaf and prick all over. Place on a floured cookie sheet. Leave to rise for 45 minutes. Bake at 400°F, for 1¼–1½ hours.

Ingredients

For the sourdough starter
1 cup rye flour
½ cup milk
½ teaspoon salt

For the dough
1 package of active dried yeast
2 cups hot water
4½ cups rye flour
2–3 teaspoons salt
2–2½ cups whole-wheat flour

Makes about one 2¼ pound loaf

Rye bread

A characteristic of rye bread is its close, moist texture. In this recipe, moistness is achieved by adding buckwheat flour and some yogurt or buttermilk to the ingredients. In the batter method of making bread used here, the whole-wheat flour is mixed with the yeast first to start the dough rising properly. The low-gluten rye flour (which does not rise as easily) is then beaten into the risen mixture. Bake in a preheated oven at 425°F, for 35 minutes. The bread is cooked if it sounds hollow when tapped lightly on the bottom.

Ingredients
1/2 package active dry yeast
2 teaspoons molasses
1 1/4 cups hot water
3 3/4 cups whole-wheat flour
pinch of salt
1 3/4 cups rye flour
1/2 cup buckwheat flour
2 teaspoons aniseeds
up to 2/3 cup yogurt or buttermilk
Makes two 1 1/4 pound loaves

Making rye bread

1 Mix together the yeast, molasses, and water. Leave in a warm place for 10 minutes until frothy. Add half the whole-wheat flour and beat in thoroughly.

2 Cover and leave to rise for 45 minutes. Beat in the remaining ingredients, adding enough yogurt or buttermilk to make a soft dough.

3 Turn out onto a floured surface and knead thoroughly until the dough feels smooth, adding more flour or liquid as necessary.

4 Shape into two round loaves and place on lightly oiled cookie sheets or in loaf pans. Leave to rise for 30 minutes before putting in the oven.

Dairy products

Yogurt can be made from any milk – cow, goat, sheep, or soy, skim or whole, – in either a wide-necked vacuum bottle or a special yogurt maker. You can even use light or heavy cream. Both yogurt and reduced fat sour cream are made using commercial starters for the first batch. These can be bought from most health food stores. If the yogurt does not set properly it can mean that the starter was not still active. In which case use a new starter. For successive batches, keep back 2 tablespoons of yogurt each time.

Homemade yogurt

To start your first batch of homemade yogurt, you will have to use either a commercially made plain yogurt, or a culture powder (advisable for anyone with an allergy to milk). For successive batches, just keep back 2 tablespoons of the yogurt each time. Yogurt can be made thicker by adding 1 tablespoon or more, of skim milk powder to the milk.

Ingredients
2½ cups skim milk
2 tablespoons plain yogurt
1–2 tablespoons skim milk powder (optional)
Makes 2½ cups yogurt

Using a vacuum bottle

1 *Bring the long-life milk to a temperature of 110–115°F, or scald the skim milk and cool to this temperature.*

2 *Stir in the yogurt starter and add the required amount of skim milk powder, if you are using it, to thicken your yogurt.*

3 *Pour into a clean, warmed vaccum bottle (the neck should be wide enough for you to get the finished yogurt out). Leave overnight, or until set.*

4 *Transfer the yogurt to a clean container and put in the refrigerator. The mixture will thicken slightly as it begins to cool.*

Using a yogurt maker

1 *Bring the long-life milk to a temperature of 110–115°F, or scald the skim milk and cool to this temperature.*

2 *Pour into clean yogurt jars, screw on the lids, and switch on the machine. Leave to set according to the manufacturer's directions.*

Thickened yogurt

Ingredients
2½ cups fresh yogurt
Makes ¾ cup thickened yogurt

By hanging fresh yogurt in cheesecloth it is possible to drain off excess whey, leaving a thick, creamy textured yogurt similar to curd cheese. The longer the yogurt is left, the thicker it will be.

Making thickened hung yogurt

1 *Suspend a cheesecloth or preserving bag over a clean bowl. Pour the fresh yogurt into it.*

2 *Leave for at least 4 hours. Turn it out into a clean container and keep in the refrigerator.*

Reduced fat sour cream

This is a low-fat soured cream made from skim milk and cream. Like sour cream and yogurt, it can be used in cakes, sauces, toppings, soups, casseroles, and loaves. When making reduced fat sour cream yourself, you will need to use a commercial brand as a starter for your first batch, using half light cream and half light skim milk. Make sure that you bring the milk to the correct temperature and incubate it for slightly longer than for yogurt.

Ingredients
1¼ cups long-life skim milk
1¼ cups light cream
2–3 tablespoons reduced fat sour cream
Makes 2½ cups

Making reduced fat sour cream

1 *Put the milk into a saucepan and stir in the light cream. Heat gently to 110–115°F.*

2 *Using a spoon, add the reduced fat sour cream to the contents of the saucepan, and mix in thoroughly.*

3 *Transfer to a clean, warm, wide-necked vacuum bottle and leave for 12 hours, or until set.*

4 *Transfer the reduced fat sour cream to a clean container and keep refrigerated for up to a week.*

Curd cheese

Ingredients
2½ cups whole milk
⅔ cup cultured buttermilk
1 tablespoon lemon juice
Makes 5 ounces curd cheese

Like yogurt, curd cheese is a versatile ingredient in healthy eating – it can be used as a thickener, a garnish, or a main ingredient. One of the best things about this lowfat, soft cheese is its freshness and creaminess – it makes commercially produced soft cheese seem cloying in comparison. Although the taste is mild, it gives plenty of scope for flavoring: add chopped chives, sage, paprika, coriander leaves, cilantro or garlic for a savory cheese, and dried or fresh fruit for a sweet one.

Once made, keep refrigerated in a sealed container for up to a week. This cheese also freezes successfully, but once thawed beat well in a blender to ensure a smooth texture.

Making curd cheese

1 *Put the milk (either cow's milk or goat's milk) into a saucepan and then scald it. Place a thermometer in the pan and allow the mixture to cool to 70°F.*

2 *Mix in the buttermilk and gently heat the mixture to a temperature of not more than 170°F. Stir the mixture every 5 minutes, being careful not to break up the curds.*

3 *Curds form at 120–140°F. Keep the mixture at this heat until the curds have separated. Add fruit juice if curds do not separate with heat alone.*

4 *Put a colander inside a large bowl and line it with two or three thicknesses of cheesecloth. Use a slotted spoon to scoop out all the curds into the cheesecloth.*

5 *When most have been removed, gently pour the remaining curds and whey down the side of the cheesecloth, taking care not to break up the curds as you pour.*

6 *Allow the curds to drain for 2 hours or until they are quite firm. Turn them out into a clean bowl and keep refrigerated. They will keep for up to a week.*

Making pastry dough

Pastry in general is not very nutritious – it is high in calories due to the fat content and, when made with white flour, is low in fiber, vitamins, and minerals. However, there are healthier ways of making pastry, using fewer fats. By switching to whole-wheat flour, you can improve the nutritional content of your pastry. This is because whole-wheat flour is higher in protein, fiber, vitamins, and minerals than refined flour, and at the same time is also free from any additives.

Until you have had some practice with whole-wheat pastry, you may find it slightly difficult to handle. Due to its fiber content, you will need to add more liquid (whether water, skim milk, oil, or eggs) than you would for refined flour, and you should allow a resting period of 30 minutes. This will give the fiber a chance to absorb the liquid and to swell. Another important point to bear in mind is that whole-wheat pastry has a much denser texture than refined pastry.

To guarantee a lighter effect to the finished pastry, it is best for beginners to add baking powder to the flour until they get used to handling the dough. Also, remember always to roll out whole-wheat pastry more thinly than normal, as a little tends to go a long way.

Lowfat pastry dough

This alternative to piecrust dough (see p. 110) uses oil, not fat, to provide the richness. It is therefore low in saturated fat and high in polyunsaturates.

Always let pastry rest before rolling it out. This allows the gluten in the flour to lose its elasticity. If this is not allowed for, the pastry will shrink once it is rolled out. It will also shrink badly during the baking process, leaving an unsightly gap around the edge of your pie.

Ingredients
1½ cups whole-wheat flour
1 tablespoon soy flour
pinch of salt
1½ teaspoons baking powder
1 tablespoon sunflower oil
skim milk to mix
Makes enough for a 9- to 10-inch
tart case

Making lowfat pastry

1 *Sift the flours, salt, and baking powder together into a mixing bowl. Use a wooden spoon to push all the flour through the strainer.*

2 *Add the oil and milk and mix to a soft dough. Let the dough rest for at least 30 minutes in a cool place before starting to roll it out.*

Basic piecrust dough

This pastry has a nuttier taste and more ingredients than white-flour pastry. It also contains more vitamins and other nutrients, as it is made with whole-wheat flour. Try using vegetable shortening for a healthier pastry.

Pastry always tastes better and has a lighter texture if it is made in cool surroundings. If your hands tend to be warm, use a pastry blender to mix the fat into the flour. Always use lightly chilled fats in pastry-making, they rub into bread crumbs without it becoming soft and greasy. A marble slab makes an ideal board for rolling out dough, as it is cool to the touch.

Ingredients
¾ cup plus 2 tablespoons
whole-wheat flour
pinch of salt
1 teaspoon baking powder
¼ cup fat (butter, solid vegetable
shortening, margarine, or a
mixture)
2 teaspoons oil
2–3 tablespoons water
squeeze of lemon juice
Makes enough for a 9- to 10-inch
crust case

Making basic piecrust dough

1 *Mix the flour and salt in a bowl and add the baking powder. Using just the tips of your fingers, rub the fat well into the flour.*

2 *Mix together the oil, water, and lemon juice in a separate bowl. Sprinkle two-thirds of this over the rubbed-in mixture.*

3 *Draw the dough together. If it is not wet enough to hold together, add the rest of the liquid.*

4 *Wrap the dough in plastic film or foil and leave for 30 minutes or so before rolling out.*

Hot-water pastry dough

Despite being the pastry traditionally used for meat pies, hot-water crust pastry is ideal for vegetarian dishes, both sweet and savory. The shortening and water are boiled together, then mixed with the flour, to produce a soft dough which is extremely pliable when hot. It must be fitted into a spring form pan or loaf pan when warm, so you should always have the filling for the pie made in advance. Once a pie is made, however, it does not matter if it stands for a few hours before being cooked. Put the pie into a hot oven, then reduce the oven temperature so that it finishes cooking properly.

Ingredients
3 cups whole-wheat flour
pinch of salt
⅔ cup vegetable shortening
½ cup water
Makes enough for a 7-inch spring form pan

Making hot-water pastry dough

1 *Put the flour and salt into a bowl. Chop the vegetable shortening into small pieces.*

2 *Put the water in a saucepan, add the shortening and bring the mixture to a steady boil.*

3 *Immediately pour the liquid onto the flour and stir it in thoroughly with a wooden spoon. Leave it for a few minutes to cool slightly.*

4 *As soon as the mixture is cool enough to handle, shape it to fit the pan. If it seems dry and crumbly, add as much boiling water as needed to keep it supple.*

Yeasted pastry dough

This cross between a bread and a pastry has a good, light texture so long as it is rolled out thinly. For an egg-free variation, use ½ cup milk and add 1 tablespoon soy flour to the fermenting yeast mixture. Then proceed as for the main recipe. Remember to leave the dough for 10 minutes before rolling it out. To prevent the bottom crust from becoming soggy, bake the dough blind. To do this, roll out the dough thinly and line a tart pan with it. Press down the bottom and sides firmly and prick the bottom all over with a fork. Bake for 5 minutes at 400°F, then put in the filling and bake as instructed.

Ingredients
6 tablespoons skim milk, warmed
1 teaspoon honey
1 teaspoon compressed yeast
1¾ cups whole-wheat flour
pinch of salt
2 tablespoons butter, melted
1 egg, beaten
Makes enough for a 9- to 10-inch tart shell

Making yeasted pastry dough

1 *Mix the milk and honey. Crumble yeast into a bowl.*

2 *Pour the milk mixture onto the yeast and beat together to blend.*

3 *Add half the flour to the bowl and stir in thoroughly.*

4 *Cover with a cloth and set aside for 30 minutes.*

5 *Add the remaining flour, salt, melted butter, and egg.*

6 *Mix to a dough and knead on a floured surface for 5–7 minutes.*

Strudel pastry dough

This is a versatile whole-wheat alternative to the traditional Greek *filo* pastry, and it can be served with both sweet and savory fillings. With practice, strudel pastry is not hard to make. The secret is to knead the dough thoroughly so that it becomes very elastic. If this is done properly, you will be able to pull and stretch it out very thinly. When stretching the dough, work on a well-floured cloth as this helps to grip the dough, and prevents it from shrinking back once stretched out. Once the dough is stretched out, leave it to dry slightly before covering with the chosen filling and carefully rolling up.

Ingredients
1¼ cups whole-wheat flour
pinch of salt
2 teaspoons sunflower oil
½ cup water
oil for brushing
Makes enough for one strudel
pastry for 4–6 people

Making strudel pastry dough

1 *Mix the flour and salt together in a bowl. Add the oil and water and mix to a soft dough. Put the dough on a board for kneading.*

2 *Knead thoroughly by picking up the dough and slapping it down on the surface. Do this until the dough becomes elastic in texture.*

3 *Brush the dough with oil to retain this elasticity. The oil will also prevent a skin from forming on the dough while it is resting.*

4 *Cover the dough with a warm dish and leave it on one side to rest for about 10–15 minutes.*

5 *Brush with oil again and place on a clean, floured cloth. Use your knuckles to flatten the dough.*

6 *Using the back of your hands, stretch the dough out gently until it is thin and almost transparent.*

Dried fruit, dried beans, and grains

Beans, peas and lentils the main staple of a whole-food vegetarian diet, are available dried. Of these, the larger beans and peas need to be soaked in water before cooking. The same is true of many dried fruits.

Although the food has usually been cleaned, it is often a good idea to rinse grains, dried fruit, and beans before reconstituting them, to remove any remaining dust or, in the case of dried fruit, traces of preservative.

Dried fruit

Dried fruit is a useful standby for the pantry. All dried fruits are high in vitamins, fiber, and minerals, and are delicious raw as snacks, in salads, or cooked for fruit salads and compotes. Try spicing the soaking water with nutmeg, cinnamon, or vanilla extract for extra flavor, but do not add any extra sugar to the water, as the sugar content of dried fruit is already highly concentrated.

Reconstituting dried fruit

1 *Put the fruit in a large bowl and cover with plenty of water. Leave to soak overnight.*

2 *The fruit will double or treble in size. Cook it in its original soaking liquid.*

Dried beans

Soaking dried beans (including peas and lentils) before cooking speeds up cooking times. Before soaking, pick over the dried beans carefully to remove any sticks or stones, and then soak in plenty of water. Some dried beans do cause flatulence, but by changing the soaking water two or three times this problem can be reduced. When you boil dried beans (step 3), flavor the water with vegetables (onions, carrots), and seasonings (caraway, fennel, aniseed, or kombu sticks) to make a good bean stock. Dried beans and peas usually take 30–50 minutes to cook (they will be soft all the way through when ready); in a pressure cooker they cook in roughly a third of the time.

Reconstituting dried beans

1 *Put the dried beans in a bowl and cover by at least 2 or 3 inches cold water. Leave overnight.*

2 *Drain away the soaking water. Rinse the beans thoroughly in cold water.*

3 *Put in a saucepan, cover with water and bring to a boil. Add any flavorings except for salt because this toughens the skins. Boil for 10 minutes, removing any white scum from the surface.*

4 *Lower the heat and cook until the beans are tender. Drain the beans, keeping the liquid for stock (see p.120). Use the beans immediately, or store, covered, in a refrigerator for up to 4 days.*

Tofu

Also known as bean curd, tofu is made from a ground soybean and water mixture which is then strained and pressed to form firm, off-white cakes. It is richer in protein than any other food of equivalent weight and is therefore a useful addition to a vegetarian diet. It is, however, more notable for its texture than its taste, which is rather bland, so dishes using it should always be well flavored. Tofu can be bought from most Chinese supermarkets, and will keep for three days in the refrigerator.

Ingredients
1 cup soybeans
juice of 2 lemons
Makes 10 ounces okara, 10 ounces tofu

Note: okara is the soybean pulp leftover from making tofu or soymilk. It can be used to add texture to soups, stews, and baked goods.

Making okara and tofu

1 *Put the beans in a bowl, cover them with water and leave them overnight in a cool place. Do not leave the beans anywhere warm, or they may start to ferment.*

2 *Drain and rinse thoroughly. Purée the beans to a creamy consistency, using 1 cup of water for each cup of beans. This mixture is called Go.*

3 *Bring 6 cups water to a boil in a large saucepan or preserving pan. When boiling, add the pureed soybeans. Bring the mixture back to a boil.*

4 *When the mixture boils up to the top of the pan, sprinkle cold water over it; this will stop the boiling and the mixture will sink back.*

5 *Repeat this 3 times, stirring occasionally. This stage is very important as it destroys any toxins present in the bean skins.*

6 *Put a colander into a clean bowl and line it with a layer of cheesecloth. Strain the mixture through the cheesecloth into the bowl.*

7 *The crumbly residue in the cheesecloth is called okara or soy bran. The liquid is soy milk.*

8 *Return the soy milk to a clean pan and bring it to a boil. Pour it into a clean bowl.*

9 *Add the lemon juice, stir, then leave the mixture to curdle. If it does not, repeat steps 8 and 9.*

10 *Using a fine strainer, press lightly against the curds in the bowl and then scoop out all the available liquid with a ladle.*

11 *Very gently tip the curds into a colander lined with cheesecloth. Allow the moisture to drain off. This is soft or silken tofu.*

12 *For a firmer tofu, wrap curds in cheesecloth and weigh down. The heavier the weight and the longer it is left, the more solid the tofu.*

Grains

Once you have measured or weighed out the amount of grain required, follow the chart on page 47 to gauge the amount of cooking water needed, and the length of time you will need to cook each type of grain.

Put the grain in a strainer and rinse thoroughly before cooking; it will not need soaking. Buckwheat and millet are best lightly roasted before boiling. For best results do not stir rice during cooking.

Roasting grains and seeds
Brush a heavy-bottomed pot lightly with oil. Heat, add the dry grains or seeds and cook until they are pale brown (about 4 minutes). Stir with a wooden spoon to prevent them sticking. Cook as normal.

Cooking grains

1 *If you weigh out the required grain, pour it into a measuring cup to establish the number of cups, and the amount of water.*

2 *Bring the correct amount of water to a boil (see the chart on p.47) and add the grain. Stir the contents of the pot once.*

3 *Bring the water back to a boil, cover and simmer until all the water has been absorbed. Add more boiling water if necessary.*

Making sauces

There are three basic sauces used in wholefood cookery which can be adapted to serve with a variety of grain, dried-bean, and vegetable dishes. They are white sauce, tomato sauce, and brown sauce, and the recipes are given here. When cooking all sauces, it is important to stir them continuously when this is indicated, to prevent them from becoming lumpy. You may wish to adjust the seasoning slightly according to your taste.

White sauce

When made with whole-wheat flour, white sauce always has a nuttier flavor than with refined flour, and a fuller texture. Not surprisingly, it also tends to be slightly browner in color.

It is best to infuse the milk to improve the flavor, especially if you are cutting down on seasoning. Use half an onion, peppercorns, a bay leaf, mace or nutmeg, or a small sprig of thyme or parsley. When using oil for the base of a roux, you must not overheat it before adding the flour, otherwise the flour fries, and cannot absorb the oil properly.

For a nutritious variation on this sauce, try adding ½–1 cup grated cheddar cheese, or 1–2 tablespoons chopped fresh herbs, such as dill, tarragon, or parsley.

If you are really concerned about your fat intake, try a lowfat white sauce instead. This recipe is low on calories because no fat is mixed with the flour to make the normal roux paste. Instead, rice flour is used as the thickening agent, mixed with skim milk.

Ingredients
1¼ cups skim milk
2 tablespoons sunflower oil
2 tablespoons whole-wheat flour
white pepper
For the infusion
½ onion
6 peppercorns
1 bay leaf
1 blade mace
Makes 1¼ cups sauce

Ingredients for a lowfat white sauce
1 tablespoon rice flour
*1¼ cups skim milk,
infused as above*
white pepper
Makes 1¼ cups sauce

Making white sauce

1 *Heat the milk with the seasoning ingredients. Bring to a boil, remove from the heat, cover and stand for 10 minutes. Strain the milk into a pitcher or into a bowl.*

2 *Gently heat the oil. When it is just hot add the flour and mix it in thoroughly, stirring all the time. Cook the oil and flour together for a few minutes.*

3 *Add the milk gradually, stirring well until completely smooth. Bring to a boil, and simmer for 3–5 minutes. Season with white pepper.*

Making lowfat white sauce

1 *Heat skim milk with infusion ingredients, see opposite. Leave to cool. Put the rice flour in a saucepan and mix to a paste with a little of the milk.*

2 *Stir in the remainder of the milk, bring to a boil and simmer for 5–7 minutes. Season to taste with the white pepper.*

Tomato sauce

This is a good example of a sauce made with vegetables and their own juices. To vary the flavor of the sauce, try adding 2 finely chopped stalks of celery to the recipe, or a couple of large, chopped broccoli flowerets (defrosted, if frozen). The herb marjoram can also be substituted instead of the oregano or fresh basil, if preferred.

Ingredients
2 teaspoons olive oil
1 small onion, finely chopped
1–2 cloves garlic, crushed
3⅓ cups peeled and roughly chopped tomatoes
1–2 tablespoons tomato purée
1 teaspoon miso (soy paste), dissolved in a little water
1 teaspoon oregano or 2 teaspoons fresh basil
black pepper
Makes 1¼ cups sauce

Making tomato sauce

1 *Heat the oil and cook the onion and garlic over a very low heat for 10–15 minutes – they should not color. Add the remaining ingredients.*

2 *Cover and simmer for 45 minutes. If you want a smooth sauce, puree the mixture in a food processor or blender. Season with black pepper.*

Brown sauce

It is much healthier to avoid all highly salted gravy mixes – vegetarian and otherwise. The points about oil and the thorough cooking of the flour (see p. 118) also apply to this recipe. Stocks made from adzuki beans or lentils provides a particularly good flavor, although you could use any dark vegetable or bean stock. Miso, which should be dissolved in a little water, and soysauce add color as well as seasoning to the sauce. Whole-wheat flour adds its own delicious taste, but must be thoroughly cooked to avoid a gummy texture.

Ingredients
1 onion, chopped
2/3 cup chopped mushrooms
2 tablespoons sunflower oil
2 tablespoons whole-wheat flour
1 1/4 cups dark stock
1 bay leaf
1 sprig fresh thyme
1/2 teaspoon dry mustard
up to 1 teaspoon miso (soy paste)
up to 1 teaspoon soysauce
black pepper
Makes 1 1/4 cups sauce

Making brown sauce

1 *Heat the oil and fry the vegetables gently for 5 minutes. Add flour, stir and cook for 3 minutes.*

2 *Pour on the stock and bring to a boil, stirring constantly to mix the ingredients thoroughly.*

3 *Add the herbs and mustard. Simmer for 7–10 minutes. Add miso, soysauce, and pepper to taste.*

Stock

Any liquid left over from cooking beans, peas, lentils, or grains can be used as the basis for a stock. Dark stocks are best made from red or black beans; for pale stocks use chickpeas or white bean cooking liquid.

To make the stock, first heat the oil and gently fry the vegetables. Add the water and simmer for 1–1 1/2 hours. Remove from heat and tip the vegetables and water into a strainer held over a clean bowl or other container. All the vitamins and minerals from the vegetables will have leached out into the water and the vegetables can be thrown away. Season the resulting stock to taste with some miso or soysauce.

Ingredients
1 tablespoon olive or sunflower oil
2 carrots, roughly chopped
1 large onion, roughly chopped
1 stick kombu
1 bay leaf
1 sprig thyme
8 1/4 cups water
miso (soy paste), soysauce, or shoyu
Makes 8 1/4 cups

Steaming and stir-frying

Steaming is an excellent way of preserving most of the minerals and vitamins in vegetables. There are two basic types of steamer; especially designed metal ones that act as container for both the food and the boiling water, and expandable steel baskets which hold the food but have to be placed inside a saucepan containing boiling water, as shown in the picture. Whichever method you use, the layer of vegetables should not be deeper than ½ to 2 inches.

Sprouting seeds

Sprouts have a very high vitamin and mineral content, and are useful if you want cheap, fresh salads and stir-fries all year round. I have found mung beans, adzuki beans, alfalfa, mustard, garden cress, and whole lentils easy to grow.

Steaming
Boil up a small amount of water in a pan and fit a steaming basket inside. Then add the chopped vegetables and steam until just tender.

Stir-frying

In this cooking technique the vegetables are cooked rapidly in the minimum amount of very hot oil so that they retain all their flavor and crisp textures. The traditional piece of equipment is a wok: a thin, round-bottomed metal pan that conducts the heat well, allowing the food to cook quickly and evenly. Peanut oil is good to use as it can be heated to high temperatures with no flavor loss.

Stir-frying vegetables

1 *Chop the vegetables into evenly sized pieces. Heat a wok over a high heat until smoke rises. Add 1½ tablespoons oil and swirl it around gently to coat the wok.*

2 *Add the chopped vegetables one at a time, putting in the ones requiring the longest cooking first, and the others at short intervals so that they will be ready together.*

3 *Just before the vegetables are cooked, add the seasoning, and then add some liquid – water or stock, to taste – to finish off cooking with a burst of steam.*

CHAPTER FIVE

HEALTHY VEGETARIAN RECIPES

This chapter contains recipe suggestions to help you toward good health. Based on the high-fiber, high-protein, lowfat principle, each recipe is accompanied by a nutritional profile (*see below*). This shows you which nutrients are contained in each dish.

HOW TO USE A NUTRITIONAL PROFILE

0000
Calories

NUTRIENTS PER PORTION
Protein 25g ● ● ●   Fiber 16g ● ● ●
Polyunsaturated fat 17g ● ● ●   Saturated fat 4g
Vitamins A, B1, B2, B6, B12, C, D, E, FA, N
Minerals Ca, Cu, Fe, Mg, Zn

Each recipe has its own nutritional profile, so that you can see at a glance, in grams, exactly how much protein, fiber, polyunsaturated fat, saturated fat, and calories each portion, or meal, contains. The profile also shows which vitamins and minerals are found in significant quantities. A dash indicates that a dish is not exceptionally high in any particular vitamin or mineral. The bullet system indicates how good the source is: three bullets show an excellent source, two bullets a very good source, and one bullet a good source. In the case of saturated fat, the amount per portion is shown in grams. This will enable you to keep a check on your daily intake.

Tempting foods
Delicious and attractive-looking dishes can be made using a wide variety of vegetarian ingredients. Top left: Vegetable terrine (see p.135); Bottom: Hot stuffed mushrooms (see p.137); Right: Eggplant dip (see p.134).

Soups

A pot of lentils or beans, pasta or rice, onions, celery or tomatoes, all simmered in a savory broth made from fresh vegetables and seasoned with soysauce, herbs and spices – this is more than a welcome hot soup: it is a meal in itself, rich in protein, full of flavor, and with a nutritious balance of beans, grains and vegetables. For summer evenings, light purées of green vegetables such as fresh peas or watercress, or chilled fruit soups, make tempting first courses.

You do not need any special skill to produce a delicious homemade soup; nor, in most of these recipes, much preparation. The bulk of the work, including presoaking peas and beans, can often be done well in advance; indeed many of the soups detailed benefit from being made the day before and given time to rest and to develop their flavor.

*Clockwise from left: Fennel soup (*see p. 126*); All Saints' broth (*see p. 126*); Pease pottage (*see p. 126*).*

All Saints' broth

Illustrated on page 125

Ingredients

*2 ounces dried chestnuts, soaked
overnight in 5 cups water, or
4 ounces fresh chestnuts
2 teaspoons sunflower oil
1 medium onion, finely grated
1/2 cup adzuki beans, soaked
overnight
1 1/3 cups peeled and chopped
celery root
2 tablespoons tomato paste
1 teaspoon dried thyme
1 tablespoon soysauce
black pepper*
Serves 4–6

120
Calories

NUTRIENTS PER PORTION
*Protein 8g ● ● ●   Fiber 10g ● ● ●
Polyunsaturated fat 2g ● ● ●   Saturated fat 0.5g
Vitamins C
Minerals –*

This soup is perfect nutritionally – high in protein and fiber, low
in fat. Serve with dishes high in minerals and vitamins.
1 Place the chestnuts and their soaking water in a saucepan.
Bring to a boil, cover, and simmer for 40–50 minutes or until
soft. Leave to cool, then purée.
2 Heat the oil in a large saucepan and gently fry the onion for
4–5 minutes or until just brown. Drain the beans.
3 Add the beans and celery root to the pan and cook for 3 minutes.
4 Pour in 3¾ cups chestnut stock. Stir in the tomato paste and
thyme. Bring to a boil and let boil for 10 minutes. Reduce the
heat, cover, and simmer for 40–50 minutes or until beans are
cooked. Season with soysauce and pepper. Serve hot.

Pease pottage

Illustrated on page 125

Ingredients

*2 teaspoons sunflower oil
1 medium onion, chopped
1 medium carrot, chopped
1 medium parsnip, chopped
1/2 cup green split peas
3¾ cups vegetable stock (see p. 120)
1 bay leaf
1/2 teaspoon dry mustard
2 teaspoons salt, or gomasio if
preferred
black pepper*
Serves 4–6

140
Calories

NUTRIENTS PER PORTION
*Protein 7g ● ● ●   Fiber 6g ● ● ●
Polyunsaturated fat 1g ● ● ●   Saturated fat 0.5g
Vitamins A, B1, C, E
Minerals Fe*

Choose brightly colored split peas for this iron-rich soup.
1 Heat the oil in a large saucepan and gently fry the onion for
4–5 minutes, or until soft.
2 Add the carrot, parsnip, and green split peas. Cook for 5
minutes, stirring frequently.
3 Stir in the stock, bay leaf, and mustard. Bring to a boil, cover,
and simmer for 50 minutes. Season with salt and pepper.

Fennel soup

Illustrated on page 124

Ingredients

*2 teaspoons sunflower oil
2¾ cups trimmed and diced fennel
1/3 cup cashew pieces
2/3 cup skim milk
1¼ cups vegetable stock (see p. 120)
1/4 teaspoon aniseeds
1–2 teaspoons lemon juice
salt, or gomasio if preferred
black pepper*
Serves 4

95
Calories

NUTRIENTS PER PORTION
*Protein 4g ● ● ●   Fiber 3g ● ●
Polyunsaturated fat 2g ● ● ●   Saturated fat 1g
Vitamins –
Minerals –*

This subtle-tasting, high-protein soup is low in saturated fat.
1 Heat the oil in a large saucepan and gently fry the fennel for
10–15 minutes, or until soft.
2 Add the cashews, milk, and stock. Bring to a boil, cover, and
simmer for 15 minutes.
3 Cool, purée until smooth, adding aniseeds and lemon juice.
Season with salt and pepper. Reheat before serving.

Minestrone alla Genovese

NUTRIENTS PER PORTION

190
Calories

Protein 11g ● ● ●   Fiber 10g ● ● ●
Polyunsaturated fat 1g ●   Saturated fat 0.5g
Vitamins A, B1, C, E, FA
Minerals Ca, Cu, Fe, Mg

Illustrated below
Ingredients
*½ cup dry cannellini or Navy
beans, soaked overnight
2 teaspoons olive oil
1 medium onion, chopped
3 cloves garlic, crushed
1 cup shredded cabbage
1½ cups sliced mushrooms
1¾ cups diced zucchini
1 small eggplant, diced
2 cups peeled and chopped tomatoes
2 tablespoons tomato paste
2 teaspoons dried oregano
3¾ cups bean stock (see p. 120)
2 ounces whole-wheat pasta
3–4 tablespoons finely chopped fresh
parsley
1–2 tablespoons soysauce
black pepper*
Serves 6–8

There is a fine distinction between a hearty soup and a casserole, and although this highly nutritious soup comes into the former category, it needs only whole-wheat bread to make it a complete and satisfying meal.

1 Drain the beans. Cover with plenty of fresh water, bring (uncovered) to a boil, and let boil for 10 minutes. Reduce the heat, skim, cover, and simmer for 45–50 minutes or until soft. Drain and reserve the cooking water for stock. Add water to measure 3¾ cups; if necessary.

2 Heat the oil in a large saucepan and gently fry the onion and garlic for 4–5 minutes or until the onion is soft. Add the cabbage, mushrooms, zucchini, eggplant, and tomatoes and cook for 5 minutes.

3 Stir in the tomato paste, oregano, beans, and the reserved bean stock. Bring to a boil, cover, and simmer for 45–50 minutes. Add more stock if necessary.

4 Add the pasta and parsley and cook for a further 10 minutes.

5 Season with soysauce and pepper. Serve hot.

Minestrone alla Genovese (see above).

*Clockwise from left:
Country vegetable broth
(see opposite); Onion
soup (see opposite);
Miso julienne (see
p. 130).*

Onion soup

120
Calories

NUTRIENTS PER PORTION
Protein 3g ● ● *Fiber 4g* ● ● ●
Polyunsaturated fat 3g ● ● ● *Saturated fat 1g*
Vitamins A, C, E, N
Minerals Ca, K

Illustrated opposite

Ingredients
1½ tablespoons sunflower oil
2¾ cups finely chopped onions
1–2 cloves garlic, crushed
1 medium carrot, roughly chopped
1 small white turnip, grated
salt and pepper
1 bay leaf
1 teaspoon celery seeds
¼ teaspoon mustard powder
2½ cups dark vegetable stock
(see p. 120)
2 tablespoons soysauce
1 teaspoon miso (soy paste)
For garnishing
2 tablespoons coriander leaves,
cilantro, or Chinese parsley finely
chopped
1 tablespoon sesame seeds
Serves 4–6

A vegetarian adaptation of the traditional French onion soup which makes a welcome start to a winter meal.
1 Heat the oil in a large, heavy-bottomed pan and add the onions, garlic, carrot and turnip. Cover the pan and cook the vegetables for 15–20 minutes over a very gentle heat. Sprinkle with a little salt to bring out extra juices.
2 Add the bay leaf, celery seeds, mustard, stock, and soysauce. Stir well, bring to a boil, cover, and simmer for 20 minutes. Remove the bay leaf and carrot (unless you prefer to leave the pieces of carrot in for extra color).
3 Blend the miso with 1 tablespoon of the soup in a small bowl. Stir it back into the soup, mixing well, and season to taste.
4 Simmer gently for another 5 minutes and serve sprinkled with the chopped parsley or chervil and the sesame seeds.

Country vegetable broth

220
Calories

NUTRIENTS PER PORTION
Protein 6g ● ● *Fiber 5g* ● ● ●
Polyunsaturated fat 4g ● ● ● *Saturated fat 1g*
Vitamins C, E, N
Minerals Ca, K, Mg, Zn

Illustrated opposite

Ingredients
2 tablespoons pot barley
2 tablespoons wheat berries
2 tablespoons green split peas
2 tablespoons red lentils
1 medium onion, finely chopped
1 medium parsnip, diced
1 medium turnip, diced
1 medium potato, diced
2 tablespoons sunflower oil
3–3¾ cups vegetable stock
(see p. 120) or water
1 tablespoon soysauce
2 teaspoons finely chopped rosemary
1 teaspoon finely chopped thyme
salt and pepper
Serves 4–6

If you do not have the individual grains, peas, and lentils readily on hand, a "soup mix," obtainable in many health food stores, makes an ideal base.
1 Steep the grains, peas, and lentils in hot water for 1 hour, then drain well.
2 Gently soften the vegetables in the oil for 10 minutes, using a large, heavy-bottomed saucepan with a lid. Add the grains, peas, and lentils to the mixture, and fry them gently for a further 5 minutes, stirring occasionally.
3 Add the stock and soysauce, bring to a boil, cover, and simmer for 50–60 minutes.
4 Stir in the herbs and season to taste. You can serve the soup immediately, just as it is, or purée it briefly in a blender if you prefer a smoother texture, but do not purée it completely or it will lose its character.

Miso julienne

Illustrated on page 128

Ingredients
¼ ounce arame
½ teaspoon sliced gingerroot
1 tablespoon peanut oil
2 teaspoons sesame oil
½ pound carrots, cut into
julienne strips
½ pound daikon (Japanese radish),
cut into julienne strips
2½ cups dark vegetable stock
(see p. 120)
2 tablespoons soysauce
1 tablespoon miso (soy paste)
Serves 4–6

NUTRIENTS PER PORTION
100 Calories
Protein 2g ● ●   Fiber 2g ● ●
Polyunsaturated fat 1g ● ● ●   Saturated fat 0.5g
Vitamins A, C
Minerals Ca, K, Mg, Zn

With its strong, salty flavor, miso makes an excellent warming basis for a clear stock. This recipe includes a julienne of carrots and daikon, the subtly flavored Japanese white radish. The sea vegetable arame contributes a rich mineral content.

1 Soak the arame in hot water for 10 minutes and drain. Either chop it finely or, if you prefer, leave it in strips.
2 In a large, heavy-bottomed pan, fry the ginger in the peanut oil for 2–3 minutes over medium heat.
3 Add the sesame oil, carrots, daikon, and arame, cover, and continue to cook over gentle heat for 15 minutes.
4 Add the stock and stir in the soysauce and miso. Bring to a boil, cover, and simmer for a further 10 minutes. Serve the soup immediately.

Cream of potato soup with garlic

Illustrated opposite

Ingredients
For the stock
2 teaspoons sunflower oil
2 medium onions, quartered
12 cloves garlic, peeled
2 medium carrots, cut into chunks
1 bay leaf
1 sprig of thyme
For the soup
2 teaspoons sunflower oil
1 medium onion, finely chopped
2 cloves garlic, crushed
1¾ cups diced potatoes
1 tablespoon soysauce
2 teaspoons miso (soy paste),
dissolved in a little water
Serves 4

NUTRIENTS PER PORTION
75 Calories
Protein 2g ●   Fiber 2g ●
Polyunsaturated fat 1g ● ● ●   Saturated fat 0g
Vitamins C
Minerals –

Do not be put off by the amount of garlic in this recipe – the cloves add a wonderfully subtle flavor to the stock. Serve with a high-protein, high-fiber dish for balance.

1 For the stock: heat the oil in a large saucepan and gently fry the onion, whole cloves of garlic and carrot for 15–20 minutes.
2 Add the bay leaf, thyme and 3¾ cups water. Bring to a boil, cover, and simmer for 1–1½ hours. Strain, and reserve all the stock.
3 For the soup: gently heat the oil in a large saucepan and fry the onion and garlic for 4–5 minutes until lightly browned, stirring frequently.
4 Add the potato and fry for a further 5–8 minutes until lightly browned.
5 Pour in the garlic stock. Bring to a boil, cover, and simmer for 20 minutes.
6 Cool slightly, then purée until smooth, adding the soysauce and miso. Reheat gently before serving.

Spiced cauliflower soup

NUTRIENTS PER PORTION
Protein 7g ● ● ●   *Fiber 7g* ● ● ●
Polyunsaturated fat 2g ● ●   *Saturated fat 2g*
Vitamins A, B₁, B₆, C, FA

170

Calories

Minerals Fe

Illustrated below

Ingredients

¼ cup pearl barley
½ cup yellow split peas
2 teaspoons sunflower oil
1 medium onion, finely chopped
1 clove garlic, crushed
1 teaspoon fresh gingerroot, grated
½ teaspoon turmeric
*½ teaspoon coriander seeds,
crushed*
½ teaspoon cumin seeds
*1 medium cooking apple, cored,
and chopped*
1 medium carrot
*1 fresh green chili, deseeded and
finely chopped*
3¾ cups vegetable stock (see p. 120)
1 cauliflower, divided into flowerets
*2 tablespoons chopped fresh
coriander leaves, cilantro, or
Chinese parsley*
salt, or gomasio if preferred
black pepper
*2 tablespoons coconut milk:
(available from Oriental
food markets)*
Serves 6–8

Although cream of coconut is high in saturated fat, the quantity used here is small enough to be allowable, and just sufficient to add a delicate, velvety texture to the soup.

1 Place the barley and yellow split peas in a bowl. Cover with hot water and leave to soak for 1 hour. Drain.

2 Heat the oil in a large saucepan and gently fry the onion and garlic for 4–5 minutes or until soft. Add the ginger, turmeric, coriander, and cumin, and cook for 3–4 minutes.

3 Add the apple, carrot, chili, barley, and yellow split peas and fry for 2–3 minutes.

4 Pour in the vegetable stock, bring to a boil, cover, and simmer gently for 1 hour.

5 Add the cauliflower and chopped coriander leaves to the soup and cook for a further 10 minutes or until the cauliflower is just tender. Season with salt and pepper.

6 Stir the coconut milk into the soup, and allow to heat thoroughly before serving.

*From left to right:
Cream of potato soup with
garlic (see opposite);
Spiced cauliflower soup
(see above).*

APPETIZERS, SAUCES, AND RELISHES

Whether you eat a formal meal with separate courses, or whether you follow the example of many vegetarians and combine several dishes at the same time, something to start with is always welcome. This can be simple, perhaps eaten with a drink before the meal – pâté spread on little crackers, raw vegetables with various dips – or more elaborate, such as a vegetable terrine or stuffed grape leaves.

Vegetarian food lends itself admirably to the occasion and offers endless possibilities. In addition to the recipes given here, you will find many dishes in other sections of the book which can be scaled down to make ideal first courses. Soufflés, quiches, or stuffed vegetables are good appetizers. For a substantial start to a meal, try a pasta dish or a risotto, while for a lighter one, salads are perfect.

Sauces need not be thickened with flour. Vegetable and fruit purées make delicious bases, as in the broccoli and sunflower sauce, or the apricot and tomato relish. Nut-based sauces play a large part in vegetarian cuisine and supply extra protein.

Clockwise from left: Leek and tomato terrine (see p. 134); Cheese devils (see p. 135).

Leek and tomato terrine

Illustrated on pages 132–33

Ingredients
*1¼ pounds leeks
1 tablespoon olive oil
1 tablespoon white wine vinegar
2 teaspoons concentrated frozen
apple juice or 1 teaspoon of sugar
½ teaspoon whole-grain mustard
1 clove garlic, crushed
salt, or gomasio if preferred
black pepper
1⅓ cups peeled and sliced tomatoes
½ teaspoon green peppercorns,
lightly crushed
For serving
radicchio, lamb's lettuce or corn
salad, endive, whole-wheat bread
(see p. 102)
Serves 4–6*

NUTRIENTS PER PORTION
85 *Calories*
*Protein 3g ● ●   Fiber 5g ● ●
Polyunsaturated fat 0.5g ● ●   Saturated fat 0.5g
Vitamins A, B₁, B₂, B₆, C, E, FA, N
Minerals Ca, Cu, Fe, Mg, Zn*

This is a colorful way to serve a leek vinaigrette, with the buttery taste and smooth texture of the leeks contrasting well with the sharp dressing. Thin slices of whole-wheat bread, rolled up with cottage cheese, would be a good accompaniment to serve with this appetizer.

1 Clean the leeks and chop them in 1-inch pieces. Steam for 5–8 minutes until soft. Drain well.
2 Mix the olive oil, vinegar, apple juice, mustard, and garlic together. Season with salt and pepper.
3 Add the dressing to the warm leeks and toss.
4 Put a layer of half the leeks in the base of a lightly oiled 9-×5-inch loaf pan. Cover with a layer of tomatoes, sprinkle with the peppercorns, then top with the remaining leeks. Weight the mixture down well. Leave to cool.
5 When cold, turn out onto a bed of salad greens. Serve in slices accompanied by whole-wheat bread.

Eggplant dip

Illustrated on page 136

Ingredients
*1 large eggplant
4 tablespoons plain yogurt
1–2 tablespoons lemon juice
3 tablespoons tahini
4 tablespoons finely chopped fresh
parsley
2 cloves garlic, crushed
salt, or gomasio if preferred
black pepper
For serving
vegetable crudités or warm pita
bread
Serves 4–6*

NUTRIENTS PER PORTION
90 *Calories*
*Protein 4g ● ● ●   Fiber 1g ●
Polyunsaturated fat 3g ● ● ●   Saturated fat 1g
Vitamins –
Minerals –*

In summer months, the eggplant in this Middle Eastern dip could be barbecued to produce a more smoky flavor. Serve with raw vegetables or whole-wheat pita bread to improve the overall fiber content.

1 Preheat the oven to 350°F.
2 Remove the eggplant stem and prick the flesh 2–3 times. Place in a baking dish and bake for about 20 minutes or until the eggplants feel soft. Let cool.
3 Peel off the skin and chop the flesh. Discard skin.
4 Put the eggplant flesh, yogurt, lemon juice, tahini, parsley, and garlic into a blender or food processor and blend until smooth. Season with salt and pepper.
5 Serve with crudités of carrot, cauliflower, radishes, corn, and snow peas, or warm pita bread.

Cheese devils

Illustrated on page 133

NUTRIENTS PER PORTION
180 Calories
Protein 14g ● ● ● Fiber 1g ●
Polyunsaturated fat 1.5g ● Saturated fat 8.5g
Vitamins A, B12, E
Minerals –

Ingredients
¾ cup low fat ricotta cheese
3 tablespoons margarine
1 (large) egg
1 teaspoon mustard
pinch of cayenne
black pepper
6 ounces asparagus
Serves 4

These delicious savories provide a high-protein start to a light, low-calorie meal.

1 Cream the ricotta with the margarine in a bowl until smooth.
2 Beat in the egg and seasonings.
3 Steam the asparagus for 6–8 minutes until just tender. Cut into small pieces.
4 Meanwhile, preheat the oven to 325°F.
5 Lightly oil 4 ramekin dishes and divide the asparagus pieces between them. Pour over the cheese mixture.
6 Bake for 30–40 minutes or until just set. Serve hot.

Vegetable terrine

Illustrated on page 136

NUTRIENTS PER PORTION
230 Calories
Protein 17g ● ● ● Fiber 3g ● ● ●
Polyunsaturated fat 5g ● ● ● Saturated fat 5g
Vitamins A, B1, B12, C
Minerals Ca

Ingredients
8 large spinach leaves, washed
1¼ cups skim milk
½ medium onion
1 bay leaf
6 peppercorns
¼ teaspoon powdered mace
2 tablespoons sunflower oil
2 tablespoons whole-wheat flour
herb salt, or salt if preferred
grated nutmeg
black pepper
6 ounces low fat ricotta cheese
1 (large) egg
4 ounces peas
⅔ cup diced carrots
4 ounces asparagus
Serves 4–6

High in both protein and fiber, and relatively low in fat, this is an impressive dish to start a meal with. It is very important, however, to make sure that the terrine is cold and well set before slicing it with a sharp knife, or the colorful effect of the layers will be lost.

1 Pour boiling water over spinach; drain after 1 minute.
2 Place the milk in a saucepan with the onion, bay leaf, peppercorns and mace. Bring almost to a boil, cover and leave to infuse for 10 minutes. Strain the milk and set aside.
3 Gently heat the oil in a saucepan. Stir in the flour to make a roux. Gradually add the seasoned milk and bring to a boil, stirring constantly. Season with herb salt, nutmeg and pepper.
4 Cool slightly, then stir in the ricotta and egg.
5 Lightly steam the peas, carrots, and asparagus in separate pans or compartments of a steamer for 6–8 minutes. Preheat the oven to 325°F.
6 Line a 9-×5-inch loaf pan with the special spinach leaves, reserving one for the top.
7 Put in a layer of sauce, then a layer of carrot. Repeat with layers of sauce, peas, sauce, asparagus, and finally sauce.
8 Fold over the leaves and place one on the top to cover the mixture completely. Place the pan in a *bain marie* or a roasting pan filled with about 1-inch hot water in the oven.
9 Bake for 1 hour. Cool completely before turning out onto a serving plate. When cold, slice and serve.

*Clockwise from top: Vegetable terrine (see p. 135);
Eggplant dip (see p. 134); Hot stuffed mushrooms
(see p. 137).*

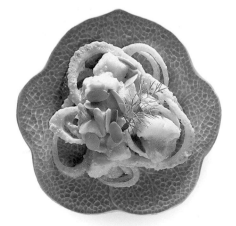

*Clockwise from left: Zyleone (see p. 138); Middle
Eastern stuffed grape leaves (see opposite).*

Hot stuffed mushrooms

Illustrated opposite

NUTRIENTS PER PORTION
165 Calories
Protein 8g ● ● ● *Fiber 3g* ● ●
Polyunsaturated fat 5g ● ● ● *Saturated fat 2g*
Vitamins C
Minerals Fe, Mg, Zn

Ingredients
4 large open mushrooms
2 teaspoons olive oil
2/3 cup diced button mushrooms
1 small green pepper, seeded and diced
2 teaspoons capers
2 cloves garlic, crushed
3/4 cup heaped fresh whole-wheat bread crumbs
1 teaspoon dried thyme
1 tablespoon lemon juice
1 tablespoon sesame seeds
salt, or gomasio if preferred
black pepper
pinch of cayenne
For the dressing
2/3 cup plain yogurt
1 tablespoon lemon juice
1 tablespoon tahini
1 clove garlic, crushed
Serves 4

Choose firm open mushrooms for this high-protein appetizer, as they have a stronger flavor than button mushrooms and are much easier to fill. The mushrooms can be broiled or baked.
1 Cut the stems out of the large mushrooms. Lightly steam the caps for 3–4 minutes until just softened. Place in a shallow baking dish, rounded sides down.
2 Preheat oven to 350°F, if baking them.
3 Heat the oil in a pan and gently fry the diced mushrooms, green pepper, capers, and garlic for 3–4 minutes or until soft.
4 Remove from the heat, mix in the bread crumbs, thyme, lemon juice, and sesame seeds. Season with salt, pepper, and a little cayenne.
5 Pile the mixture into the mushroom caps. Either place under a pre-heated broiler for 4–5 minutes, or, if you prefer, bake for 10–15 minutes.
6 Mix the dressing ingredients together thoroughly. Serve with the hot stuffed mushrooms.

Middle Eastern stuffed grape leaves

Illustrated opposite

NUTRIENTS PER PORTION
160 Calories
Protein 5g ● ● *Fiber 3g* ● ●
Polyunsaturated fat 5g ● ● ● *Saturated fat 1g*
Vitamins A, C
Minerals Ca, Cu, Fe

Ingredients
1/2 cup bulgur wheat
2/3 cup vegetable stock
20 grape leaves
2 teaspoons olive oil
1 medium onion, finely chopped
1 clove garlic, crushed
2 tablespoons diced dried apricots
1/2 cup chopped walnuts
2 teaspoons crushed coriander seeds
1 teaspoon soysauce
salt, or gomasio if preferred
black pepper
Serves 4–6

Based on a classic Middle Eastern hors d'oeuvre, this lowfat dish uses fruit and nuts for substance, and bulgur wheat.
1 Soak the bulgur wheat in the stock for 15 minutes. Drain and then squeeze out any excess moisture. Spread on a clean dish towel to dry out slightly.
2 Rinse the grape leaves and set aside.
3 Heat the oil in a saucepan and fry the onion and garlic for 4–5 minutes or until the onion is soft.
4 Add the apricots, walnuts, soaked bulgur wheat, and coriander to the pan and mix well. Cook for 10 minutes, adding a little more stock if the mixture begins to look dry. Season with soysauce, salt, and pepper.
5 Preheat the oven to 350°F.
6 Take a grape leaf and place with the stem nearest you. Put about 1 tablespoon of the mixture into the center of each grape leaf. Fold in both sides to the center, then roll the leaf up from the bottom. Place the grape leaves in a lightly oiled baking dish. Cover with foil. Bake for 10–15 minutes. Serve hot.

Illustrated on page 136

Ingredients
1/3 cup blanched almonds, ground
1 tablespoon white-wine vinegar
1/2 cup peeled and roughly chopped
cucumber
1 tablespoon sunflower oil
1 large or 2 small pears
1 1/3 cups diced fennel
For garnishing
1 tablespoon toasted slivered
almonds
fennel leaves
Serves 4

Zyleone

NUTRIENTS PER PORTION
150 Calories
Protein 4g ● Fiber 6g ● ● ●
Polyunsaturated fat 4g ● ● ● Saturated fat 1g
Vitamins C, E
Minerals –

Meaning "green" in Russian, this is a refreshing and unusual high-fiber, lowfat appetizer.
1 Put the almonds, vinegar, and cucumber in a grinder, blender, or food processor and blend thoroughly.
2 Add the oil drop by drop as if making mayonnaise. The mixture will thicken slightly.
3 Chop the pear into bite-sized pieces. Mix with the fennel.
4 Stir the pear and fennel into the dressing until well coated.
5 Pile into individual dishes and garnish with toasted almonds and fennel leaves. Serve chilled.

Illustrated opposite

Ingredients
6 finger avocados, peeled and
chopped
4 ounces cucumber, peeled and cut
into half-moons
1/2 cantaloupe, scooped into balls
4 ounces grapes
4 kumquats, halved
For the dressing
2 tablespoons orange juice
2 tablespoons lemon juice
1 tablespoon sunflower oil
For garnishing
fresh mint
Serves 4

Cocktail kabobs

NUTRIENTS PER PORTION
150 Calories
Protein 2g ● Fiber 1.5g ●
Polyunsaturated fat 3g ● ● ● Saturated fat 1g
Vitamins A, C, FA
Minerals Ca, Mg

This refreshing, lowfat appetizer should be served with a high-protein, high-fiber main course.
1 Place prepared fruit in a bowl. Put the dressing ingredients together in a screw-top jar and mix by shaking well. Pour over fruit and leave the fruit to marinate for 2 hours.
2 Thread the cucumber, melon, and kumquats alternately onto kabob skewers, ending with the avocado.

Illustrated opposite

Ingredients
2/3 cup sunflower seeds
10 ounces silken tofu
1 tablespoon olive oil
3 tablespoons wheat germ
1 cup finely grated carrots
1/2 teaspoon fresh dill
1/2 teaspoon paprika
salt, or gomasio if preferred
black pepper
For serving
4–6 large tomatoes or vegetable
crudités
Serves 4–6

Golden tofu pâté

NUTRIENTS PER PORTION
330 Calories
Protein 12g ● ● Fiber 4g ● ●
Polyunsaturated fat 9g ● ● Saturated fat 6g
Vitamins A, E
Minerals Ca

Use this high-protein pâté as a stuffing or served as a dip.
1 Grind half the sunflower seeds into a fine powder in a blender, or food processor.
2 Add the tofu, olive oil, and wheat germ, and blend until smooth. Transfer to a serving dish if using crudités.
3 Stir in the grated carrot, remaining whole sunflower seeds, dill, paprika, and season with salt and pepper.
4 Cut the tops off the tomatoes, scoop out the flesh and seeds, and stuff with the tofu mixture, or serve with crudités.

From left to right: Golden tofu pâté (see opposite); Cocktail kabobs (see opposite).

Peanut and sesame sauce

Illustrated on page 140

NUTRIENTS PER PORTION
Protein 3g ● ● *Fiber 1g* ●
Polyunsaturated fat 5g ● ● ● *Saturated fat 2g*
Vitamins –
Minerals –

125 Calories

Relatively low in fat, this simple sauce is like a nut mayonnaise.
1 Purée all the ingredients, except the peppers.
2 Gradually add ¾ cup plus 2 tablespoons water, puréeing until the sauce is smooth.
3 Season with cayenne and black pepper.

Ingredients
2 tablespoons tahini
1 tablespoon peanut butter
1 tablespoon sesame oil
1 tablespoon red-wine vinegar
2 teaspoons concentrated frozen apple juice or 1 teaspoon of sugar
2 teaspoons soysauce, or salt if preferred
1-inch piece fresh gingerroot, grated
pinch of cayenne
black pepper
Makes about 1¼ cups

Sharp mushroom sauce

Illustrated on page 140

NUTRIENTS PER PORTION
Protein 2g ● ● *Fiber 1g* ●
Polyunsaturated fat 0.5g ● ● *Saturated fat 0.5g*
Vitamins C
Minerals –

65 Calories

Low in saturated fat, this is a versatile sauce which can be served with both pasta and vegetable dishes.
1 Heat the oil in a saucepan and gently fry the onions for about 5–6 minutes until just brown.
2 Stir the remaining ingredients into the pan, mixing well. Bring to a boil, cover and simmer for 20 minutes, stirring occasionally. Season with extra soysauce if necessary, and pepper.

Ingredients
2 teaspoons olive oil
½ pound pearl onions
½ pound button mushrooms
⅔ cup tomato juice
⅔ cup apple juice
1 tablespoon red-wine vinegar
1 teaspoon soysauce
pinch of dried thyme
soysauce, or salt if preferred
black pepper
Makes about 2 cups

Clockwise from left: Peanut and sesame sauce (see p. 139); Carob sauce (see below); Sharp mushroom sauce (see p. 139); Ankake sauce (see opposite); Broccoli and sunflower sauce (see opposite); Apricot and tomato relish (see opposite).

Illustrated above

Ingredients
2 ounces dried pitted dates
1 tablespoon rice flour
1¼ cups milk
1–2 teaspoons carob powder
4–6 drops vanilla extract
Makes about 1¼ cups

Carob sauce

95
Calories

NUTRIENTS PER PORTION
Protein 3g ● ● *Fiber 1g* ●
Polyunsaturated fat 0g ● ● ● *Saturated fat 2g*
Vitamins –
Minerals –

As you lose your taste for sugar you may find that desserts need no flavoring other than vanilla. To start with, however, try this sauce sweetened with dates and carob.

1 Gently stew the dates in a little water for about 10–15 minutes until soft. Beat to a stiff purée.

2 Combine the rice flour with a little of the milk to dissolve. Then stir in the remaining milk.

3 Bring to a boil and cook gently for 5 minutes, stirring. (The rice flour will thicken the milk as it cools.)

4 Purée the milk with the dates, carob, and vanilla until the sauce is quite smooth.

5 Reheat gently before serving.

Ankake sauce

NUTRIENTS PER PORTION
Protein 3g ● *Fiber 0g*
Polyunsaturated fat 0.5g ● *Saturated fat 0.5g*
Vitamins C
Minerals –

65
Calories

Illustrated opposite
Ingredients
7 ounces pineapple juice
1 teaspoon honey
1 teaspoon red-wine vinegar
1 tablespoon miso (soy paste)
1 teaspoon cornstarch
Makes about 1¼ cups

This sweet-and-sour fruit sauce has a strong but pleasant miso flavor.
1 Mix all the ingredients together in a saucepan.
2 Bring to a boil and simmer for 2–3 minutes until the sauce thickens, stirring all the time.

Broccoli and sunflower sauce

NUTRIENTS PER PORTION
Protein 4g ● ● ● *Fiber 3g* ●
Polyunsaturated fat 4g ● ● ● *Saturated fat 1g*
Vitamins C, E
Minerals –

60
Calories

Illustrated on page 140
Ingredients
½ pound broccoli flowerets
2 tablespoons sunflower seeds
4 tablespoons silken tofu or
reduced fat sour cream
2 teaspoons lemon juice
salt, or gomasio if preferred
black pepper
Makes about 2 cups

A light, creamy sauce with a slightly nutty flavor. Serve with baked dishes or pasta.
1 Steam the broccoli flowerets for 8–10 minutes until tender.
2 Grind all of the sunflower seeds in a grinder, blender or food processor.
3 Purée the broccoli with 1¼ cups of the steaming water. Add the tofu, lemon juice, and sunflower seeds and purée again. Season to taste with salt and pepper.
4 Reheat very gently before serving.

Apricot and tomato relish

NUTRIENTS PER PORTION
Protein 9g ● ● *Fiber 7g* ● ● ●
Polyunsaturated fat 0g ● ● ● *Saturated fat 0g*
Vitamins A, C
Minerals –

250
Calories

Illustrated on page 140
Ingredients
⅔ cup thinly sliced dried apricots
1 teaspoon coriander seeds
1⅓ cups peeled and chopped
tomatoes
1 small onion, diced
1 medium green pepper, seeded and
chopped
¼ cup orange juice
juice of ½ lemon
1 tablespoon tomato paste
1 tablespoon white-wine vinegar
1 tablespoon frozen concentrated
apple juice or ½ tablespoon of sugar
1 teaspoon soysauce, or salt if
preferred
½-inch piece fresh gingerroot,
grated
Makes about 1¼ cups

A tasty high-fiber fruit-and-vegetable relish to serve as an accompaniment to stir-fries and steamed vegetables, or baked dishes.
1 Place the apricots in a saucepan with 1¼ cups of water. Cook until soft. Drain, reserving juice.
2 Dry roast the seeds (see p. 117). Cool and crush. Mix with remaining ingredients and ¼ cup of juice. Cover and simmer for 1–1½ hours.

SALADS

Salads of fresh, raw vegetables are a rich source of vitamins and minerals and as such play an important part in any healthy diet. Ideally, they should be part of at least one meal a day and can be the meal itself.

A growing number of supermarkets and vegetable stands are supplying a wider and wider range of vegetables and salad ingredients, and it is worth searching these out, or growing your own fresh produce if you can. For extra nutrients, add fresh or dried fruit, nuts, or sprouts. For a substantial main dish, try a salad with cooked dried beans or peas, pasta, or grains. The range of dressings can be varied beyond mayonnaise and vinaigrette. Lettuce and other leafy salads can be prepared slightly ahead of time, but should be dressed just before serving.

*Clockwise from top: Fiesta salad (see p. 145);
Tomato salad (see p. 144); Greek salad (see p. 144);
Fattoush (see p. 144).*

Tomato salad

Illustrated on page 143
Ingredients
12 cherry tomatoes
1 avocado, halved, pitted, and peeled
4 ounces low fat ricotta cheese
juice of 1 lemon
1 clove garlic, crushed
1 tablespoon finely chopped fresh basil
salt, or gomasio if preferred
black pepper
1 bunch watercress, divided into sprigs
lamb's lettuce or corn salad
6 scallions, sliced lengthwise
juice of ½ lemon
Serves 4

NUTRIENTS PER PORTION
Protein 9g ● ● ● *Fiber 4g* ● ●
Polyunsaturated fat 1.5g ● ● *Saturated fat 3.5g*
Vitamins – A, B6, C, E, FA
Minerals Ca, Fe

170 Calories

This salad is high in protein and iron, and low in saturated fat.
1 Cut a lid off the bottom of each tomato. Spoon out the seeds and take out the flesh.
2 Purée the avocado, ricotta, lemon juice, garlic, and basil. Season, then fill the tomatoes.
3 Toss salad ingredients in the lemon juice, and arrange the tomatoes on top.

Greek salad

Illustrated on page 143
Ingredients
½ pound tomatoes
3-inch piece of cucumber
¼–½ pound feta cheese
12 Spanish or ripe olives
For the dressing
1 tablespoon olive oil
1 tablespoon lemon juice
2 tablespoons chopped fresh parsley
1 clove garlic, crushed
1 tablespoon chopped fresh basil
black pepper
Serves 4

NUTRIENTS PER PORTION
Protein 7g ● ● ● *Fiber 1g* ●
Polyunsaturated fat 1g ● ● *Saturated fat 4g*
Vitamins A, B12, C
Minerals Ca

145 Calories

This classic Greek salad gets its protein from the feta cheese.
1 Chop the tomatoes, cucumber and feta cheese into even, bite-sized pieces.
2 Mix together with the olives in a bowl.
3 Put the dressing ingredients together in a screw-top jar and mix by shaking well.
4 Pour the dressing over the salad and toss.

Fattoush

Illustrated on page 143
Ingredients
1 romaine or iceberg lettuce
1 red pepper, seeded and diced
4 hard-boiled eggs, shelled
4 tomatoes, sliced
2 teaspoons capers
16 ripe olives
4 thinly cut slices whole-wheat bread
2 cloves garlic
1 tablespoon walnut or olive oil
For the dressing
1 tablespoon walnut or olive oil
2 teaspoons white-wine vinegar
1 tablespoon chopped fresh parsley
1 teaspoon dried tarragon
salt and black pepper
Serves 4

NUTRIENTS PER PORTION
Protein 11g ● ● ● *Fiber 6g* ● ● ●
Polyunsaturated fat 2g ● ● ● *Saturated fat 3g*
Vitamins A, B1, B2, B12, C, D, E, FA
Minerals Fe, Mg, Zn

235 Calories

This substantial peasant dish from Syria is a rich source of protein and fiber.
1 Prepare all the salad ingredients and place in a bowl.
2 Toast the whole-wheat bread and rub with the cut cloves of garlic. Lightly sprinkle with oil. Break into small pieces.
3 Put the dressing ingredients together in a screw-top jar and mix by shaking well.
4 Toss the garlic toast and dressing into the salad.

Fiesta salad

Illustrated on page 142

NUTRIENTS PER PORTION
115
Calories

Protein 4g ● ● *Fiber 4g* ● ●
Polyunsaturated fat 0.5g ● ● *Saturated fat 0g*
Vitamins A, C
Minerals –

Ingredients

1 cup long-grain brown rice
1 papaya
1 mango
¼ cucumber, sliced
⅔ cup peas, lightly steamed
salt
black pepper
For the dressing
2 teaspoons sesame oil
juice of ½ lime
*juice of ½ orange or 2 tablespoons
mango juice*
½ teaspoon ground cinnamon
*1 tablespoon finely chopped fresh
mint*
For garnishing
sprigs of mint
Serves 4

The saturated fat level of the dressing is kept low by using only
2 teaspoons sesame oil.

1 Measure the rice and bring twice the volume of water, about
2 cups, to a boil. Add the rice, cover and simmer for about
25 minutes or until tender.

2 Put the dressing ingredients together in a screw-top jar and
mix by shaking well.

3 Pour the dressing over the rice while it is still warm, and
combine together. Allow to cool completely.

4 To prepare the papaya, cut it in half lengthwise. Remove the
seeds and skin. Slice the flesh. To prepare the mango, cut the
flesh away from the pit, then peel.

5 Mix the fruit and vegetables into the rice.

6 Season with salt and pepper. Garnish with sprigs of
fresh mint.

Spiced rice salad (see p. 146).

Illustrated on page 145

Ingredients

1 onion, finely chopped
1 tablespoon sunflower oil
1 teaspoon turmeric
1/4 teaspoon cayenne
3/4 cup long-grain brown rice
1 3/4 cups boiling water
2/3 cup chopped green beans
2/3 cup diced pineapple
3 tablespoons coconut milk
(available from Oriental food
markets)
10–12 radishes, quartered
For the dressing
2 tablespoons sunflower oil
1 tablespoon white-wine vinegar
3 tablespoons pineapple juice
1/2 teaspoon grated gingerroot
salt and pepper
Serves 4

Spiced rice salad

NUTRIENTS PER PORTION
Protein 5g ● Fiber 3g ● ●
Polyunsaturated fat 7g ● ● ● Saturated fat 4g
Vitamins B1, B6, C, E, N
Minerals K

305 Calories

This is an ideal dish for a summer buffet. The high fiber in the rice and vegetables balances the fat content of the coconut.
1 Gently fry the onion in the oil for 3–4 minutes until soft.
2 Put in the spices and rice and fry for another 2–3 minutes.
3 Pour the boiling water over, bring back to a boil and simmer until all the water is absorbed and the rice is tender – about 25–30 minutes.
4 Meanwhile, steam the green beans for 3–4 minutes until barely tender.
5 Mix all the dressing ingredients together and pour over the warm rice. Season well and leave to cool.
6 When the rice is cool, mix with the remaining ingredients.

Illustrated opposite

Ingredients

1 1/3 cups cooked red kidney beans
1 1/3 cups cooked chickpeas
1 1/2 cups fresh peas, lightly steamed
6 scallions, diced
salt
black pepper
For the dressing
1/4 cup orange juice
2 tablespoons lemon juice
1 tablespoon sunflower oil
1 clove garlic, crushed
2 teaspoons soysauce
1 teaspoon frozen concentrated
apple juice or 1/2 teaspoon of sugar
1 teaspoon dried thyme
1 teaspoon dried oregano
1 1/2 cups thinly sliced mushrooms
Serves 6–8

Tangy bean salad

NUTRIENTS PER PORTION
Protein 13g ● ● ● Fiber 12g ● ● ●
Polyunsaturated fat 3g ● ● ● Saturated fat 1g
Vitamins B1, B2, C, E, FA, N
Minerals Ca, Cu, Fe, Mg, Zn

215 Calories

With beans and peas as the major ingredients, this salad is an ideal source of both protein and fiber. The sharp citrus dressing adds a deliciously refreshing tang to the other ingredients.
1 Mix the cooked beans, chickpeas, and peas together with the scallions.
2 Mix all the dressing ingredients together, except the mushrooms, then stir in the mushrooms. Let stand for 30 minutes to let the flavors blend together.
3 Pour the dressing over the bean salad and toss. Season with salt and pepper if desired.

Clockwise from top: Potato salad (see p. 148); Tangy bean salad (opposite); Pasta and lentil salad (see p. 149).

Illustrated on page 147

Potato salad

Ingredients

1 pound potatoes
½ cucumber, diced
3 artichoke hearts, sliced
3 scallions, diced
2 tablespoons finely chopped fresh parsley
1 tablespoon sunflower seeds
1 teaspoon dillweed
For the dressing
¼ cup mayonnaise
¼ cup plain yogurt
1 teaspoon lemon juice
1 teaspoon whole-grain mustard
herb salt, or salt if preferred
Serves 4

NUTRIENTS PER PORTION
260 Calories
Protein 5g ● Fiber 3g ● ●
Polyunsaturated fat 6g ● ● ● Saturated fat 2g
Vitamins B6, C, E
Minerals –

Potato salads are often coated in heavy, high-fat, creamy dressings. Here, mayonnaise has been mixed with yogurt, but you could also use all yogurt.

1 Scrub and cube the potatoes. Bring a large saucepan of water to boil. Add the potatoes, cover and simmer for 15–20 minutes until tender. Drain and place in a bowl.

2 Mix the dressing ingredients together. Spoon the dressing over the potatoes while they are still warm and toss together. Leave the salad to cool completely.

3 When cold, mix in the remaining salad ingredients.

Mixed bean salad (see opposite).

Pasta and lentil salad

Illustrated on page 147

NUTRIENTS PER PORTION
Protein 11g ● ● ● *Fiber 5g* ●
Polyunsaturated fat 1g ● ● *Saturated fat 1g*
Vitamins A, C, E
Minerals Fe, Mg

260 *Calories*

Ingredients
½ cup green lentils, cleaned
4 ounces whole-wheat pasta shells
1 pound tomatoes, quartered
For the dressing
2 tablespoons white-wine vinegar
2 tablespoons olive oil
4 tablespoons finely chopped fresh parsley
4 scallions, very finely chopped
1 tablespoon capers, chopped
2 gherkins, chopped
herb salt, or salt if preferred
black pepper
Serves 4–6

Unusual for a salad, this is substantially high in protein.
1 Bring the lentils to a boil in a saucepan of water. Cover and simmer for 30–40 minutes. Drain. Cook the pasta in boiling water for 8–10 minutes. Drain. Mix with the lentils and tomatoes.
2 Put the dressing ingredients together in a screw-top jar and mix by shaking well. Pour the dressing over salad and toss. Serve on a bed of lettuce leaves.

Mixed bean salad

Illustrated opposite

NUTRIENTS PER PORTION
Protein 8g ● ● *Fiber 9g* ● ● ●
Polyunsaturated fat 7g ● ● ● *Saturated fat 3g*
Vitamins B1, B6, FA, N
Minerals Fe, K, Mg

290 *Calories*

Ingredients
⅓ cup red kidney beans, soaked overnight
⅓ cup chickpeas, soaked overnight
⅓ cup lima or cannellini beans, soaked overnight
4 ounces green beans, cut into ½-inch pieces
For the marinade
¼ cup white-wine vinegar
6 tablespoon mixed olive and sunflower oil
1 tablespoon lemon juice
1 teaspoon grated lemon peel
2 cloves garlic, crushed
1 tablespoon white wine
1 dried red chili, very finely chopped
1 bunch scallions, chopped
Serves 4

The kidney beans should be soaked and cooked separately unless you want the whole salad to be pink.
1 Drain the beans and peas. Cover with fresh water, bring to a boil and boil rapidly for 10 minutes. Reduce the heat and simmer until tender. The kidney beans will take 35–40 minutes, the chickpeas and lima beans up to 1 hour, depending on how fresh they are. Drain.
2 Steam the green beans for 3–4 minutes. They should be still quite crunchy, only just beginning to be tender.
3 Mix together all the marinade ingredients.
4 Mix all the beans and peas together and pour the marinade over them. Leave for several hours in a cool place before serving. Drain off any excess dressing.

VEGETABLES

Vegetable dishes are very versatile. They can form the centerpiece of a meal or act as a side dish to complement a substantial main course. A recipe for one vegetable can often be adapted for another: for example, the grape leaf stuffing given here also goes well with peppers or zucchini. A simple preparation can be made more elaborate by adding pastry, or a topping of cornbread or nut crumble.

A meal of vegetables alone will be low in protein, so try to have a dish based on grains or beans as well. Some of the recipes here already include high-protein ingredients: for example, the nuts in the green vegetable and almond stir-fry or the tofu stir-fry.

Clockwise from left: Fennel and red pepper stir-fry (see p. 152); Bean sprout and sesame stir-fry (see p. 153); Tofu stir-fry with Ankake sauce (see p. 152); Green vegetable and almond stir-fry (see p. 152).

Fennel and red pepper stir-fry

Illustrated on page 150

Ingredients

12 ounces fennel, about 1 large bulb
1 large red pepper, seeded
2 teaspoons sunflower oil
black pepper
Serves 3–4

NUTRIENTS PER PORTION

35 Calories

Protein 1g ● ●   Fiber 2g ●
Polyunsaturated fat 1g ● ● ●   Saturated fat 0g
Vitamins C, E
Minerals –

High in Vitamins C and E, these vegetables also have the benefit of being low in saturated fat.
1 Trim the fennel and chop into matchstick-sized pieces.
2 Slice the pepper into thin strips.
3 Heat the oil in a wok or large skillet. When hot, stir-fry the pepper and fennel for 4–5 minutes over a high heat, stirring constantly. Season with pepper. Serve immediately.

Tofu stir-fry with Ankake sauce

Illustrated on page 151

Ingredients

1 quantity of Ankake sauce (see p. 141)
½ pound carrots
½ pound daikon
6 stalks of celery
6 scallions
12 ounces–1 pound firm tofu
2 teaspoons sunflower oil
Serves 3–4

NUTRIENTS PER PORTION

205 Calories

Protein 10g ● ● ●   Fiber 3g ● ●
Polyunsaturated fat 2g ● ● ●   Saturated fat 1g
Vitamins A, C
Minerals Ca, Cu, Fe, Mg

This high-protein stir-fry dish is served with a tangy, sweet and sour sauce.
1 Cut the carrots, daikon, celery, and scallions into matchstick-sized pieces. Slice the tofu.
2 Heat the oil in a wok or large skillet. When hot, stir-fry the vegetables for 3–4 minutes over a high heat, stirring constantly, until they are just soft. Add the tofu and cook for another 2 minutes.
3 Heat the Ankake sauce and serve immediately with the stir-fried tofu and vegetables.

Green vegetable and almond stir-fry

Illustrated on page 151

Ingredients

2 teaspoons sesame oil
½ cup blanched almonds halved
1 dried red chili
2 cups sliced green beans
2½ cups broccoli flowerets
6 cups shredded Chinese cabbage leaves
1 tablespoon dry sherry
juice of 1 lemon
1 tablespoon water
salt, or gomasio if preferred
Serves 3–4

NUTRIENTS PER PORTION

145 Calories

Protein 9g ● ● ●   Fiber 7g ● ● ●
Polyunsaturated fat 2g ● ● ●   Saturated fat 1g
Vitamins A, C, E, FA
Minerals Ca, Fe, Mg

The liquid added at the end of the recipe provides a burst of steam to finish the cooking.
1 Heat the oil in a wok or large skillet. When hot, toast the almonds and chili for 2 minutes. Remove and discard the chili.
2 Add the vegetables and stir-fry for 3–4 minutes.
3 Mix the sherry, lemon juice and 1 tablespoon water together. Pour over the vegetables, then stir in the toasted almonds. Cook for 1 minute.
4 Serve immediately. Sprinkle with salt, if desired.

Stuffed tomatoes (see p. 154).

Bean sprout and sesame stir-fry

Illustrated on page 151

155
Calories

NUTRIENTS PER PORTION
Protein 9g ● ● ●   Fiber 3g ● ●
Polyunsaturated fat 5g ● ● ●   Saturated fat 1g
Vitamins C, FA, N
Minerals Fe, Mg, Zn

Ingredients
For the sauce
3 tablespoons tahini
2 tablespoons water
1 tablespoon soysauce
2 tablespoons dry sherry
1 teaspoon of frozen concentrated
apple juice or ½ teaspoon of sugar
1 teaspoon red-wine vinegar
2 tablespoon chopped fresh
coriander leaves, cilantro or
Chinese parsley
For the stir-fry
½ pound bean sprouts, rinsed
3 cups sliced oyster mushrooms
1 cauliflower, divided into flowerets
1 medium red pepper, seeded and
diced
1 clove garlic, crushed
2 teaspoons sesame oil
Serves 4

If you cannot find fresh oyster mushrooms, use another type of mushroom instead.
1 Mix the sauce ingredients together. Leave to stand for 1 hour before making the stir-fry.
2 Meanwhile, prepare the bean sprouts, mushrooms, cauliflower, pepper, and garlic.
3 Heat the oil in a wok or large skillet. When hot, stir-fry the vegetables for 3–4 minutes over a high heat, stirring constantly, until just soft.
4 Serve immediately, accompanied by the sauce.

Stuffed tomatoes

Illustrated on page 153

Ingredients

*½ cup flageolet or cannellini beans,
soaked overnight
2 teaspoons olive oil
3 scallions, very finely chopped
2 cloves garlic, crushed
1⅓ cups peeled and chopped
tomatoes
2 tablespoons tomato paste
12 stuffed Spanish olives, sliced
2 teaspoons dried oregano
2 tablespoons dried chervil
1 teaspoon miso (soy paste),
dissolved in a little water
½ avocado, peeled, seeded, and
cubed
black pepper
4 large tomatoes
2 ounces mozzarella cheese
(optional)
Serves 4*

225 Calories

NUTRIENTS PER PORTION
*Protein 11g ● ● ●   Fiber 10g ● ● ●
Polyunsaturated fat 1g ● ●   Saturated fat 3g
Vitamins A, B₁, B₆, C, E, FA
Minerals Ca, Fe, Mg, Zn*

The bean filling provides the major source of protein and fiber in this dish, which is complemented by a tomato and avocado sauce. For a lower fat content, omit the mozzarella topping.
1 Drain the beans. Cover with plenty of fresh water, bring to boil, uncovered, and boil fast for 10 minutes. Reduce the heat, skim, cover, and simmer for another 20–25 minutes or until the beans are soft. Drain.
2 Heat the oil in a large saucepan and gently fry the scallions and garlic for 2–3 minutes.
3 Add the tomatoes, paste, olives, oregano, chervil, and miso. Cover and cook for 25 minutes.
4 Stir in the cooked beans and avocado. Season with pepper.
5 Preheat the oven to 350°F.
6 To prepare the tomatoes, slice off the base and scoop out the seeds and flesh. Season the tomato shells with pepper.
7 Fill the tomato shells with the mixture. Cover with slices of mozzarella, or simply replace the tomato "lids."
8 Place in a baking dish with 2–3 tablespoons bean stock or water. Cover and bake for 30–35 minutes.

Stuffed squash

Illustrated opposite

Ingredients

*1 squash, weighing about 2 pounds
2 teaspoons sunflower oil
12 ounces leeks, cleaned and finely
sliced
3 sticks celery, chopped
2⅓ cups chopped carrots
⅔ cups rolled oats
2 tablespoons sunflower seeds
2 tablespoons pumpkin seeds
1 tablespoon tahini
1 teaspoon miso, dissolved in a little
water
salt, or gomasio if preferred
black pepper
For serving
Tomato sauce (see p. 119)
Serves 6*

260 Calories

NUTRIENTS PER PORTION
*Protein 9g ● ●   Fiber 8g ● ● ●
Polyunsaturated fat 6g ● ● ●   Saturated fat 2g
Vitamins A, B₆, C, E, FA
Minerals Ca, Fe*

In this dish, which is an excellent source of fiber, iron, calcium, and vitamins, it is important to cook the vegetables slowly so that they have a chance to blend together well. The seeds add a contrast in taste and texture.
1 Cut the squash in half lengthwise. Scoop out and discard the seeds. Take out enough flesh to make 3½ cups chopped.
2 Heat the oil in a skillet and fry the leeks very gently for 10 minutes.
3 Add the celery, carrot, and squash. Cover and cook for 20 minutes or until the vegetables are soft, stirring frequently.
4 Preheat the oven to 350°F.
5 Remove the pan from the heat and add the remaining ingredients. Mix well and season with salt and pepper.
6 Fill the squash halves with the mixture, cover and bake for 45–55 minutes or until cooked.
7 Serve hot, accompanied by tomato sauce.

Spiced zucchini and apple (see below).

Spiced zucchini and apple

NUTRIENTS PER PORTION

75 Calories

Protein 2g ● Fiber 1g ●
Polyunsaturated fat 2g ● ● ● Saturated fat 0.5g
Vitamins C, E
Minerals –

Illustrated above

Ingredients
½ pound zucchini
1 medium dessert apple
2 teaspoons sunflower oil
2 teaspoons lemon juice
1 tablespoon of frozen concentrated apple juice or ½ tablespoon sugar
½ teaspoon ground cinnamon
½ teaspoon grated nutmeg
2 tablespoons hazelnuts or filberts, finely chopped
salt, or gomasio if preferred
black pepper
Serves 3–4

Despite being fried, this dish remains low in saturated fat.
1 Chop the zucchini and apple into finger-sized pieces (chunky matchsticks).
2 Heat the oil in a large saucepan and fry the zucchini and apple pieces for 3 minutes.
3 Mix in the other ingredients. Cover and cook for 10–15 minutes until the zucchini and apple are just soft. Season with salt and black pepper.

Stuffed squash
(see opposite).

RICE AND PASTA DISHES

R ice and pasta can be used to form the base for many vegetarian dishes. Risottos and pilafs are filling and nutritious rice dishes. Mushrooms, fresh or dried, go well with rice; so do fresh peas, broccoli, and zucchini. Different chopped nuts can be used to make a good contrast of textures.

Pasta, fresh or dried, is a great standby. It can be made from whole-wheat or refined flour, with or without eggs, plain or colored green with spinach. If you prefer it homemade, there are machines to help you to turn it out in various shapes and sizes. Whole-wheat pasta has a denser texture than regular pasta. Some kind of sauce or filling is always used with pasta. It may be as simple as an oil and garlic sauce for spaghetti, or it may be as robust as a mushroom lasagne.

From top to bottom: Mushroom lasagne (see p. 158); Walnut ravioli (see p. 159).

Illustrated on pages 156–57

Mushroom lasagne

Ingredients
2 teaspoons olive oil
1 medium onion, finely chopped
2 cloves garlic, crushed
1 bay leaf
½ teaspoon dried thyme
3¼ cups sliced mushrooms
2 tablespoons cornstarch
1¼ cups skim milk
1¼ cups plain yogurt
salt, or gomasio if preferred
2½ cups broccoli flowerets
⅔ cups diced carrots
2 tablespoons pine nuts
black pepper
9 pieces whole-wheat lasagne
2 teaspoons cornstarch
2 tablespoons freshly grated
Parmesan cheese
Serves 4

385
Calories

NUTRIENTS PER PORTION
Protein 20g ● ● ●   Fiber 6g ● ● ●
Polyunsaturated fat 3g ● ●   Saturated fat 3g
Vitamins A, B₁, B₂, C, FA
Minerals Ca, Cu, Fe, Mg, Zn

In this lasagne, which is high in protein and fiber but low in saturated fat, a tangy yogurt sauce is used to flavor the layers of pasta. For a milder version, use more milk and less of the yogurt.

1 Heat the oil in a saucepan and gently fry the onion and garlic for 4–5 minutes or until the onion is soft.

2 Add the bay leaf, thyme, and mushrooms and simmer the sauce over a low heat for 10 minutes. Dissolve 2 tablespoons of cornstarch in a little of the milk.

3 Pour the remaining milk over the mushrooms. When heated through, stir in the dissolved cornstarch. Cook for 5 minutes until thickened, stirring all the time. Remove the bay leaf. Remove pan from the heat and stir in ⅔ cup of the yogurt. Season with the salt and pepper.

4 Steam the broccoli and carrot until fairly soft. Place in a bowl, then mix in the pine nuts and season well with salt and black pepper.

5 Preheat the oven to 350°F.

6 Meanwhile, separate the lasagne pieces and cook in a large saucepan of boiling salted water for 8–10 minutes or until they are just *al dente*.

7 Put a layer of mushroom sauce in the bottom of a lightly oiled oblong baking dish. Cover with a layer of lasagne, then the broccoli mixture, then the sauce. Repeat the layers, ending, finally, with lasagne.

8 Mix the 2 teaspoons of cornstarch with the remaining yogurt. Pour this over the lasagne. Sprinkle the top with Parmesan cheese.

9 Bake for 25–30 minutes. Serve hot.

Walnut ravioli

Illustrated on page 156

NUTRIENTS PER PORTION
595 *Protein 25g ● ● ● Fiber 16g ● ● ●*
Polyunsaturated fat 17g ● ● ● Saturated fat 4g
Vitamins A, B1, B2, B6, B12, C, D, E, FA, N
Calories Minerals Ca, Cu, Fe, Mg, Zn

Ingredients
For the dough
3 cups whole-wheat flour
pinch of salt
2 eggs
1¼ cups cooked and puréed spinach
For the filling
1 medium onion, finely chopped or minced
4 stalks celery, finely chopped or minced
1½ cups walnuts, very finely chopped
2 tablespoons finely chopped fresh basil
3 tablespoons finely chopped fresh parsley
3 cloves garlic, crushed
2 tablespoons tomato paste
soysauce, or salt if preferred
black pepper
beaten egg for sealing
Serves 4 as a main course or 6 as a starter

This dish manages to reach a nutritious ideal – it is high in protein and fiber, low in saturated fat, and is an excellent source of all the essential vitamins and minerals. Buy good-quality walnuts for this dish and store in an airtight container, otherwise the taste will be bitter.

1 For the pasta dough, mix the flour and salt together in a large bowl or on a work surface. Make a well in the center and add the eggs and spinach. Using your fingers, or a fork, gradually draw the flour into the center to make a dough. Knead thoroughly until the dough mixture no longer feels sticky. Cover and let to rest for half an hour.

2 Mix the filling ingredients together in a large bowl. Season with soysauce and pepper.

3 Roll out the pasta dough very thinly into a rectangle. Mark half into 1- to 2-inch squares. Dot 1 teaspoon of filling on each square. Brush the edges and in between the rows of filling with beaten egg. Cover with the remaining dough. Press firmly along the edges and between the rows to seal. Use a pastry wheel to cut out the ravioli squares. Let dry for 30 minutes.

4 Cook the ravioli in a large saucepan of boiling salted water for 8–10 minutes or until *al dente*. Drain. Serve hot with tomato sauce (see p. 119) or mushroom sauce (see p. 139).

Three grain pilaf (see p. 160).

Paella de la Huerta

Illustrated opposite

Ingredients
2 teaspoons olive oil
1 medium onion, finely chopped
2 cloves garlic, crushed
²⁄₃ cup peas
1 cup sliced green beans
4 artichoke hearts, halved
1 cup heaped short-grain brown rice
6 strands saffron
8 ounces tomatoes, peeled and chopped
1 teaspoon dried oregano
1 teaspoon dried thyme
2 tablespoons finely chopped fresh parsley
soysauce
black pepper
juice of ½ lemon
For garnishing
12 ripe or Spanish olives
lemon slices
coriander leaves, cilantro, or Chinese parsley
Serves 4

NUTRIENTS PER PORTION
280 Calories
Protein 6g ● *Fiber 5g* ● ●
Polyunsaturated fat 0.5g ● *Saturated fat 1g*
Vitamins B₁, C
Minerals Mg

Short-grain rice is used for this Valencian peasant dish as it provides the creamiest texture. Although low in saturated fats, paella needs to be served with a high-protein dish for full nutritional balance.

1 Heat the oil in a large saucepan and gently fry the onion and garlic for 4–5 minutes or until soft.

2 Add the peas, beans, and artichoke hearts, stirring in well, and cook over a very low heat for 5 minutes.

3 Measure the rice and have ready twice the volume of boiling water.

4 Add the rice to the pan of vegetables and cook gently for 3–4 minutes, without browning.

5 Dissolve the saffron in the boiling water, then add to the pan with the tomatoes and herbs. Bring to a boil and cook uncovered for 35–45 minutes. Stir occasionally and adjust the liquid if necessary. Season with soysauce and pepper and add the lemon juice. Garnish with olives, lemon slices, and coriander leaves.

Three grain pilaf

Illustrated on page 159

Ingredients
¼ cup wheat berries
¼ cup long-grain brown rice
¼ cup roasted buckwheat
For the sauce
2 teaspoons olive oil
1 onion, finely chopped
1 clove garlic, crushed
6½ cups quartered mushrooms
1 green pepper, seeded and cut in rings
1 pound tomatoes, skinned and chopped
2 tablespoons tomato paste
2 teaspoons dried oregano
1 bay leaf
miso (soypaste), or salt if preferred
black pepper
Serves 4

NUTRIENTS PER PORTION
175 Calories
Protein 7g ● ● ● *Fiber 6g* ● ● ●
Polyunsaturated fat 1g ● ● *Saturated fat 0.5g*
Vitamins B₁, B₂, C, FA, N
Minerals Cu, Fe

Cooked together, the grains used in this nutritious dish – rice, wheatgrains and buckwheat – allow you to taste their different flavors without one becoming dominant.

1 Rinse the grains. Bring the wheat to a boil in 2 cups water, cover and simmer for 30 minutes.

2 Add the rice and buckwheat with another 2 cups boiling water. Continue to simmer for a further 25–30 minutes or until the water is absorbed and the grains are soft.

3 For the sauce, heat the oil in a saucepan and gently fry the onion and garlic for 4–5 minutes or until soft. Add the mushrooms and green pepper and cook for 3 minutes.

4 Stir in the remaining sauce ingredients, cover and simmer for 35–40 minutes. Season with miso and pepper.

5 Put the grains into a serving dish and pour the sauce over.

Paella de la Huerta (see opposite).

Peanut pilaf with stir-fried vegetables

Illustrated below

Ingredients
1¼ cups long-grain brown rice
For the sauce
1 tablespoon peanut oil
1 medium onion, finely chopped
1 clove garlic, crushed
1 green chili, seeded and diced
½-inch piece fresh gingerroot,
grated
10 ounces silken tofu plus ⅔ cups
water or 1¼ cups skim milk
⅔ cups roasted peanuts, ground
1 teaspoon soysauce
For the stir-fry
1 tablespoon peanut oil
2 cups shredded cabbage
1½ cups sliced fresh green beans
1¾ cups mung bean sprouts
½ cucumber, diced
⅓ cup peanuts
1 teaspoon soysauce
Serves 4

590
Calories

NUTRIENTS PER PORTION
Protein 23g ● ● ●   Fiber 9g ● ● ●
Polyunsaturated fat 8g ● ● ●   Saturated fat 5g
Vitamins B1, B6, C, E, FA, N
Minerals Ca, Cu, Fe, Mg, Zn

This dish, with its crispy stir-fried vegetables coated in a creamy peanut sauce, is a perfect combination of tastes and textures. It is also an excellent source of protein and fiber.

1 Measure the rice and bring twice the volume of water to a boil. Add the rice and stir once. Cover and simmer for about 25 minutes or until cooked. Add a little extra water at the end if necessary.

2 For the sauce, heat the oil in a saucepan and gently fry the onion and garlic for 4–5 minutes or until soft. Add the chili and ginger and cook for 3 minutes.

3 Purée the onion mixture with the remaining sauce ingredients. Heat through gently.

4 For the stir-fry, heat the oil in a wok or large skillet. When hot, stir-fry the cabbage, beans, bean sprouts, and cucumber over high heat for 3 minutes, stirring constantly. Stir in the peanuts and soysauce.

5 To serve, pile the long-grain rice onto a warm serving dish. Top with all the stir-fry vegetables and carefully pour over the hot, spicy sauce.

Peanut pilaf with stir-fried vegetables (see above).

Beet Kasha (see below).

Beet kasha

NUTRIENTS PER PORTION
355 Calories
Protein 12g ● ● *Fiber 4g* ● ●
Polyunsaturated fat 6g ● ● ● *Saturated fat 2g*
Vitamins B1, E, N
Minerals Ca, Fe, Mg, Zn

Illustrated above

Ingredients
2 teaspoons sunflower oil
1 medium onion, finely chopped
4 stalks celery, chopped
heaped 2 cups buckwheat
3¾ cups hot water
1 tablespoon soysauce
2–3 teaspoons grated horseradish
black pepper
1 pound baby beets
For the sauce
7 ounces skim milk
1 onion
1 bay leaf
4 peppercorns
2 tablespoons sunflower oil
1 heaped tablespoon whole-wheat flour
4–5 tablespoons yogurt or reduced fat sour cream
1–2 teaspoons grated horseradish
black pepper
Serves 4

This dish is low in saturated fat, and is a good source of all minerals except calcium.

1 Heat the oil in a large saucepan and gently fry the onion for 4–5 minutes or until soft.

2 Add the celery and cook for 2–3 minutes. Stir in the buckwheat and stir-fry for 3 minutes until lightly roasted.

3 Pour in the water, stir once, bring to a boil, cover, and cook for 20–25 minutes. Add a little boiling water if the mixture looks rather dry.

4 Stir in the soysauce and horseradish. Season with pepper.

5 Either bake the baby beets in a preheated oven at 350°F for about 45 minutes, or steam for 20 minutes or until tender. When cool enough to handle, peel and set aside.

6 For the sauce, place the milk, onion, bay leaf, and peppercorns in a saucepan. Bring almost to a boil, remove from the heat and let stand for 10 minutes. Strain.

7 Heat the oil in a saucepan and stir in the flour. Cook for 3 minutes, stirring.

8 Pour in the milk, stirring constantly. Bring the sauce to a boiling point and simmer for 5 minutes, stirring. Cool slightly, then blend in the yogurt or reduced fat sour cream. Season with horseradish and pepper.

9 To serve, pile the kasha onto a warm serving plate. Slice or arrange the baby beets on top. Serve the sauce separately.

From top to bottom: Spaghetti with lentil Bolognaise (see opposite); Tagliatelle (see opposite).

Spaghetti with lentil Bolognaise

NUTRIENTS PER PORTION
Protein 26g ● ● ●   Fiber 9g ● ● ●
530
Polyunsaturated fat 1g ●   Saturated fat 2g
Vitamins A, B1, B2, B6, C, E, FA, N
Calories   *Minerals Ca, Cu, Fe, Mg, Zn*

Illustrated opposite
Ingredients
Scant 1 cup brown or green lentils
1 tablespoon olive oil
1 medium onion, finely chopped
2 cloves garlic, crushed
5 cups diced mushrooms
1 teaspoon dried marjoram
1 bay leaf
2½ cups peeled and chopped tomatoes
2 tablespoons tomato paste
soysauce, or salt if preferred
black pepper
For serving
12 ounces whole wheat spaghetti
1–2 tablespoons grated Parmesan cheese
Serves 4

Either green or brown lentils can be used for this recipe's sauce. Lentils make an excellent introduction for a non-vegetarian to the dried bean and pea family because they are high in protein, very adaptable, easy to digest and, because of their small size, do not overpower the dish.

1 Place the lentils in a saucepan of water. Bring, uncovered, to a boil, skim, cover, and simmer for about 40 minutes or until soft. Drain.

2 Heat the oil in a large saucepan and fry the onion and garlic for 4–5 minutes or until the onion is soft.

3 Add the mushrooms, cooked lentils, marjoram, and bay leaf and cook for 10 minutes.

4 Stir in the tomatoes and purée. Cover and cook for 20–25 minutes. Remove the bay leaf. Season with soysauce and pepper.

5 Cook the spaghetti in a large saucepan of boiling salted water for about 8–10 minutes until just tender. Drain. Pour the Bolognaise sauce over the cooked spaghetti. Add Parmesan.

Tagliatelle

NUTRIENTS PER PORTION
Protein 13g ● ● ●   Fiber 3g ● ●
145
Polyunsaturated fat 1.5g ●   Saturated fat 2.5g
Vitamins B1, B12
Calories   *Minerals –*

Illustrated opposite
Ingredients
2 teaspoons olive oil
3 scallions, chopped
1 small red pepper, seeded and chopped
4 canned or cooked artichoke hearts, quartered
1¼ cups peas
6 ounces low fat ricotta cheese
⅔ cup skim milk
salt, or gomasio if preferred
black pepper
8 ounces fresh whole wheat tagliatelle
Serves 4

Blending the ricotta cheese with skim milk, produces a creamy sauce, lower in fat than light cream.

1 Heat the oil in a saucepan and gently fry the chopped scallions for 4–5 minutes.

2 Add the red pepper, artichoke hearts, and peas, cover, and cook for 10 minutes, adding a little water if the mixture begins to look a bit dry.

3 Purée the ricotta cheese with the skim milk until it is a smooth cream. Pour this into the vegetables and heat through gently. Season with salt and pepper.

4 Cook the tagliatelle in a large saucepan of boiling salted water for 3–4 minutes or until *al dente*. Drain.

5 Toss the tagliatelle well with the sauce. Serve immediately.

CASSEROLES AND LOAVES

As with dried beans and peas, the vegetarian pantry comes into its own with grains. Apart from rice there are many others, such as wheat, barley, millet, buckwheat, and bulgur wheat, to give different textures and varied flavors. Cook grains as casseroles, with fresh vegetables or dried beans and lentils, or serve them as accompaniments to other dishes, perhaps with a nut or vegetable sauce. Most grains can be used interchangeably, although the delicate taste of wild rice is probably best appreciated when it is simply boiled.

Grain dishes are generally simple and quick and easy to make, often using only one pan. Many can be cooked in advance and frozen. Thaw overnight in the refrigerator and reheat gently, either in the oven covered with waxed paper and foil, by steaming or using the microwave. There are more ideas for cold grain dishes in the Salad section (see pp. 142–49).

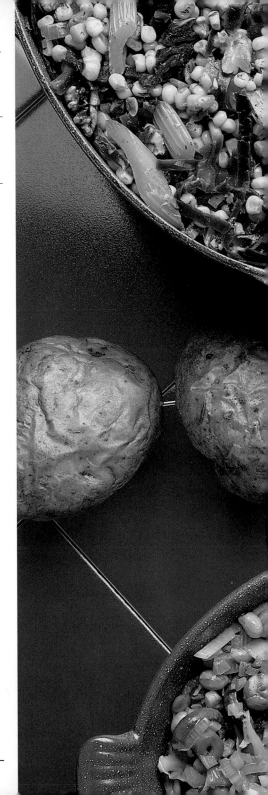

Clockwise from top: Ghiuvetch (see p. 168); Barley Bourguignon (see p. 169); Peanut Stroganov (see p. 168).

Ghiuvetch

Illustrated on pages 166–67

Ingredients

2 teaspoons sunflower oil
1 medium onion, finely chopped
4 stalks celery, sliced diagonally
1 tablespoon grated horseradish
1 tablespoon paprika
1 pound frozen corn kernels
1 cup coarsely chopped walnuts
2 tablespoons finely chopped fresh parsley
1 teaspoon fresh dill
²⁄₃ cup vegetable stock
2¹⁄₂ cups shredded red cabbage
soysauce, or salt if preferred
black pepper
For garnishing
yogurt or reduced fat sour cream (optional)
For serving
baked potatoes
Serves 4–6

315 Calories

NUTRIENTS PER PORTION
Protein 9g ● ●   Fiber 8g ● ● ●
Polyunsaturated fat 12g ● ● ●   Saturated fat 2g
Vitamins B₁, B₆, C, E, FA
Minerals Fe, Mg, Zn

A quickly made, colorful vegetable stew inspired by Romanian cuisine. Extra protein and flavor are provided by the inclusion of corn and walnuts.

1 Heat the oil in a large saucepan and gently fry the onion for 4–5 minutes or until soft.

2 Add the celery, horseradish, and paprika to the pan and cook for 2–3 minutes.

3 Stir in the corn, walnuts, herbs, and stock. Cover and simmer for 10 minutes.

4 Add the red cabbage and cook for a further 10–15 minutes. Season with soysauce and pepper.

5 Serve hot, garnished with yogurt or reduced fat sour cream (optional), and accompanied by baked potatoes.

Peanut Stroganov

Illustrated on page 167

Ingredients

2 teaspoons sunflower oil
1 medium onion, finely chopped
4 cups shredded Chinese cabbage
6 stalks celery, finely chopped
³⁄₄ pound button mushrooms
1¹⁄₂ cups roasted unsalted peanuts
¹⁄₂ teaspoon caraway seeds
1 teaspoon mustard
²⁄₃ cup red wine
soysauce, or salt if preferred
black pepper
yogurt or reduced fat sour cream
For serving
whole-wheat noodles
Serves 4

430 Calories

NUTRIENTS PER PORTION
Protein 21g ● ● ●   Fiber 7g ● ● ●
Polyunsaturated fat 10g ● ●   Saturated fat 6g
Vitamins A, B₁, B₂, B₆, C, E, FA, N
Minerals Ca, Cu, Fe, Mg, Zn

The seasonings of caraway and mustard complement the flavors of the Chinese cabbage and celery well, and the reduced fat sour cream provides the traditional creaminess of this dish without the addition of a lot of fat.

1 Heat the oil in a saucepan and gently fry the onion for 4–5 minutes or until soft.

2 Add the Chinese cabbage, celery, mushrooms, and peanuts and cook for 5 minutes, stirring frequently. Stir in the caraway seeds, mustard, and red wine.

3 Cover and cook for 10 minutes.

4 Remove from the heat and season with soysauce and pepper. Cool slightly, then stir in the reduced fat sour cream. Serve immediately with boiled whole-wheat noodles.

Barley Bourguignon

NUTRIENTS PER PORTION
230 Calories
Protein 9g ● ● ● *Fiber 11g* ● ● ●
Polyunsaturated fat 2g ● ● ● *Saturated fat 0.5g*
Vitamins A, B1, B2, B6, C, E, FA, N
Minerals Ca, Cu, Fe, Zn

Illustrated on page 167

Ingredients
½ cup pearl barley
2 teaspoons sunflower oil
1 cup finely chopped leeks
5 cups quartered button
mushrooms
1½ cups chopped parsnips
1 teaspoon dried thyme
1 teaspoon dried sage
1 bay leaf
⅔ cup red wine
2½ cups peeled and chopped
tomatoes
2 tablespoons tomato paste
soysauce, or salt if preferred
black pepper
1½ cups broccoli flowerets
Serves 4

Always be careful when adding barley to a casserole or soup as a little goes a long way. It is a chewy grain which absorbs flavors well, so it benefits from standing overnight. Serve with cooked, dried beans, or fresh green peas or snowpeas, and a low-fat pudding for a balanced meal.
1 Dry roast the barley for 2–3 minutes in a heavy-bottomed pan. Add enough boiling water to cover by 1-inch and cook for 40–45 minutes. Drain, reserving the cooking liquid.
2 Heat the oil in a large saucepan and gently fry the leeks for about 5 minutes until soft.
3 Add the mushrooms, parsnips, herbs, and cooked barley. Stir in well and cook for 2–3 minutes.
4 Add the wine, tomatoes, paste, and up to ⅔ cup reserved stock. Bring to a boil, cover, and cook gently for 35 minutes. Add a little reserved stock if the mixture begins to look dry. Season with soysauce and pepper.
5 Add the broccoli flowerets and cook for a further 8–10 minutes or until tender. Remove the bay leaf before serving.

Georgian casserole

NUTRIENTS PER PORTION
210 Calories
Protein 14g ● ● ● *Fiber 18g* ● ● ●
Polyunsaturated fat 2g ● ● *Saturated fat 0.5g*
Vitamins A, B1, B6, C, E, FA
Minerals Ca, Fe

Illustrated on page 170

Ingredients
1 cup black kidney beans, soaked
overnight
2 teaspoons sunflower oil
½ pound pearl onions or
shallots, peeled
½ teaspoon ground allspice
½ teaspoon ground cinnamon
½ teaspoon dried thyme
4 ounces button mushrooms
4 ounces prunes
1⅓ cups peeled and chopped
tomatoes
⅔ cup tomato juice
juice and peel of 1 orange
1 tablespoon red-wine vinegar
soysauce or salt if preferred
black pepper
For serving
buckwheat or brown rice
Serves 4

High in protein because of the beans, this rich, dark casserole with its tangy sauce contains whole tiny vegetables for a contrast in textures.
1 Drain the beans. Cover with plenty of fresh water, bring to a boil and boil fast, uncovered, for 10 minutes. Reduce the heat, skim, cover, and simmer for another 35–40 minutes or until soft. Drain well.
2 Heat the oil in a large saucepan and gently fry the onions for 4–5 minutes or until just brown. Add the spices and thyme and cook for 2–3 minutes.
3 Stir in the remaining ingredients, including the beans, cover, and cook for 40 minutes. Season with soysauce and pepper. Serve with boiled buckwheat or brown rice.

From left to right: Georgian casserole (see p. 169); Spicy bean goulash (see below).

Spicy bean goulash

Illustrated above

Ingredients
*1 cup red kidney beans,
    soaked overnight
1 tablespoon olive oil
1 medium onion, finely chopped
1 clove garlic, crushed
1 small red chili, finely chopped
3 large red peppers, chopped
3 cups chopped mushrooms
1 medium potato, diced
2–3 teaspoons paprika
1 teaspoon thyme
2 tablespoons tomato paste
1 teaspoon miso (soy paste),
    dissolved in a little water
salt, or gomasio if preferred
black pepper
For serving
brown rice or whole-wheat noodles*
Serves 4

NUTRIENTS PER PORTION
*Protein 13g ● ● ● Fiber 14g ● ● ●
Polyunsaturated fat 1g ● ● Saturated fat 0.5g
Vitamins B₁, B₂, B₆, C, FA, N
Minerals Ca, Cu, Fe, Mg, Zn*

205 *Calories*

The red beans used here provide most of the high protein and fiber contained in this tasty stew.
1 Drain the beans, cover with plenty of fresh water, bring to a boil, uncovered, and boil fast for 10 minutes. Reduce the heat, cover, and simmer for 40 minutes or until soft. Drain, reserving the liquid.
2 Heat the oil in a large saucepan and gently fry the onion in the oil for 4–5 minutes or until soft.
3 Add the garlic, chili, peppers, and mushrooms and cook for 5 minutes. Cover and cook the mixture for 15–20 minutes over a very gentle heat.
4 Add the cooked beans, potato, paprika, thyme, tomato purée, and miso to the stew.
5 Simmer gently for 30 minutes, adding a little bean liquid if necessary. Season with salt and pepper and serve hot with brown rice or whole-wheat noodles.

Health loaf (see below).

Health Loaf

425
Calories

NUTRIENTS PER PORTION
Protein 10g ● ● *Fiber 7g* ● ● ●
Polyunsaturated fat 7g ● ● ● *Saturated fat 3g*
Vitamins C, E, N
Minerals Fe, Mg

Illustrated above

Ingredients
1 cup long-grain brown rice
2 teaspoons olive oil
1 medium onion, finely chopped
1½ cups sliced zucchini
1 small eggplant, diced
½ cup pine nuts
1⅓ cups peeled and chopped
tomatoes
½ cup mixed nuts (cashews and
almonds), ground
2 teaspoons ground cinnamon
6 cloves or ¼ teaspoon ground
cloves
salt, or gomasio if preferred
black pepper
Serves 4

Only a small amount of pine nuts is needed to flavor this high-fiber, lowfat dish.
1 Weigh out the rice and cook according to the instructions given in the chart on p.47.
2 Preheat the oven to 350°F.
3 Heat the oil in a large saucepan and gently fry the onion for 4–5 minutes or until soft. Add the zucchini, eggplant, and pine nuts and cook for 10 minutes.
4 Remove from the heat and mix in the remaining ingredients and cooked rice. Season with salt and pepper.
5 Put the mixture in a lightly oiled 9-×5-inch loaf pan, pressing it down firmly. Bake for about 50 minutes.

Buckwheat loaf

Illustrated below

Ingredients

1 tablespoon sunflower oil
¾ cup buckwheat
2 cups boiling water
1 medium onion, finely chopped
2 teaspoons paprika
1 teaspoon ground ginger
1 teaspoon curry powder
pinch of cayenne
2½ cups shredded red cabbage
1 ounce arame, soaked in warm
water for 15 minutes
3 tablespoons wheat germ
soysauce or salt if preferred
black pepper
For serving
sharp mushroom sauce (see p. 139)
Serves 4

NUTRIENTS PER PORTION
220 Calories

Protein 9g ● ● ●   *Fiber 2g* ●
Polyunsaturated fat 2g ● ● ●   *Saturated fat 0.5g*
Vitamins E
Minerals –

Buckwheat, with its strong flavor, can be an acquired taste, so try boiling and tasting the grain separately first. For balance, serve this meal with a high-fiber appetizer or side dish.

1 Brown the buckwheat in a little oil (see p. 47). Pour over the boiling water, bring back to the boil, cover, and simmer until tender. Drain.

2 Preheat the oven to 375°F.

3 Heat the remaining oil in a large saucepan and gently fry the onion for 4–5 minutes, or until just soft. Add the spices and cook for a few minutes.

4 Stir in the red cabbage, drained arame, and cooked buckwheat. Cook over a gentle heat for 10 minutes, stirring all the ingredients frequently. Add the wheat germ and season with soysauce and pepper.

5 Pack the mixture into a lightly oiled 9-×5-inch loaf pan. Bake for 45–50 minutes.

6 Let cool for 10 minutes, then remove from pan. Serve hot with sharp mushroom sauce (see p. 139).

Buckwheat loaf (see above).

Vegetable casserole (see below).

Vegetable casserole

380

Calories

NUTRIENTS PER PORTION
Protein 10g ● ● *Fiber 8g* ● ● ●
Polyunsaturated fat 7g ● ● ● *Saturated fat 3g*
Vitamins A, B1, B6, C, E, FA, N
Minerals Ca, Cu, Mg

Illustrated above
Ingredients
For the topping
²/₃ cup rolled oats
2 tablespoons brown rice flour
¹/₃ cup finely chopped cashews
2 tablespoons sunflower oil
1 teaspoon dried rosemary
For the filling
2 pounds root vegetables (carrots,
parsnips, rutabaga, turnip)
For the sauce
2 teaspoons sunflower oil
1 medium onion, finely chopped
2 tablespoons cashews
2 tablespoons brown rice flour
²/₃ cup skim milk
1¹/₄ cups vegetable stock
1 teaspoon dried rosemary
salt, or gomasio if preferred
black pepper
Serves 4

This dish is a root vegetable casserole, covered with a nutty sauce and sprinkled with a crunchy topping. It is high in fiber, and low in saturated fat.

1 For the topping, put the oats, rice flour, and cashews into a bowl. Mix in the oil and rosemary with your fingertips to form a light, crunchy crumble topping.

2 For the filling, scrub or peel the vegetables and cut into bite-sized pieces. Steam for 10–12 minutes until just tender. Reserve the steaming water for stock.

3 Preheat the oven to 375°F.

4 Heat the oil in a large saucepan and gently fry the onion for 4–5 minutes or until soft. Add the cashews and lightly brown for 3–4 minutes.

5 Mix the rice flour to a smooth paste with a little of the milk.

6 Pour the milk and reserved stock into the pan and add the rice flour paste and rosemary. Bring to a boil and simmer until thickened, stirring constantly. Season with salt and pepper.

7 Cool slightly, then purée the sauce until smooth.

8 Put the steamed vegetables into a lightly oiled baking dish. Pour over the sauce, then cover with the topping. Bake for 30 minutes and serve hot.

DESSERTS

From a health food point of view, if not strictly a vegetarian one, desserts make a very positive contribution to a meal. If the main course has been light and lacking in protein, serve cheesecake made with tofu, a soufflé, mousse or roulade using eggs, or a custard. If you prefer to avoid cream, try a cashew "cream" (made with cottage cheese), yogurt, or custard made with cornmeal as an accompaniment, and use yogurt also to make delicious "ice cream".

Fresh fruit salad is one of the best possible endings to a meal. Base it on a color theme – green and white looks cool and refreshing, red berries with peaches or nectarines is lovely for a party – as is a combination of fruits, such as pomegranate and banana. Dried fruits really come into their own in desserts, whether individually, as mixed fruit compotes, or puréed, and give a nutritious as well as delectable final touch to a meal.

From top to bottom: Tropical trifle (see p. 176); Baked tofu cheesecake (see p. 176).

Tropical trifle

Illustrated on page 174–75

Ingredients
For the cake
2 eggs
2 tablespoons apple butter
½ cup whole-wheat flour
For the trifle
3 tablespoons sugar-free jam
2 tablespoons medium-dry sherry
1¼ cups fruit juice
1 papaya
2 bananas, sliced
6 ounces low fat ricotta cheese
6 tablespoons skimmed milk
For garnishing
toasted slivered almonds
Serves 6

255 Calories

NUTRIENTS PER PORTION
Protein 14g ● ● ● *Fiber 1g* ●
Polyunsaturated fat 1g ● *Saturated fat 1g*
Vitamins B12, C, D
Minerals Ca

It is quite possible to make this lowfat, seemingly rich dessert without sugar by using a well-flavored, sugar-free jam.
1 Preheat the oven to 375°F.
2 Beat the eggs and fruit spread until very thick and creamy. Fold in half the flour, then fold in the remainder very carefully.
3 Butter and flour a 7-inch cake pan. Carefully spoon in the mixture evenly.
4 Bake for 20 minutes. Turn out of the pan and cool the cake on a wire rack.
5 Cut the cake in half, spread with jam and sandwich together again. Cut into 1-inch cubes. Place in the bottom of a glass dish.
6 Sprinkle with the sherry. Pour the fruit juice in.
7 Cut the papaya in half lengthwise. Remove the seeds and skin. Slice the flesh.
8 Arrange the banana and papaya slices in alternate layers over the cake.
9 Purée the ricotta cheese with the milk and spread evenly over the fruit.
10 Decorate with some toasted slivered almonds.

Baked tofu cheesecake

Illustrated on page 175

Ingredients
For the base
¼ cup butter or sunflower margarine
2 teaspoons apple butter
⅔ cup rolled oats
½ cup whole-wheat flour
For the filling
peel and juice of 1 orange
4 ripe bananas
21 ounces silken tofu
For garnishing
grapes and orange segments
Serves 6–8

180 Calories

NUTRIENTS PER PORTION
Protein 8g ● ● ● *Fiber 3g* ● ●
Polyunsaturated fat 2g ● ● ● *Saturated fat 4g*
Vitamins A, B1, C
Minerals Ca, Cu, Fe, Mg, Zn

Cheesecake is a slight misnomer as no cheese is used in this dish; protein-rich tofu is used instead. If you are trying tofu for the first time, you may wish to blend in a little cottage cheese or sweetening such as honey or maple syrup.
1 Preheat the oven to 350°F.
2 For the base, cream the butter or margarine and fruit spread together until smooth. Stir in the oats and flour and mix well.
3 Spread the mixture over the bottom of a lightly oiled 7-inch spring-form cake pan. Bake for 10 minutes.
4 For the filling, purée the orange peel, orange juice, bananas, and tofu until smooth. Pour over the baked base.
5 Bake for about 45 minutes until just set.
6 Leave to cool in the pan before removing. Decorate with grapes and orange segments. Chill before serving.

Cranachan

Illustrated on page 178

NUTRIENTS PER PORTION
450 Calories
Protein 16g ● ● *Fiber 9g* ● ● ●
Polyunsaturated fat 4g ● ● *Saturated fat 3g*
Vitamins B1, B2, B6, C, E, FA
Minerals Ca, Fe, Mg, Zn

Ingredients
*½ cup hazelnuts or filberts,
coarsely ground
3 ounces steel-cut oats
1¼ cups thickened yogurt (see
p.106) and ⅔ cup lowfat yogurt or
2 cups homemade lowfat thickened
yogurt (p.106)
½ pound black grapes, halved and
seeded
1½ cups sliced strawberries
For garnishing
a few small whole strawberries*
Serves 4

This high-fiber dessert can be varied depending on the fruit that is in season at the time.
1 Preheat the oven to 350°F.
2 Mix the hazelnuts with the oats and place in a shallow baking dish or on a cookie sheet. Toast in the oven for 10–15 minutes until golden.
3 Using 4 wide tumbler glasses, make layers of the yogurt, fruit-and-oat mixture. Finish with a layer of yogurt and decorate with whole strawberries. Serve chilled.

Chestnut purée

Illustrated on page 178

NUTRIENTS PER PORTION
170 Calories
Protein 14g ● ● ● *Fiber 2g* ●
Polyunsaturated fat 6g ● ● ● *Saturated fat 4g*
Vitamins C
Minerals Fe, Mg

Ingredients
*4 ounces dried chestnuts, soaked
overnight in 1 cup orange juice
2 tablespoons lemon juice
2 teaspoons carob powder
4 tablespoons tahini
6 ounces lowfat ricotta cheese
12 drops almond extract
2 teaspoons maple syrup
For garnishing
grated carob chocolate and
grated orange peel*
Serves 4

This high-protein dessert owes its unusual taste to the inclusion of tahini and sesame.
1 Place the chestnuts and their soaking liquid in a saucepan. Bring to a boil, cover, and simmer for 35–40 minutes or until they are soft. Drain.
2 Purée the chestnuts with the remaining ingredients.
3 Pour into 4 glasses and chill. Garnish with grated carob and orange peel.

Clockwise from top: Cranachan (see p. 177); Chestnut purée (see p. 177).

Illustrated opposite

Ingredients
½ cup chopped pitted dried dates
1 teaspoon grated orange peel
1¼ cups orange juice
3 tablespoons butter or sunflower
margarine
2 tablespoons whole-wheat flour
2 eggs, separated
Serves 4

Date and orange frazzan

215
Calories

NUTRIENTS PER PORTION
Protein 5g ● Fiber 3g ● ●
Polyunsaturated fat 0.5g ● Saturated fat 0.6g
Vitamins B1, B12, C, D
Minerals –

Sweet, without added sugar, these fruit slices should be served
to follow high-protein, lowfat dishes.
1 Place the dates in a small saucepan.
2 Add the orange peel and orange juice and cook for 10–15
minutes or until the dates are soft.
3 Meanwhile, preheat the oven to 350°F.
4 Melt the butter or margarine in a large saucepan and stir in
the flour until smooth. Stir in the date mixture, bring to a boil
and simmer for 2–3 minutes, stirring. Cool.
5 Beat the egg yolks into the date mixture. Beat the egg whites
until stiff, then fold into the mixture. Spoon the mixture into a
lightly oiled baking dish and bake for 30 minutes.

Whole-wheat crêpes

NUTRIENTS PER PORTION
135 Calories
Protein 6g ● ● ● *Fiber 3g* ● ●
Polyunsaturated fat 1g ● ● *Saturated fat 1g*
Vitamins B12
Minerals Ca

Ingredients
*¾ cup plus 2 tablespoons
whole-wheat flour
pinch of salt
1 egg
1¼ cups milk
1 teaspoon oil
oil or butter for frying*
Makes 8–10 pancakes

This recipe can be used for sweet or savory crêpes. Serve sweet crêpes with maple syrup, or just with a generous squeeze of lemon juice and brown sugar to taste. If you are going to eat the crêpes right away, stack them on top of one another on a lightly oiled plate and keep warm in a moderately hot oven or under a low broiler. If you are going to keep them to use later, place each one onto a cool surface as it is cooked. If they are stacked before cooling, their own steam will moisten them and make them soggy.

1 Mix the flour and salt in a bowl. Beat together the egg, milk, and oil. Pour this into the flour, stirring constantly and mixing in the flour until you have a smooth batter. If you use a blender, first blend the milk, egg, salt, and oil for 15–30 seconds, then add the flour and blend for a further 30 seconds until a smooth, creamy batter is produced.

2 Let the batter stand for 30 minutes or more before making the crêpes. Blend or beat again just before using, because some of the flour will almost certainly have settled at the bottom.

3 Heat about teaspoon oil or butter in a skillet until it smokes. Pour in 2 tablespoons of batter, quickly tipping the pan so that the batter spreads out thinly and evenly into a circle.

4 Cook for 2–3 minutes. Toss or flip over with a pancake turner and cook the other side for a further 2–3 minutes.

Date and orange frazzan (see opposite).

Fruity oatcakes

Illustrated opposite
Ingredients
½ cup butter or sunflower margarine
¼ cup date or apricot purée
¾ cup plus 2 tablespoons whole-wheat flour
1¼ cups rolled oats
Makes 12

NUTRIENTS PER PORTION
130 Calories
Protein 2g ● *Fiber 5g* ● ●
Polyunsaturated fat 0.5g ● ● *Saturated fat 4g*
Vitamins A, B1
Minerals Fe, Mg

These iron-rich cookies are easy to make, and the use of a purée instead of sugar means that they have a fruity flavor.
1 Preheat the oven to 350°F.
2 Cream the butter or margarine and fruit purée together in a large bowl until light. Mix in the flour and rolled oats and beat together until a stiff dough is formed.
3 Press or roll out the dough and cut into small circles – so that you make about 12 oatcakes.
4 Bake for 15 minutes or until just firm and lightly browned. Cool on a wire rack.

Carob cookies

Illustrated opposite
Ingredients
2–3 ounces dates
⅓ cup unsalted peanuts
2 teaspoons aniseed
2 teaspoons sesame seeds
½ cup olive or sunflower oil
peel and juice of 1 orange
2 cups flour
1 teaspoon cinnamon
1 tablespoon carob powder
1 small egg
For the topping:
1 egg white
2 tablespoons finely chopped peanuts
Makes 18

NUTRIENTS PER PORTION
130 Calories
Protein 3g ● *Fiber 2g* ●
Polyunsaturated fat 4g ● ● ● *Saturated fat 1g*
Vitamins B1, E, FA, N
Minerals Fe, Mg

These simple, lowfat cookies have a good texture and subtle flavor, naturally sweetened by dates.
1 Preheat the oven to 350°F.
2 Cook the dates gently in a little water until soft, drain and beat to a stiff purée with a fork.
3 Grind the peanuts, aniseed, and sesame seeds, and place in a large mixing bowl.
4 Slowly mix in the olive oil, then add the orange peel and juice, and the puréed dates.
5 Add the flour, cinnamon, and carob powder. Blend well, making sure to stir the mixture thoroughly.
6 Beat in the egg and mix to a stiff dough.
7 Turn onto a floured work surface. Roll out and cut into cookie shapes, or divide the mixture into walnut-sized pieces and press into individual circles.
8 Brush the cookies with egg white and then sprinkle with peanuts.
9 Bake on a greased cookie sheet for 25–30 minutes.
10 Cool on a wire rack.

Clockwise from left: Fruity oatcakes (opposite), Fruit and nut bars (below); Carob cookies (opposite).

Fruit and nut bars

315
Calories

NUTRIENTS PER PORTION
Protein 7g ● Fiber 11g ● ● ●
Polyunsaturated fat 2g ● ● Saturated fat 1g
Vitamins B1, E
Minerals Ca, Fe, Mg

Illustrated above
Ingredients
2 ounces dried apricots
2 ounces dried dates
2 ounces dried figs
⅓ cup golden raisins
⅓ cup sunflower seeds
⅓ cup hazelnuts or filberts
1½ cups rolled oats
1–2 tablespoons lemon juice
1 tablespoon frozen concentrated
apple juice or ½ tablespoon of sugar
Makes 12 slices

This recipe is a nutritious alternative to the standard high-fat and high-sugar snacks.
1 Preheat the oven to 350°F.
2 Finely chop or grind the fruit and nuts, and mix thoroughly with the other ingredients.
3 Press into a lightly greased 7-inch square baking pan. Bake for 15 minutes. Cut into slices while still warm.

· CHAPTER SIX ·

MENU IDEAS FOR SPECIAL OCCASIONS

This part of the book is designed to help you prepare varied and interesting meals, well balanced in tastes, textures, and nutrients. These meals are also high in fiber and protein but low in saturated fat, and provide a good source of vitamins and minerals.

HOW TO USE A NUTRITIONAL PROFILE

0000
Calories

NUTRIENTS PER PORTION
Protein 25g ● ● ●   Fiber 16g ● ● ●
Polyunsaturated fat 17g ● ● ●   Saturated fat 4g
Vitamins A, B1, B2, B6, B12, C, D, E, FA, N
Minerals Ca, Cu, Fe, Mg, Zn

Each recipe has its own nutritional profile, so that you can see at a glance, in grams, exactly how much protein, fiber, polyunsaturated fat, saturated fat, and calories each portion, or meal, contains. The profile also shows which vitamins and minerals are found in significant quantities. A dash indicates that a dish is not exceptionally high in any particular vitamin or mineral. The bullet system indicates how good the source is: three bullets show an excellent source, two bullets a very good source, and one bullet a good source. In the case of saturated fat, the amount per portion is shown in grams. This will enable you to keep a check on your daily intake.

Appetizing meals
Opposite: Summer Dinner Party menu (see pp.192–95). By combining different tastes and textures, and balancing the levels of protein, fiber, and fat, you can create interesting, special meals for all events.

Sunday Lunch

A delicious blend of taste and texture makes this an ideal
Sunday lunch for the family. Low-protein dishes like beet salad
and golden fruit salad are balanced by the high-protein, high-
fiber celebration loaf and spinach soup.

NUTRIENTS PER PORTION
1350 Calories
Protein 37g ● ● ●   Fiber 39g ● ● ●
Polyunsaturated fat 32g ● ● ●   Saturated fat 11g
Vitamins A, B1, B2, C. E, FA, N
Minerals Ca, Cu, Fe, Mg

Celebration loaf

Tomato sauce

Wine

Baked parsnips in orange

Hazel's potatoes

Spinach soup

This nutritious, high-protein, high-fiber, lowfat soup is based on a spiced fruit stock made from fruit juices, coriander, and ginger. The last two ingredients provide just the right amount of tang to the soup.

Celebration loaf

This high-protein, high-fiber dish contrasts a creamy nut mixture with a dark, moist layer of mushrooms and walnuts.

Tomato sauce

The tomato sauce is served here to enhance the flavor of the celebration loaf, not to moisten it. (See p. 119 for the recipe.)

Hazel's potatoes

Roast potatoes need not become a forbidden food once you have turned to a healthy regime of eating, as this dish proves. The potatoes here, baked lightly with a minimum amount of olive oil, are delicious, and yet low in saturated fat.

Baked parsnips in orange

After steaming, baking is the best way to preserve nutrients in cooked vegetables. The natural sweetness of the parsnips is well complemented here by the fresh orange juice.

Beet salad

Raw beets have a far better flavor than canned, pre-cooked varieties, which have often had preservatives and sugar added to them. Here, the beets are mixed with celeryroot and turnip and tossed in an oil, lemon, mustard, onion and pepper dressing. This produces a clean-tasting salad to follow the main course.

Golden fruit salad

Using tropical fruits such as mango, passionfruit, pomegranate, and dates, this fruit salad is an ideal way to end a meal – light, naturally sweet, and fat-free.

Wine

A glass of dry, white wine will add 75 calories to the nutritional profile of this meal.

Golden fruit salad

Beet salad

Spinach soup

Spinach soup

Illustrated on page 185

Ingredients

*2 teaspoons olive oil
1 medium onion, chopped
1 clove garlic, crushed
6½ cups washed and shredded
spinach
2 cups mixed apple and orange juice
2-inch piece fresh gingerroot, grated
1 teaspoon ground coriander
⅔ cup plain yogurt or reduced fat
sour cream
salt, or gomasio if preferred
black pepper*
Serves 4

110
Calories

NUTRIENTS PER PORTION
*Protein 7g ● ● ●   Fiber 6g ● ● ●
Polyunsaturated fat 0.5g ● ●   Saturated fat 1g
Vitamins A, C, E
Minerals Ca, Cu, Fe, Mg*

A good source of vitamins A, C, and E, and high in minerals, protein, and fiber, this soup uses a spiced fruit stock to add another dimension to the spinach flavor.

1 Heat the oil in a large saucepan and gently fry the onion and garlic for 4–5 minutes, or until the onion is soft.

2 Add the spinach and stir-fry for 2–3 minutes over a high heat until it becomes limp.

3 Pour over the fruit juices, ginger, and coriander. Bring to a boil, cover, and simmer for 20 minutes.

4 Cool slightly, then purée until smooth. Stir in the yogurt or sour cream. Season with salt and pepper. Reheat the soup gently before serving.

Celebration loaf

Illustrated on page 184

Ingredients

*2 tablespoons sunflower oil
1 medium onion, finely chopped
5 stalks celery, finely chopped
1 tablespoon whole-wheat flour
1¼ cups white wine or stock
1½ cups blanched almonds,
ground
1 cup whole-wheat bread crumbs
⅔ cup rolled oats
1 apple, grated
2 eggs
juice of ½ lemon
salt, or gomasio if preferred
black pepper*
For the filling
*2 teaspoons sunflower oil
1 medium onion, finely chopped
5 cups diced mushrooms
1 clove garlic, crushed
1¼ cups chopped walnuts*
Serves 6–8

775
Calories

NUTRIENTS PER PORTION
*Protein 41g ● ●   Fiber 15g ● ● ●
Polyunsaturated fat 7g ● ● ●   Saturated fat 2.5g
Vitamins B$_1$, B$_2$, B$_6$, B$_{12}$, C, D, E, FA, N
Minerals Ca, Cu, Fe, Mg, Zn*

Successful nut loaves should be moist. They should include plenty of vegetables, otherwise the nut-and-bread-crumb mix becomes too reminiscent of stuffing. This attractive dish, made with a creamy nut "meat" filled with a contrasting layer of mushrooms and walnuts, provides a near perfect nutritional balance for a meal.

1 Heat the oil in a large saucepan and gently fry the onion for 4–5 minutes, or until soft. Add the celery and fry for 5 minutes.

2 Sprinkle on the flour. Cook for 1–2 minutes, stirring, then pour in the wine or stock. Cook and stir for 1–2 minutes.

3 Mix the almonds, bread crumbs, oats, grated apple, and eggs together in a large bowl. Add the sauce and lemon juice. Season.

4 Preheat the oven to 375°F.

5 For the filling, heat the oil in a saucepan and gently fry the onion until soft. Add other ingredients and cook for about 10 minutes, stirring.

6 Lightly oil and line a 2½-to-3¾ cup savarin or ring mold with parchment paper. Spoon in a third of the creamy nut mixture, add the dark filling, then cover the top of the dish with the remaining nut mixture.

7 Bake for 50–55 minutes. Cool in the pan for 10 minutes.

Hazel's potatoes

NUTRIENTS PER PORTION
165 Calories
Protein 3g ● Fiber 2g ●
Polyunsaturated fat 1g ● ● Saturated fat 1g
Vitamins C
Minerals –

Illustrated on page 184
Ingredients
1 pound potatoes
2–3 tablespoons olive oil
juice of ½ lemon
Serves 4

These roast potatoes are low in saturated fat.
1 Preheat the oven to 400°F.
2 Peel and cut the potatoes into pieces. Place in a saucepan of water, bring to a boil, and parboil for 10–15 minutes until almost cooked. Drain.
3 Heat the olive oil in a baking dish in the oven for a few minutes.
4 Put the potatoes in the dish and sprinkle with lemon juice. Bake for 20–25 minutes until well cooked and lightly browned.

Baked parsnips in orange

NUTRIENTS PER PORTION
80 Calories
Protein 2g ● ● Fiber 5g ● ●
Polyunsaturated fat 1g ● ● ● Saturated fat 0g
Vitamins C, E, N
Minerals –

Illustrated on page 184
Ingredients
1 pound parsnips
juice of 1 orange
2–3 tablespoons water
2 teaspoons sunflower oil
Serves 4

After steaming, baking is the best way to preserve nutrients.
1 Preheat the oven to 400°F.
2 Scrub or peel the parsnips and cut lengthwise. Put in a lightly oiled baking dish.
3 Mix together the orange juice, water and oil. Pour this over the parsnips.
4 Bake for 40–50 minutes, adding more water or orange juice during the cooking if the parsnips begin to look dry. Serve hot.

Golden fruit salad

NUTRIENTS PER PORTION
120 Calories
Protein 2g ● Fiber 6g ● ● ●
Polyunsaturated fat 0.5g ● Saturated fat 0.5g
Vitamins A, C
Minerals –

Illustrated on page 185
Ingredients
1 mango
1 ugli fruit or pink grapefruit
2 passion fruit
1 pomegranate
8 fresh dates
6 yellow plums
1 teaspoon lemon juice
1 tablespoon white grape juice
Serves 4

In a healthy diet fruit salads come into their own – naturally sweet and fat-free.
1 Peel the mango and chop the pulp into bite-sized pieces.
2 Peel the ugli fruit or grapefruit and segment the flesh.
3 Cut the passion fruit and pomegranate in half and scrape out the seeds, taking care to remove the bitter white pith from the pomegranate.
4 Pit the dates and plums and chop into bite-sized pieces.
5 Mix fruits together with the juices. Leave for 2–3 hours.

Quick and Tasty Supper

This delicious supper menu is for when time is at a premium, just allow time for the ice cream to set. The buffet-style dishes happily mix together. The meal also shows how the addition of whole-wheat noodles and zucchini can improve the level of fiber.

NUTRIENTS PER PORTION
875
Calories

Protein 34g ● ● ●   *Fiber 17g* ● ● ●
Polyunsaturated fat 12g ● ● ●   *Saturated fat 9g*
Vitamins A, B₁, B₂, C, E, FA
Minerals Ca, Cu, Fe, Mg, Zn

Papaya and lime salad with mint
This light, easy-to-prepare appetizer uses papaya (a tropical fruit containing the digestive enzyme pepain) at its simplest – just peel and sprinkle with lime juice to offset its natural sweetness.

Tofu bobotie
This spicy fruit casserole is an adaptation of the traditional South African dish. This version makes excellent use of tofu, a high-protein soybean product. Although tofu has little taste of its own when uncooked, it absorbs the flavors of whatever it is cooked with.

Whole-wheat noodles
Whole-wheat noodles are a good standby item to keep in the pantry. They have been used here as an alternative to potatoes or rice. They are a good way of increasing the fiber levels in a meal which may otherwise be too low.

Steamed zucchini
Steaming is one of the best ways of preserving the nutrients in vegetables. Salt should ideally not be added – or kept to a minimum. If you find you cannot do without a dab of butter on the vegetables, try using a margarine or a dollop of yogurt mixed with chives, instead.

*Papaya and lime
salad with mint*

Corn salad with bean sprouts
This crisp salad is a good choice to make when serving a substantial dish like tofu bobotie because its lightness and range of ingredients make such a pleasing and varied contrast.

Iced cashew cream
Containing no heavy cream, this dessert owes its richness to the puréed nuts and fruit. The fat level in this dish is impressively low.

Mineral water
Mineral water, whether still or carbonated, is a refreshing, calorie-free accompaniment to meals. Read the bottle's label to check for the specific mineral content.

Iced cashew cream

Corn salad
with bean sprouts

Steamed zucchini

Whole-wheat noodles

Mineral water

Tofu bobotie

Papaya and lime salad with mint

Illustrated on page 188

Ingredients
2 papayas
1 lime
Chinese cabbage leaves and
watercress sprigs
For garnishing
sprig fresh mint
Serves 4

NUTRIENTS PER PORTION
50 Calories
Protein 0.5g ● Fiber 0g
Polyunsaturated fat 0g ● ● ● Saturated fat 0g
Vitamins –
Minerals –

Also known as pawpaw or papaw, this tropical fruit contains the digestive enzyme pepain.

1 Cut the papaya in half lengthwise and discard the seeds.

2 Squeeze the juice of half the lime over the papaya flesh. Use the remaining half as garnish, cut into very thin slices, together with the sprig of mint.

3 Arrange the papaya halves on a bed of Chinese cabbage leaves and watercress sprigs.

Tofu bobotie

Illustrated on page 189

Ingredients
2 teaspoons peanut oil
1 medium onion, finely chopped
1 pound firm tofu, cut in chunks
1 teaspoon ground allspice
1 teaspoon ground cumin
½ teaspoon ground ginger
½ teaspoon turmeric
pinch of cayenne
1 pound tomatoes, skinned and
chopped
1 medium red pepper, seeded and
cut into strips
1 medium green pepper, seeded and
cut into strips
1 large eggplant, chopped
⅔ cup golden raisins
soysauce, or salt if preferred
black pepper
For the topping
½ teaspoon cumin seeds
1¼ cups plain yogurt
1 egg
juice of ½ lemon
Serves 4

NUTRIENTS PER PORTION
265 Calories
Protein 16g ● ● ● Fiber 6g ● ● ●
Polyunsaturated fat 3g ● ● ● Saturated fat 2g
Vitamins A, B₁, B₂, B₆, C, E, FA
Minerals Ca, Cu, Fe, Mg, Zn

This dish is an adaptation of the South African spiced fruit casserole. It is perfect for tofu, which absorbs the flavor and color of the vegetables and spices, while providing a good source of lowfat, low-calorie protein.

1 Heat the oil in a saucepan and gently fry the onion for 4–5 minutes, or until soft. Add the tofu and spices to the pan and fry for 5 minutes.

2 Stir in the remaining ingredients, cover and cook for 30 minutes. Season with soysauce and pepper.

3 Preheat the oven to 350°F.

4 Spoon the mixture into a lightly oiled baking dish.

5 Dry roast the cumin seeds in a heavy-bottomed pan (see p. 117) for 3–4 minutes, or until lightly browned. Mix the topping ingredients together and pour over the bobotie.

6 Bake for 30 minutes. Serve hot.

Corn salad with bean sprouts

110
Calories

NUTRIENTS PER PORTION
Protein 5g ● ● ● *Fiber 4g* ● ●
Polyunsaturated fat 2g ● ● ● *Saturated fat 0.5g*
Vitamins C, E
Minerals Fe

Illustrated on page 189

Ingredients
*1¼ cups fresh or frozen corn
kernels
8 ounces bean sprouts (adzuki
or lentil)
⅔ cup scrubbed and chopped
Daikon (Japenese radish)
1 medium green pepper, seeded
and diced
12 radishes, sliced
For the dressing
1 tablespoon sunflower oil
1 teaspoon white-wine vinegar
1 teaspoon fennel seeds
½ teaspoon paprika*
Serves 4

This crisp and colorful salad provides a good source of protein, fiber, and iron.
1 Cook the corn in a saucepan of boiling water for about 5 minutes, or until lightly cooked.
2 Combine the salad ingredients together in a bowl.
3 Put the dressing ingredients together in a screw-top jar and mix by shaking well. Pour the dressing over the salad and toss.

Iced cashew cream

230
Calories

NUTRIENTS PER PORTION
Protein 5g ● *Fiber 1g* ●
Polyunsaturated fat 4g ● ● ● *Saturated fat 3g*
Vitamins C, E
Minerals Mg

Illustrated on page 189

Ingredients
*⅔ cup cashews
⅔ cup soy milk (unsweetened)
2 teaspoons honey
½ teaspoon vanilla extract
1 tablespoon rum (optional)
1 tablespoon sunflower oil
½ medium pineapple, diced*
Serves 6

The richness and flavor of this unusual ice cream come from the nuts and fruit.
1 Grind the cashews in a grinder, blender, or food processor until they become a very fine powder.
2 Blend the milk, honey, vanilla extract, ground cashews, rum (if using), and oil together until quite smooth.
3 Add the pineapple and blend briefly so that the pineapple still provides some texture.
4 Transfer to a freezerproof container and freeze for about 2 hours until the cream is firm.

Summer Dinner Party

The whole-wheat crêpes with their assorted, colorful fillings help to give substance to this party menu for a summer's evening. Extra protein is provided by the tofu in the mushroom salad and the avocado in the avocado and kiwi salad, which is also full of vitamins. A light, lowfat "ice cream" dessert is the perfect dish to finish with after a filling main course.

NUTRIENTS PER PORTION
Protein 40g ● ● ● Fibre 20g ● ● ●
Polyunsaturated fats 9g ● ● Saturated fats 28g ●
Vitamins A, B, B₁, B₂, B₆, B₁₂, C, E
Minerals Ca, Fe, K, Mg, Zn

1200 Calories

Artichokes with lemon sauce
Globe artichoke served with individual bowls of lemon and garlic sauce is a quick-and-easy first course which can be prepared well in advance.

Galette
A layereed galette of whole-wheat crêpes with three different vegetable fillings – spinach, fennel, and tomato and onion. The crêpes (see pp.176–77) can be made in advance and frozen; the fillings will keep for 1–2 days in the refrigerator. Serve sprinkled with grated Parmesan cheese.

Mushroom salad
Button mushrooms are garnished with walnuts and scallions in a tofu and lemon dressing.

Avocado and kiwi salad
A salad of avocado and kiwi fruit with a julienne of celery and cucumber, tossed in a herb vinaigrette.

Black currant yogurt ice cream
This looks rich and creamy, but is low in fat and sugar. Its clean, sharp taste is enhanced with orange.

Mushroom salad in tofu

Galette

Black currant yogurt
ice cream

Avocado and
kiwi salad

Artichokes with
lemon sauce

Artichokes with lemon sauce

Illustrated on page 193

Ingredients
4 globe artichokes
6 tablespoons butter
1 tablespoon wheat flour
1¼ cups boiling water
2 teaspoons lemon juice
grated peel of ½ lemon
3 cloves garlic, crushed
salt and pepper
1 tablespoon snipped chives
Serves 4

NUTRIENTS PER PORTION
155 Calories
Protein 2g Fiber 1g
Polyunsaturated fat Trace Saturated fat 9g
Vitamins A, N
Minerals –

A more elaborate variation is to prepare and cook the artichokes, cool them, remove the soft inner leaves, scoop out the inedible chokes with a teaspoon and fill them with sauce.
1 Wash the artichokes thoroughly. Remove the stems and trim the bottoms so that the artichokes will sit flat. Trim the points off the leaves with scissors.
2 Bring a large pan of water to a boil and cook the artichokes, covered, for 30–40 minutes or until a leaf pulls out easily.
3 Meanwhile, melt half the butter in a pan. Add the flour and cook, stirring, over gentle heat for 2–3 minutes. Pour in the boiling water, stirring vigorously, and as soon as the mixture is smooth, beat in the remaining butter. Stir in the lemon juice, grated lemon peel and garlic. Season to taste. Keep warm, stirring from time to time, on a very low heat.
4 Drain the artichokes as soon as they are cooked and arrange them on a serving dish or on individual plates. Pour the sauce into a heated sauceboat and sprinkle it with chives.

Galette

Illustrated on page 192

Ingredients
8 crêpes (see pp. 178–79)
For the fennel filling
2⅔ cups finely sliced fennel
¼ cup butter
½ cup freshly grated Parmesan cheese
salt and pepper
For the spinach filling
1 pound fresh spinach, washed
½ teaspoon grated nutmeg
black pepper
For the tomato filling
2 tablespoons olive oil
1 onion, chopped
1 clove garlic, crushed
2½ cups peeled and chopped tomatoes
3 stalks celery, diced
½ teaspoon aniseeds
1 tablespoon tomato paste
salt and pepper
For serving
extra grated Parmesan cheese
Serves 4

NUTRIENTS PER PORTION
475 Calories
Protein 22g ● ● ● Fiber 7g ● ● ●
Polyunsaturated fat 2g ● Saturated fat 14g
Vitamins A, B1, B2, B12, C, E, FA, N
Minerals Ca, Fe, K, Mg, Zn

This makes a spectacular dish for a dinner party.
1 Blanch the fennel for 10 minutes in boiling water. Drain well.
2 Melt the butter in a small pan, put the fennel in, cover, and stew for 10 minutes over low heat. Purée the fennel with the grated Parmesan cheese and add salt and pepper to taste.
3 Preheat the oven to 350°F.
4 Cook the spinach in its own juices for 7–8 minutes in a covered pan. Chop and season with nutmeg and pepper.
5 Heat the olive oil in a saucepan and gently fry the onion and garlic for 3–4 minutes. Stir in the tomatoes, celery, aniseeds, and tomato paste and cook, uncovered, over moderate heat, for 10–15 minutes, or until you have a thick sauce. Season well.
6 Assemble the galette in a lightly greased 7-inch springform pan. Put in one crêpe, then sandwich in the different fillings (reserving some of the tomato sauce) between the crêpes. End with a crêpe.
7 Bake in the oven for 10–15 minutes. Turn out and serve with the remaining tomato sauce and extra grated Parmesan cheese.

Mushroom salad

75
Calories

NUTRIENTS PER PORTION
Protein 5g ● Fiber 3g ●
Polyunsaturated fat 2g ● ● Saturated fat 1g
Vitamins B2, N
Minerals Ca, Fe, K, Mg

The lemon dressing adds a pleasant tang to the salad.
1 Toss the mushrooms in the oil with the garlic.
2 Toast the walnuts for 2–3 minutes under a hot broiler. Chop.
3 Mix together the tofu and lemon juice. Season well and stir into the mushroom slices.
4 Either mix in the scallions and toasted walnuts or arrange them on top as a garnish.

Illustrated on page 192
Ingredients
5 cups sliced button mushrooms
1 tablespoon oil
1 clove garlic, crushed
½ cup shelled walnuts
5 ounces silken tofu
1 tablespoon lemon juice
salt and pepper
3–4 scallions, sliced lengthwise
Serves 4

Avocado and kiwi salad

330
Calories

NUTRIENTS PER PORTION
Protein 5g ● Fiber 4g ● ●
Polyunsaturated fat 4g ● ● Saturated fat 3g
Vitamins A, C, FA, N
Minerals Fe, K

To give contrast to the salad, use red raddicchio leaves instead of the green lettuce.
1 Toss avocados, kiwi fruit, and herbs in half the vinaigrette.
2 Toss the cucumber and celery in the remaining vinaigrette.
3 To serve, arrange the lettuce leaves and watercress in a dish. Pile on the avocado and kiwi fruit and arrange the cucumber and celery julienne on top.

Illustrated on page 193
Ingredients
2 large avocados, diced
4 kiwi fruit, peeled and sliced
1 tablespoon finely chopped parsley
1 tablespoon snipped chives
6 tablespoons vinaigrette (see p.219)
½ small cucumber, cut into julienne strips
2 stalks celery, cut into julienne strips
1 head of lettuce
1 bunch watercress, cleaned – about 2 ounces
Serves 4

Black currant yogurt ice cream

90
Calories

NUTRIENTS PER PORTION
Protein 6g ● ● Fiber 2g ●
Polyunsaturated fat 1g ● ● ● Saturated fat 1g
Vitamins B2, C, N
Minerals Ca, K

Red currants, blackberries, bilberries, or gooseberries could also be used, as could pitted sweet cherries.
1 Mix together the yogurt, vanilla extract and honey and freeze until mushy – about 1 hour.
2 Put the black currants in a pan with the orange juice and sugar. Cover and simmer over low heat for 5 minutes (gooseberries would take about 10 minutes).
3 Remove from the heat and let the fruit to steep for 30 minutes. Strain and allow to cool completely.
4 Stir the fruit into the yogurt. Freeze for 1 hour. Beat the egg whites until stiff, fold them in and freeze for 1–2 hours or until ice cream is firm.

Illustrated on page 193
Ingredients
2½ cups plain yogurt
1 teaspoon vanilla extract
2 tablespoons honey
4–6 ounces black currants, topped and tailed
2 tablespoons orange juice
2 tablespoons light raw sugar
2 egg whites
Serves 6

Outdoor Lunch

A wholesome meal that can easily be packed to take on a picnic.
The major source of protein is the celery and green pepper
quiche, with the wild rice salad, fruit pie, and bread being the
major sources of fiber.

NUTRIENTS PER PORTION
1095 Calories
Protein 37g ● ● ●   *Fiber 23g* ● ● ●
Polyunsaturated fat 17g ● ● ●   *Saturated fat 9g*
Vitamins A, B1, B2, B6, B12, E, FA, N
Minerals Ca, Cu, Fe, Mg, Zn

Whole-wheat bread

Summer soup

*Green bean
julienne*

*Celery and green
pepper quiche*

Summer soup
Served chilled, this high-protein soup, based on lettuce and Chinese cabbage leaves, is an ideal appetizer for a summer meal. The cardamom and yogurt add to the delicate flavor of the main ingredients.

Celery and green pepper quiche
This high-protein, lowfat quiche is a simple combination of vegetables in a well-flavored, sauce. The horseradish and celery seeds add a special tang to the taste of the filling. The whole-wheat pastry crust is an excellent source of fiber and, because it has to be rolled out thinly, is light and delicate in texture.

Green bean julienne
Salads are often used to provide a contrast in texture, as well as taste, and this is certainly true of this dish, where raw green beans and fresh celery have been used to complement the soft filling of the quiche.

Wild rice salad
This salad is an interesting combination of textures and tastes – the firmness of the rice is set off by the peppery taste of the watercress and the spiciness of the fresh gingerroot.

Whole-wheat bread
This type of bread is one of the best sources of fiber in our diet. It is important not to use refined flours, as most of their nutrients and roughage have been removed in manufacture.

Fresh fruit pie
Pies need not be unhealthy so long as you use the freshest ingredients. Use a good whole-wheat pastry dough and do not use sugar. In this pie, the fresh peaches and pears are sweetened with golden raisins, and they are enclosed in a light yeasted pastry.

Apple juice
High in vitamin C, apple juice is available both filtered and "raw". Always choose natural juices, and read the label to check that there is no preservatives or added colorings. Unfiltered juice is higher in fiber.

Apple juice

Wild rice salad

Fresh fruit pie

Summer soup

Illustrated on page 196

Ingredients
2 teaspoons sunflower oil
3 scallions, chopped
1 round head of lettuce, shredded
2 cups shredded Chinese cabbage
⅔ cup skim milk
1¼ cups yogurt
8 cardamom seeds, crushed
a little lemon juice
salt, or gomasio if preferred
black pepper
Serves 4

NUTRIENTS PER PORTION
50 Calories
Protein 3g ● ● ●   Fiber 1g ●
Polyunsaturated fat 1g ● ● ●   Saturated fat 0g
Vitamins A, C, E
Minerals Ca, Mg

Large portions of soup can be daunting, so try serving just enough to whet the appetite. This chilled soup is high in protein and low in fat.
1 Heat the oil in a large saucepan and gently fry the onions for about 3 minutes.
2 Add the lettuce and Chinese cabbage leaves to the pan, cover, and cook for 5–8 minutes.
3 Transfer the lettuce mixture to a blender or food processor and add the milk and yogurt. Purée until smooth.
4 Mix in the cardamom seeds and lemon juice. Season with salt and pepper.
5 Chill thoroughly before serving.

Celery and green pepper quiche

Illustrated on page 196

Ingredients
1 quantity of lowfat or piecrust
dough (see p.109)
2 cups skim milk
½ onion
4 peppercorns
¼ teaspoon powdered mace
2 tablespoons sunflower oil
6 stalks celery, chopped
1 large green pepper, seeded and diced
½ teaspoon celery seeds
2 tablespoons whole-wheat flour
2 eggs
1 tablespoon grated horseradish
½ teaspoon paprika
salt, or gomasio if preferred
black pepper
For garnishing
½ teaspoon paprika
Serves 6

NUTRIENTS PER PORTION
360 Calories
Protein 13g ● ● ●   Fiber 2g ●
Polyunsaturated fat 7g ● ● ●   Saturated fat 3g
Vitamins B2, B6, B12, C, E, FA, N
Minerals Ca, Cu, Fe, Mg, Zn

Quiches are often synonymous with rich cheese fillings and are, therefore, high in fat. It is best to use simple vegetable combinations which, when bound together with a well-flavored sauce, produce delicious, tasty, light, and lowfat results.
1 Preheat the oven to 400°F.
2 Roll out the pastry dough and line a 8-inch tart pan. Prick the bottom and bake blind for 4 minutes.
3 Meanwhile, place the milk in a saucepan with the onion, peppercorns, and mace. Bring almost to a boil, remove from the heat and let stand for 10 minutes. Strain and reserve the flavored milk.
4 Heat the oil in a large saucepan and cook the celery, green pepper, and celery seeds very slowly for 10–15 minutes.
5 Add the flour and cook for 3 minutes, stirring well.
6 Pour in the flavored milk and mix well. Bring the sauce to a boil and simmer for 5 minutes, stirring. Cool slightly.
7 Beat in the eggs, then add the horseradish, paprika, salt, and the pepper.
8 Pour the filling into the crust and dust with paprika.
9 Bake for 30–35 minutes. Serve warm.

Green bean julienne

NUTRIENTS PER PORTION
80
Calories

Protein 2g ● *Fiber 3g* ● ●
Polyunsaturated fat 5g ● ● ● *Saturated fat 1g*
Vitamins C, E
Minerals –

Illustrated on page 196
Ingredients
½ pound French-style green beans
8 stalks celery
2 tablespoon sunflower seeds
For the dressing
juice of ½ lemon
1 tablespoon sunflower oil
1 teaspoon of frozen concentrated
apple juice or ½ teaspoon of sugar
salt, or gomasio if preferred
black pepper
Serves 4

Green beans are excellent raw, but if you prefer them cooked, steam them to preserve their nutrients.
1 Slice the beans into matchstick-sized pieces. Cut the celery into julienne strips. Place in a bowl and mix together.
2 Put the dressing ingredients in a screw-top jar and mix thoroughly. Pour over salad, toss well, and add sunflower seeds.

Wild rice salad

NUTRIENTS PER PORTION
110
Calories

Protein 2g ● *Fiber 3g* ● ● ●
Polyunsaturated fat 2g ● ● ● *Saturated fat 0.5g*
Vitamins A, C, E
Minerals –

Illustrated on page 197
Ingredients
¾ cup wild rice
1 cup grated carrot
1 large bunch watercress
For the dressing
1 tablespoon sunflower oil
peel and juice of ½ orange
1 teaspoon frozen concentrated
apple juice or ½ teaspoon of sugar
½-inch piece fresh gingerroot,
grated
soysauce, or salt if preferred
black pepper
Serves 4

This salad is delicious served with a high-protein bean dish.
1 Measure the rice. Bring twice the volume of water to a boil. Add the rice, cover and simmer for 35–40 minutes, or until just tender. Drain.
2 Put dressing ingredients in a screw-top jar; mix well. Pour over the warm rice and mix. Cool. Add carrots and watercress.

Fresh fruit pie

NUTRIENTS PER PORTION
385
Calories

Protein 11g ● ● *Fiber 8g* ● ● ●
Polyunsaturated fat 1g ● *Saturated fat 5g*
Vitamins A, B₁, B₂, B₁₂, C, D, N
Minerals Fe, Mg, Zn

Illustrated on page 197
Ingredients
1 pound dessert pears (Williams
or Comice)
3 medium peaches, skinned
⅓ cup golden raisins
⅔ cup white wine or apple juice
½ teaspoon ground coriander
12 cardamom seeds
1 teaspoon cornstarch
1 quantity of yeasted
pastry (see p.112)
1 egg, beaten
Serves 4–6

It takes time to adjust to eating sugar-free fruit dishes. Pick ripe fruit for the best flavor and use dried fruit for extra sweetness. This pie is high in most vitamins, iron, and zinc.
1 Coarsely chop the fruit. Place in a saucepan with the golden raisins, wine, or apple juice, coriander and cardamom seeds. Cook, uncovered, over a gentle heat for 15–20 minutes. Remove seeds. Preheat oven to 400°F.
2 Dissolve the cornstarch in a little water and add to the fruit. Bring to a boil, stirring, and simmer for 2–3 minutes.
3 Divide pastry dough in half. Roll out one portion and line an 8-inch pie plate. Spoon in the fruit. Moisten the edges with water.
4 Roll out the remaining dough for the lid. Seal and crimp the dough edges. Brush with beaten egg.
5 Bake for 25–30 minutes, or until the pie is golden.

Light Lunch

This meal, with its creamy soup, moist main course, and eggplant side dish, looks filling but is light on calories, and it is, in fact, low in saturated fat. The lentil stew and sweet red pepper soup are the major sources of protein, with snowpeas being served to improve the overall balance of fiber.

NUTRIENTS PER PORTION
Protein 27g ● ● ●   *Fiber 24g* ● ● ●
Polyunsaturated fat 5g ● ● ●   *Saturated fat 3g*
Vitamins C, B₁, FA
Minerals Ca, Fe

620
Calories

Sweet red pepper soup

Red and white salad

Lentil stew

Sweet red pepper soup
A rich soup, deriving its creaminess from high-protein, lowfat tofu.

Lentil stew
This simple, fragrant-tasting Middle Eastern dish is a combination of bulgur wheat, lentils and zucchini. It is served with yogurt, which adds moisture to the dish.

Eggplant bake
This dish is low in saturated fats, largely because the eggplant is baked and not fried. The corn provides an appealing, crunchy texture. The moistness of the dish ensures that the intrinsic dryness of the bulgur wheat does not overpower the whole meal.

Steamed snowpeas
These sweet-tasting pea pods should be so tender when raw that they need only the briefest steaming.

Red and white salad
A light way to end a substantial meal, this salad contrasts the smoothness of the lychees with the bite of the strawberries.

Wine
Healthy living need not preclude alcohol in moderation, and many white wines such as hock and Riesling have a low alcohol content – look for those around 9° to 10° proof. Remember, a glass of wine will add 75 calories to the meal.

Eggplant bake

Wine

Steamed snowpeas

Illustrated on page 200
Ingredients
*2 medium red peppers, halved
and seeded
2 teaspoons olive oil
1 medium onion, finely chopped
1 clove garlic, crushed
1⅓ cups peeled and chopped
tomatoes
2 tablespoons tomato paste
1¼ cups vegetable stock (see p.120)
1 teaspoon dried marjoram
10 ounces silken tofu
salt, or gomasio if preferred
black pepper
Serves 4*

Sweet red pepper soup

NUTRIENTS PER PORTION
*Protein 7g ● ● ●   Fiber 2g ●
Polyunsaturated fat 2g ● ● ●   Saturated fat 1g
Vitamins A, B1, B2, C, FA, N
Minerals Ca, Cu, Fe*

100
Calories

This soup derives its richness from the tofu – a good way of providing a creamy texture while keeping fats low and protein content high.
1 Preheat the oven to 350°F. Place the peppers in a baking dish and bake for 15–20 minutes, turning them over occasionally so that the skin chars. Cool, then peel off the skin and dice the flesh finely.
2 Heat the oil in a large saucepan and gently fry the onion and garlic for 4–5 minutes, or until soft.
3 Add the red pepper, tomatoes, paste, stock, and marjoram. Bring to a boil, cover, and simmer for 30 minutes.
4 Cut the tofu into pieces and purée until smooth. Pour into the soup and stir well. Season with salt and pepper. Heat through gently and serve hot.

Illustrated on page 200
Ingredients
*2 teaspoons olive oil
½ cup green lentils, cleaned
1 teaspoon ground allspice
12 cardamom pods, cracked
1⅓ cups bulgur wheat
2 tablespoons currants
4 cups sliced zucchini
salt, or gomasio if preferred
black pepper
For garnishing
2 tablespoons sesame seeds
1 teaspoon coriander seeds
For serving
thickened yogurt
steamed snowpeas
Serves 4*

Lentil stew

NUTRIENTS PER PORTION
*Protein 14g ● ● ●   Fiber 3g ● ●
Polyunsaturated fat 1g ●   Saturated fat 1g
Vitamins C, FA
Minerals Fe, Mg*

340
Calories

This simple, fragrant Middle Eastern dish is high in protein, low in saturated fat, and is a good source of iron.
1 Heat the oil in a large saucepan and gently fry the lentils and spices for 3–4 minutes.
2 Add 2½ cups cold water. Cover and simmer for about 30 minutes.
3 Add the bulgur wheat and currants and a little extra water if the mixture begins to look too dry. Cook for 10 minutes, stirring frequently.
4 Meanwhile, steam the zucchini for about 6 minutes. Mix the zucchini into the lentil mix. Season with some salt and pepper.
5 For the garnish, dry roast the seeds in a heavy-bottomed saucepan for 3–4 minutes. Crush them to a fine powder using a mortar and pestle or a coffee grinder.
6 Spoon the stew onto a warm serving dish and sprinkle with garnish. Serve with the thickened yogurt and steamed snowpeas.

Eggplant bake

Illustrated on page 201

NUTRIENTS PER PORTION
141 Calories
Protein 2g ● ● *Fiber 3g* ● ●
Polyunsaturated fat 2g ● ● ● *Saturated fat 0.5g*
Vitamins C, E
Minerals –

Ingredients
1 medium eggplant
2 teaspoons sunflower oil
1 medium onion, finely chopped
½ teaspoon cumin seeds
½ teaspoon turmeric
1 teaspoon ground coriander
1 teaspoon curry powder
1 medium green pepper, seeded and diced
4 ounces baby corn
1 tablespoon tomato paste
⅔ cup vegetable stock or water
2 teaspoons soysauce
black pepper
Serves 4

The eggplant in this recipe is baked and not fried, so the fat content remains desirably low. It can be served with other baked dishes, like the Health loaf (see p. 171).

1 Preheat the oven to 400°F.
2 Remove the eggplant stem. Prick the skin 2–3 times. Bake for 15–20 minutes or until soft. Cool and chop the pulp into bite-sized pieces.
3 Heat the oil in a large saucepan and gently fry the onion for 4–5 minutes. Stir in the spices and fry for 3 minutes.
4 Add the baked eggplant pieces, green pepper, and corn, and mix in well.
5 Dissolve the tomato paste in the stock. Pour over the vegetables.
6 Transfer to a baking dish. Reduce the oven temperature to 350°F. Cover the dish and bake for 45 minutes. Season with soysauce and pepper. Serve hot.

Red and white salad

Illustrated on page 200

NUTRIENTS PER PORTION
80 Calories
Protein 2g ● *Fiber 4g* ● ●
Polyunsaturated fat 0g ● ● ● *Saturated fat 0g*
Vitamins C
Minerals –

Ingredients
12 ounces lychees
½ pound red fruit (strawberries, cherries, or raspberries)
1 tablespoon kirsch
Serves 4

With the fruits used here, the dish is high in Vitamin C.
1 Peel the lychees. Using a small, sharp knife, cut in half and remove the pit. It is easier to try to find the top of the pit and work down toward the stem end, splitting open the fruit.
2 To prepare the berries, hull and slice the strawberries, pit the cherries, but leave the raspberries whole.
3 Mix the fruits together in a bowl and toss in the kirsch. Leave to stand for 2 hours before serving.

Celebration Dinner Party

This is a filling and impressive meal, and most of the dishes can be prepared in advance for easy planning. It provides plenty of fiber and protein as well as essential vitamins and minerals.

The fat content is relatively high but there is a greater proportion of polyunsaturated fat than saturated fat. The thick mushroom soup is low in calories to prepare you for the spicy and substantial Byzantine millet pilaf, which is balanced by the flavor of the lighter, tangy bean sprout salad. The spinach is a wonderful source of fiber, protein, vitamins, and minerals, and the winter fruit compote keeps its calories down with a delicious lowfat cashew cream sauce made with lowfat cottage cheese, cashews, and honey.

NUTRIENTS PER PORTION
Protein 25g ● ● ●   Fiber 23g ● ● ●
Polyunsaturated fat 23g ● ● ●   Saturated fat 9g
Vitamins A, B, B2, C, E, FA, N
Minerals Ca, Fe, K, Mg, Zn

1085 Calories

Mushroom soup with herbs
This soup with mushrooms, and red wine, flavored with parsley, bay, marjoram, and tarragon, can be made in advance and frozen.

Byzantine millet pilaf
A pilaf with coriander, apricots, and eggplant in sesame sauce, this dish can be prepared in advance and frozen.

Spinach darioles
Spinach leaves are stuffed with tomatoes and flavored with basil (or oregano, if preferred) and scallions.

Bean sprout salad
Mung bean sprouts are combined with sweet peppers, button mushrooms, and celery. They are then tossed in a dressing made from oil, vinegar, soysauce and seasoning, to make a colorful salad, which is chilled before serving.

Rhubarb with cashew cream
Rhubarb, pink grapefruit, and pears in wine can be served hot or cold. The "cream" to go with them is based on cashews and cottage cheese.

Spinach darioles

Bean sprout salad

Rhubarb with
cashew cream

Mushroom soup
with herbs

Byzantine millet
pilaf

Illustrated in page 205

Ingredients

3 tablespoons sunflower oil
1 medium onion, finely chopped
2 bay leaves
1 teaspoon chopped marjoram
1 teaspoon chopped tarragon
3¼ cups chopped mushrooms
2 cups dark vegetable stock
(see p.120)
¼ cup red wine
2 tablespoons tomato paste
2 tablespoons chopped parsley
Serves 4

Mushroom soup with herbs

NUTRIENTS PER PORTION
130 Calories
Protein 2g Fiber 3g ● ●
Polyunsaturated fat 6g ● ●   Saturated fat 2g
Vitamins A, C, E, FA, N
Minerals K

For extra flavor, you can include some dried mushrooms and use their soaking water in the vegetable stock.
1 Heat the oil in a large, heavy-bottomed pan and sauté the onion and herbs gently for about 5 minutes.
2 Add the mushrooms and cook for another 5 minutes or until they are well browned.
3 Stir in the stock, wine, tomato paste, and parsley. Bring to a boil, cover, and simmer for 30–45 minutes.
4 Remove the bay leaves, season to taste and serve hot. Croutons or crackers go well with this soup.

Illustrated on page 205

Ingredients

2 medium eggplants, thickly sliced
olive oil for frying
2 tablespoons tahini
2 tablespoons water
juice of ½ lemon
1 clove garlic, crushed
1 teaspoon soysauce
For the millet pilaf
1 small onion, finely chopped
1 tablespoon olive oil
1 large clove garlic, crushed
1 teaspoon ground coriander
6 ounces millet
4 ounces dried apricots, washed
4 cloves
1 cup white wine or cider
2 cups boiling water
salt and pepper
fresh, chopped coriander leaves,
cilantro, or Chinese parsley
Serves 4

Byzantine millet pilaf

NUTRIENTS PER PORTION
470 Calories
Protein 8g ● ●   Fiber 11g ● ● ●
Polyunsaturated fat 2g ● ● ●   Saturated fat 3g
Vitamins A, B1, B2, B6, FA, N
Minerals Ca, Fe, K, Mg, Zn

The combination of apricots and grains, topped with eggplants baked in a sesame sauce, is greatly influenced by Middle Eastern cookery.
1 Preheat the oven to 350°F.
2 Lightly sauté the eggplant slices in the olive oil until just browned and softened. Arrange them in layers in a shallow baking dish.
3 Mix the tahini with the water in a bowl. Add the lemon juice, garlic, and soysauce and blend together thoroughly. Pour this over the eggplant slices and bake, uncovered, for 20 minutes. Keep warm.
4 Meanwhile, gently fry the onion in 1 tablespoon olive oil for 3–4 minutes until soft. Add the garlic, coriander, and millet and fry for another 2–3 minutes.
5 Cut the apricots into thin slivers. Add them to the skillet together with the cloves, white wine or cider, and boiling water. Bring back to a boil and simmer for 20 minutes or until the millet is cooked. Season well and serve hot with the eggplant, sprinkled with fresh coriander leaves.

Spinach darioles

Illustrated on page 204

NUTRIENTS PER PORTION
Protein 3g ● Fiber 2g ●
Polyunsaturated fat Trace Saturated fat Trace
Vitamins A, C, FA
Minerals Ca, Fe, K, Mg

50
Calories

Ingredients
½ pound spinach
1⅓ cups peeled and sliced tomatoes
3–4 teaspoon chopped basil
2–3 scallions, finely chopped
pepper
a little vegetable oil
1 tomato, sliced
Serves 4

Delicious with most egg dishes, the spinach also complements bakes, roasts or pilafs such as Buckwheat loaf (see p.172) or Peanut Stroganov. This dish looks particularly attractive in the individual molds.

1 Preheat the oven to 350°F, and bring a large pan of water to a boil.

2 Blanch the spinach for a minute in the boiling water so that it becomes slightly wilted. Drain, refresh under cold, running water, and remove any coarse stems.

3 Lightly grease 8 dariole molds or a 7-inch quiche dish. Line with a little over half the spinach leaves, allowing them to overlap the top.

4 Fill with layers of tomato slices, sprinkling each layer with basil, scallions, and pepper. Fold the edges of the spinach over the top and cover with the remaining spinach.

5 Put a small ovenproof plate or weight on top, brush any exposed leaves with a little vegetable oil, and bake for 35–40 minutes. Turn out and serve decorated with tomato slices.

Rhubarb with cashew cream

Illustrated on page 205

NUTRIENTS PER PORTION
Protein 9g ● ● Fiber 5g ● ●
Polyunsaturated fat 8g ● ● Saturated fat 2g
Vitamins C, E
Minerals Ca, Fe, K, Mg, Zn

270
Calories

Ingredients
1 large, firm pear
1 tablespoon sugar
¾ cup red wine
5 cups rhubarb chopped into 1–inch pieces
1 pink grapefruit, peeled and chopped
2 tablespoons honey
For the cashew cream
⅔ cup cashews
½ cup cottage cheese
1–2 tablespoons honey
⅔ cup water
Serves 4

Made with lowfat cottage cheese, the nut "cream" makes a perfect accompaniment to cooked fruit – and a healthy alternative to cream.

1 Peel the pear and cut it into chunks. Dissolve the sugar in the wine in a small pan and stew the pear, covered, over very low heat for 15 minutes. Strain, reserving the juice.

2 In a separate pan, stew the rhubarb and grapefruit with the honey over low heat for 10 minutes or until the rhubarb is tender but not disintegrating. Strain, reserving the juice.

3 Put the pear juice and rhubarb juice in a pan together and boil until reduced by at least half and beginning to thicken. Combine the pear, rhubarb, and grapefruit in a serving bowl and pour the juice over. Leave to cool.

4 To make the cashew cream, blend all the ingredients together until very smooth. Serve with the rhubarb.

Exotic Evening Meal

This light but filling meal is an excellent balance of protein, fiber, polyunsaturated and, to a lesser extent, saturated fat. It also provides a subtle range of spicy and delicate tastes – from the earthy artichoke soup to the leafy green packages and julienne of vegetables through to the fruity and light taste of the mango and orange sorbet.

NUTRIENTS PER PORTION
880
Calories
Protein 21g ● ● ● *Fiber 30g* ● ● ●
Polyunsaturated fat 14g ● ● ● *Saturated fat 5g*
Vitamins A, C, E, FA
Minerals Ca, Cu, Fe, Mg, Zn

Chinese cabbage and grapefruit salad

Julienne of winter vegetables

Artichoke soup

Artichoke soup
Artichokes are high in protein, and they have been used in this dish to produce a thick, substantial soup which, although creamy in taste, is low in saturated fats.

Leafy green packages
These spinach and cabbage leaf packages, enclosing a tasty cilantro-flavored mixture of hazelnuts and spinach, are high in fiber and low in saturated fats. Their flavor is complemented by the fruity taste of the apricot and tomato relish.

Julienne of winter vegetables
The carrots, parsnips, and turnips used here have been baked, both to preserve as many nutrients as possible and to retain the vegetables' firm textures and shapes.

Chinese cabbage and grapefruit salad
This salad combines the tangy taste of grapefruit with the crispness of the Chinese cabbage, and it is offset by a yogurt dressing.

Apricot and tomato relish
This tasty, high-fiber, lowfat fruit and vegetable relish (see p.141) is a versatile accompaniment to baked dishes, stir-fries, and steamed vegetables.

Mango and orange sorbet
Sorbets provide a refreshing, lowfat end to a meal, and when including the fruits used here, will be high in vitamins A and C.

Grape juice
It is possible to buy non-alcoholic juices which nevertheless have a similar taste to light, white wines. These are ideal alternatives for those who choose not to drink. A glass will contain about 70 calories.

Grape juice

Mango and orange sorbet

Apricot and tomato relish (see p.141)

Leafy green packages

Illustrated on page 208

Ingredients

2 teaspoons sunflower oil
1 medium onion, finely chopped
1 pound Jerusalem artichokes,
peeled and diced
1 small potato, peeled and diced
1¼ cups skim milk
1¼ cups vegetable stock (see p. 120)
salt, or gomasio if preferred
white pepper
Serves 4–6

Artichoke soup

NUTRIENTS PER PORTION

95 *Calories*

Protein 5g ● ● ●   *Fiber 1g* ●
Polyunsaturated fat 1g ● ● ●   *Saturated fat 0g*
Vitamins C
Minerals Ca

Artichokes are high in protein and are used here to produce a delicious creamy soup.

1 Heat the oil in a large saucepan and gently fry the onion for 4–5 minutes, or until soft.

2 Add the artichokes and potato and cook lightly for about 5 minutes but do not allow to color.

3 Pour in the milk and stock. Bring to a boil, cover, and simmer for 25–30 minutes.

4 Cool slightly, then purée until smooth. Season with salt and pepper and reheat before serving.

Illustrated on page 209

Ingredients

8 large spinach leaves
8 young cabbage leaves
For the filling
½ pound spinach, washed
2 teaspoons sunflower oil
1 medium onion, finely chopped
1¼ cups hazelnuts or filberts,
ground
1 cup whole-wheat bread crumbs
2 tablespoons finely chopped fresh
coriander leaves, cilantro, or
Chinese parsley
2 tablespoons finely chopped fresh
parsley
1 egg
1 tablespoon soysauce
black pepper
Serves 4

Leafy green packages

NUTRIENTS PER PORTION

270 *Calories*

Protein 9g ● ●   *Fiber 10g* ● ● ●
Polyunsaturated fat 4g ● ● ●   *Saturated fat 2g*
Vitamins A, B6, C, E, FA
Minerals Ca, Fe, Mg, Zn

These attractive parcels are an excellent source of fiber and iron. Serve with tomato and apricot relish (see p. 141).

1 Wash then blanch the spinach and cabbage leaves for 2 minutes in a little boiling water. Drain.

2 For the filling, shred the spinach finely. Place in a saucepan, cover and cook, with only the water still adhering to the leaves, for 6 minutes.

3 Heat the oil in another saucepan and gently fry the onion for 4–5 minutes, or until soft. Add the hazelnuts and bread crumbs and cook for 2 minutes.

4 Remove from the heat, add the herbs, cooked spinach, egg, and soysauce. Season with pepper.

5 Preheat the oven to 350°F.

6 Take 1 cabbage and 1 spinach leaf. Place 2–3 tablespoons of the filling on each. Fold in the sides to the center and roll up into a parcel. Continue using cabbage and spinach leaves alternately until you have used all the leaves.

7 Place in a lightly oiled baking dish. Add 2–3 tablespoons water. Cover and bake for 30 minutes.

Julienne of winter vegetables

Illustrated on page 208

Ingredients
2 tablespoons sunflower oil
2 teaspoons maple syrup
2 teaspoons whole-grain mustard
1¼ pounds mixed root vegetables,
cut into matchstick-sized pieces
salt, or gomasio if preferred
black pepper
Serves 4

NUTRIENTS PER PORTION
180 Calories
Protein 2g • Fiber 4g • •
Polyunsaturated fat 4g • • • Saturated fat 1g
Vitamins A, C, E
Minerals –

Serve with a high-protein and high-mineral dish.
1 Preheat the oven to 400°F.
2 Heat the oil in a baking dish. Mix syrup and mustard together.
3 Add the vegetables, add mustard mix and toss well.
4 Cover and bake for 25–30 minutes. Add water if vegetables begin to look dry. Season with salt and pepper. Serve hot.

Chinese leaf and grapefruit salad

Illustrated on page 208

Ingredients
1 grapefruit
3½ cups shredded Chinese cabbage
For the dressing
1 egg yolk
3 tablespoons sunflower oil
1 tablespoon grapefruit juice
2 tablespoons thickened yogurt
(see p.106)
For garnishing
salad cress
Serves 4

NUTRIENTS PER PORTION
160 Calories
Protein 5g • • Fiber 1g •
Polyunsaturated fat 6g • • • Saturated fat 2g
Vitamins A, C, E, FA
Minerals Ca, Fe, Mg

If you are watching your fat intake, use plain not thickened yogurt.
1 Place the grapefruit on a board and cut downward to remove the peel and pith. To separate each segment from its membrane, hold the grapefruit over a bowl to catch the juice and cut on each side of the membranes to release skinless segments. Dice the segments. Reserve 1 tablespoon of juice.
2 For the dressing, beat the egg yolk. Add the oil a drop at a time to make a mayonnaise. When 2 tablespoons have been added, mix in the grapefruit juice.
3 Add remaining oil, 1 teaspoon at a time, then the yogurt.
4 Combine the Chinese cabbage and grapefruit in a bowl.
5 Mix dressing into salad, toss and garnish with cress.

Mango and orange sorbet

Illustrated on page 209

Ingredients
2 mangos
juice of 1 orange
1 teaspoon grated orange peel
1 tablespoon Cointreau (optional)
1 egg white, beaten
Serves 4

NUTRIENTS PER PORTION
110 Calories
Protein 2g • Fiber 2g •
Polyunsaturated fat 0g • • • Saturated fat 0g
Vitamins A, C
Minerals –

Use a blender to blend the frozen purée and egg white.
1 Peel the mangos and cut the flesh away from the seed.
2 Put the mango pulp, orange juice and peel, Cointreau, if using, into a blender and blend until smooth. Transfer to a freezerproof container and freeze for 1–2 hours.
3 Remove from freezer and blend until broken up.
4 Beat the egg white until stiff and fold into the fruit purée. Freeze again for 2–3 hours.

Weekday Supper

This substantial meal is both satisfying and simple to prepare. It provides both protein and fiber, but remains low in fat. The relatively low protein levels of the strudel and salads are balanced out by the meal as a whole, which, apart from the nutritional element, is a happy blend of colors, textures, and tastes.

NUTRIENTS PER PORTION
1175 *Calories*
Protein 36g ● ● ● *Fiber 27g* ● ● ●
Polyunsaturated fat 17g ● ● ● *Saturated fat 7g*
Vitamins A, B₁, B₆, C, E, FA, N
Minerals Ca, Cu, Fe, Mg, Zn

Crunchy green salad

Fennel risotto

Spiced bean pâté and banana raita
Beans make excellent bases for vegetarian pâtés because they are high in protein and fiber but low in fat. The bean pâté shown here was well flavored with coriander and cumin, and made slightly hot with the addition of ginger and chili. The spiciness is complemented by a cooling raita, and the whole dish is served with crisp yellow pepper, cucumber, and celery sticks.

Fennel risotto
High in fiber and low in fat, this tangy-tasting rice dish has all the creaminess of a classic risotto. The walnuts add a crunchiness to the overall texture of the dish.

Crunchy green salad
Despite a creamy mayonnaise dressing, this salad remains low in saturated fat. This is largely because yogurt and fruit juice have been used instead of oil. Chinese cabbage were used for this salad, but crispy cabbage would also be delicious.

Radicchio salad
In a meal that already has ample sources of protein and fiber, this salad is used to provide additional variety of texture and color. Radicchio was used here, and mixed with carrot, endive, mustard, and garden cress before being tossed in an olive oil, lemon juice, mustard, and black pepper dressing. Chinese cabbage or other greens can be used instead of the radicchio.

Apple strudel
This light fruit dessert, based on the classic European pastry, is high in fiber and, for pastry, low in fat, especially when served with yogurt or reduced fat sour cream (see p.107).

Fruit juice
Avoid artificially flavored drinks and those with added preservatives. Choose fresh fruit juice or water instead. (A glass of orange juice contains about 65 calories.) For a refreshing drink, add some sparkling water to the juice.

Fruit juice

Spiced bean pâté and banana raita

Radicchio salad

Apple strudel

Illustrated on page 213

Ingredients

*½ cup fava beans or ful medames,
soaked overnight
1 teaspoon coriander seeds
½ teaspoon cumin seeds
1 teaspoon black mustard seeds
2 tablespoons sunflower oil
1 medium onion, finely chopped
1 clove garlic, crushed
1 fresh green chili, seeded and diced
½-inch piece fresh gingerroot,
peeled and grated
¼ teaspoon curry powder
¼ teaspoon turmeric
1 tablespoon tomato paste
juice of 1 lemon
salt, or gomasio if preferred
black pepper*
For the banana raita
*1 banana, sliced
⅔ cup plain yogurt
½ teaspoon roasted cumin seeds*
Serves 4–6

Spiced bean pâté

NUTRIENTS PER PORTION

190 Calories

*Protein 9g ● ● ●   Fiber 8g ● ● ●
Polyunsaturated fat 4g ● ● ●   Saturated fat 1g
Vitamins B₁, C, N
Minerals Ca, Fe, Mg*

Beans make excellent bases for vegetarian pâtés because they are high in protein and fiber but low in fat. They do, however, need to be well flavored with spices or herbs. The taste improves if the pâté is kept covered in the refrigerator for a few days before serving.

1 Drain the beans. Cover with plenty of fresh water, bring uncovered to a boil, and boil fast for 10 minutes. Reduce the heat, skim, cover, and simmer for about 40 minutes, or until soft. Drain.

2 Dry roast the coriander, cumin and mustard seeds in a heavy-bottomed pan for about 3–4 minutes, until they start to pop, shaking the pan from time to time.

3 Add the oil to the pan and lightly fry the onion and garlic for 4–5 minutes until soft. Stir in the chili, ginger, curry powder, and turmeric and cook for 3–4 minutes. Add the cooked beans and stir well.

4 Purée the mixture until smooth, adding the tomato paste and lemon juice. Season with salt and pepper. Leave overnight for the flavors to blend.

5 To make the banana raita, mix the banana, yogurt, and cumin seeds together. Serve with the pâté.

Illustrated on page 212

Ingredients

*2 teaspoons sunflower oil
1 medium onion, finely chopped
1 teaspoon grated lemon peel
2½ cups diced fennel
1¼ cups short-grain brown rice
1½ cups boiling water
2 cups peeled and chopped tomatoes
juice of ½ lemon
½ cup coarsely chopped walnuts
salt, or gomasio if preferred
black pepper*
For garnishing
a fennel leaf
Serves 4

Fennel risotto

NUTRIENTS PER PORTION

320 Calories

*Protein 7g ●   Fiber 7g ● ● ●
Polyunsaturated fat 6g ● ● ●   Saturated fat 1g
Vitamins B₆, C, E, FA
Minerals Cu*

This tangy rice dish is high in fiber and low in fat, despite having all the creaminess of a classic risotto.

1 Heat the oil in a large saucepan and gently fry the onion for 4–5 minutes, or until soft.

2 Add the lemon peel and fennel and cook for 2–3 minutes.

3 Add the rice and 1 cup of the boiling water. Stir, bring to a boil and cook covered, until all the water has been absorbed, stirring occasionally.

4 Add the tomatoes, lemon juice, walnuts and ½ cup boiling water. Stir again and cook until all the liquid is absorbed. If the rice is not yet cooked, add a little more boiling water if necessary.

5 Once cooked, the risotto should be creamy. Season with salt and pepper. Garnish with a fennel leaf. Serve hot.

Crunchy green salad

Illustrated on page 212

NUTRIENTS PER PORTION
100 Calories
Protein 2g ● Fiber 2g ●
Polyunsaturated fat 3g ● ● ● Saturated fat 1g
Vitamins C
Minerals –

Ingredients
2½ cups shredded white cabbage or Chinese cabbage
1 small green pepper, seeded and diced
3 stalks celery, chopped
3 scallions, diced
For the dressing
3 tablespoons mayonnaise
2 tablespoons yogurt
1 tablespoon orange juice
1 teaspoon grated orange peel
herb salt, or salt if preferred
For garnishing
½ bunch watercress
Serves 4

This is the ideal salad to serve with a rich grain or dried bean dish.
1 Prepare and mix the vegetables together in a large bowl.
2 Stir the dressing ingredients together to make a thin cream.
3 Mix the dressing, pour over the salad and toss. Garnish with watercress. Serve chilled.

Apple strudel

Illustrated on page 213

NUTRIENTS PER PORTION
410 Calories
Protein 8g ● Fiber 7g ● ● ●
Polyunsaturated fat 3g ● ● Saturated fat 2g
Vitamins B₁, E
Minerals Ca, Cu, Fe, Mg

Ingredients
1 quantity of strudel pastry dough (see p. 113)
For the filling
1 tablespoon butter
1 cup fresh whole-wheat bread crumbs
1 pound crisp dessert apples
⅔ cup raisins
4 tablespoons slivered almonds
2 teaspoons ground cinnamon
1 teaspoon grated lemon peel
1 teaspoon maple syrup
little melted butter
For the glaze
1 teaspoon malt extract
1 teaspoon of frozen concentrated apple juice or ½ teaspoon of sugar
Serves 6–8

This version of the classic pastry is slightly less sweet, being virtually sugar-free. As it is high in fiber it is ideal to serve after a low-fiber main course. Bread crumbs are incorporated here to absorb some of the fruit juices, and to prevent the pastry from becoming soggy.
1 Melt the butter in a pan and gently fry the bread crumbs for about 3 minutes until very lightly toasted.
2 Preheat the oven to 400°F.
3 Finely slice the apples and mix with the raisins, slivered almonds, cinnamon, lemon peel, and maple syrup.
4 Stretch the dough very thinly on a floured surface to form a rectangular shape.
5 Sprinkle on the bread crumbs. Cover with the apple filling to within ½-inch of the edges.
6 Brush the edges of the dough with melted butter. Fold in the long side edges over the filling so that they meet in the center. Roll up the strudel like a jelly roll.
7 Put on a lightly oiled cookie sheet. Brush the top with a little melted butter. Bake for 45–50 minutes.
8 Remove from the oven. Mix the malt extract and frozen concentrated apple juice together and brush over the strudel.

Impromptu Dinner Party

A colorful meal that is quick to prepare. The main pasta dish is
an excellent source of carbohydrate, protein, and fiber. The
vegetable dishes add essential vitamins and minerals.

NUTRIENTS PER PORTION
1380
Calories
Protein 32g ● ● ● *Fiber 17g* ● ● ●
Polyunsaturated fat 10g ● ● ● *Saturated fat 21g* ● ●
Vitamins A, B, B1, B2, B6, B12, C, D, E
Minerals Ca, Fe, K, Mg, Zn

Spaghetti with oil, garlic, and chili sauce
*Spaghetti aglio, olio, e peperoncino is the Italian name for this quickly
made dish of pasta with garlic and chili. Grated cheese is an optional extra.*

Broccoli roulade
*A roulade always looks impressive, but in fact is easy to make once you
have mastered the technique.*

Tomato sauce
*Tomato sauce is easy to make in quantity and keeps well, whether
frozen or stored in the refrigerator (see p.119).*

Snowpea and mushroom salad
*Make an impromptu salad with whatever you have to
hand: use leftover grains or beans, and nuts or raisins,
as well as fresh salad vegetables, dressed with a
vinaigrette sauce.*

Tomato sauce

Steamed potatoes
*Potatoes, lightly steamed and
sprinkled with toasted almonds, are a
good accompaniment to the roulade,
but steamed carrots or celery would be
good, too (see Cooking times for
vegetables, pp. 74–75).*

Marinated oranges
*Fresh oranges can be sliced
and marinated in orange and
lemon juices with honey and
Grand Marnier to taste, and
then decorated with some
orange zest.*

Steamed potatoes

*Snowpea and
mushroom salad*

Broccoli roulade

Marinated oranges

*Spaghetti with oil,
garlic, and chili sauce*

Illustrated on page 217

Ingredients

*500g (1lb 2oz) fresh wholewheat
spaghetti
30ml (2 tbsp) olive oil
2–3 cloves garlic, crushed
1 dried chilli, very finely diced
2–3 tbsp finely chopped parsley
salt and pepper*
Serves 4–6

Spaghetti with oil, garlic, and chili sauce

460

Calories

NUTRIENTS PER PORTION
*Protein 18g ● ● ● Fiber 9g ● ● ●
Polyunsaturated fat 3g ● ● .051 Saturated fat 5g
Vitamins A, B1, B2, B12, C, E, FA, N
Minerals Fe, K, Mg, Zn*

Pasta must always be freshly cooked. Bring a large pot of water to a boil and put in plenty of salt. If the pot is big enough, there is no need to add a little oil as some cooks do to prevent the pasta from sticking together. It should be cooked *al dente* – until just tender but offering a very slight resistance to the bite. The only way to be sure of this is to taste a piece. Whole-wheat spaghetti will take from 8–10 minutes to cook. This is one of the quickest of all pasta sauces. It can be made while the spaghetti is cooking.
1 Using a large, heavy-based pot, heat the oil and sauté the garlic and chili over medium heat for 2–3 minutes. The garlic should turn golden, but must on no account burn.
2 As soon as the pasta is cooked, drain it, turn it into the pan and mix quickly to coat it with the oil. Mix in the parsley and season with salt (and pepper if necessary). Serve immediately.

Illustrated on page 217

Ingredients

*1½ cups broccoli flowerets
5 tablespoons butter
4½ tablespoons whole-wheat flour
⅔ cup milk
3 eggs, separated
salt and pepper*
Filling
tomato sauce (see p.119)
For garnishing
*2–3 tablespoons freshly grated
Parmesan cheese
tomato slices (optional)*
Serves 4–6

Broccoli roulade

250

Calories

NUTRIENTS PER PORTION
*Protein 12g ● ● ● Fiber 2g ●
Polyunsaturated fat 1g ● ● Saturated fat 8g
Vitamins A, B2, B12, C, D, FA, N
Minerals Ca, K*

To vary the dish, substitute ½ cup green or brown lentils for the broccoli. Simmer them in plenty of water for 35–40 minutes and drain.
1 Preheat the oven to 375°F, and line a 13-×9-inch cookie sheet with waxed paper.
2 Steam the broccoli lightly for 5–6 minutes. Chop it finely.
3 Melt the butter, stir in the flour and cook over low heat for 2 minutes. Add the milk and bring to a boil, stirring well to avoid lumps. Simmer for 2–3 minutes.
4 Remove from heat, beat the egg yolks into the sauce, one at a time. Season well, and mix in the broccoli.
5 Beat the egg whites until stiff but not dry and gently fold them into the broccoli mixture.
6 Spread this over the prepared cookie sheet, and bake for 17–20 minutes.
7 Turn out onto a clean dish towel covered with a fresh sheet of waxed paper. Peel off the old sheet. Spread the filling over the roulade and roll it up, using the dish towel. Do not worry if it cracks slightly. Sprinkle with grated cheese and put back in oven for 5 minutes before serving garnished with tomato slices.

Basic vinaigrette

NUTRIENTS PER PORTION
550 Calories
Protein Trace Fiber 0g
Polyunsaturated fat 6g Saturated fat 8g
Vitamins –
Minerals –

Ingredients
4–6 tablespoons oil (olive or sunflower or a mixture to taste)
1 tablespoon wine or cider vinegar
1 tablespoon lemon juice
1 large clove garlic, crushed
large pinch of dry mustard
salt and pepper
Makes 6–8 tablespoons

Although in itself this vinaigrette dressing is not high in nutrients, combined with the ingredients of the snowpea and mushroom salad it will add the perfect finishing touch to the main course.

To vary this recipe, add a peeled and mashed avocado and blend until smooth. The result, more like a mayonnaise than a vinaigrette, is also good with a simple green or tomato salad, or with coleslaw. Another alternative is to add 1–2 tablespoons soy flour and 1 teaspoon honey and blend until smooth. This looks similar to egg mayonnaise. Both are useful recipes for those who prefer not to eat dairy products.

Mix all the ingredients together in a jar with a screw top and shake well.

Marinated oranges

NUTRIENTS PER PORTION
90 Calories
Protein 1g ● Fiber 0g
Polyunsaturated fat 0g ● ● ● Saturated fat 0g
Vitamins C
Minerals –

Illustrated on page 217
Ingredients
5 large oranges
1 lemon
2 teaspoons honey
2 tablespoons Grand Marnier
Serves 4

Cointreau may be substituted for Grand Marnier.

1 Peel four of the oranges, using a sharp knife to remove the pith. Cut into thin slices and place in a shallow dish.

2 Squeeze the juice from the remaining orange (save the peel) and the lemon and pour into a bowl. Add the honey and Grand Marnier and mix thoroughly. Pour over the orange slices.

3 Cut the zest of the squeezed orange into very fine julienne strips and sprinkle over the orange slices.

INDEX

Page numbers in italics refer to illustrations

ACKNOWLEDGMENTS

Designer: Sue Hall
Editors: Sydney Francis, Mary Lambert
Typesetter: Bournetype, Bournemouth
Reproduction: Colourscan, Singapore

Dorling Kindersley
Managing editor: Jemima Dunne
Managing art editor: Derek Coombes
Americanization: Elizabeth Wolf-Cohen
US contributing editor: Barbara Jacksier
Editor: Julia Harris-Voss
Designer: Camilla Fox
Production: Helen Creeke

Reader's Digest Fund for the Blind is publisher of the Large-Type Edition of *Reader's Digest.* For subscription information about this magazine, please contact Reader's Digest Fund for the Blind, Inc., Dept 250, Pleasantville, N.Y. 10570.

Photographic credits All photography by Philip Dowell except: pp 8/9 David Bradfield and p 42 Peter Myers